On Translation of Laws and Regulations in China

Xiaobo Dong • Yafang Zhang

On Translation of Laws and Regulations in China

A National Governance Perspective

Springer

Xiaobo Dong
Nanjing Normal University
Nanjing, Jiangsu, China

Yafang Zhang
Southwest Univerisity of Political Science and Law
Chongqing, China

ISBN 978-981-95-9405-4 ISBN 978-981-95-9406-1 (eBook)
https://doi.org/10.1007/978-981-95-9406-1

This Springer imprint is published by the registered company Springer Nature Singapore Pte Ltd.
The registered company address is: 152 Beach Road, #21-01/04 Gateway East, Singapore 189721, Singapore

Preface

In an era of deepening globalization and evolving international governance paradigms, China's legal system has emerged as a pivotal force in shaping contemporary rule-of-law discourse worldwide. The translation of Chinese laws and regulations, however, extends far beyond linguistic conversion; it represents a critical conduit for cross-cultural legal dialogue and a strategic instrument of national governance in a multipolar world. This book, *On Translation of Laws and Regulations in China: A National Governance Perspective*, seeks to systematically address the complexities, challenges, and opportunities inherent in rendering China's legislative texts into English with accuracy, consistency, and authority.

This work explores legal translation within the broader framework of China's governance modernization, examining how translated laws function not only as textual artifacts but as vehicles of sovereign expression and international engagement. Subsequent chapters undertake a meticulous, layer-by-layer analysis of the concrete challenges of translating legislative titles, terminology, fixed syntactic structures, and culturally specific expressions. Each segment combines theoretical reflection with empirical case studies, illustrating both persistent difficulties and practicable strategies for standardization. At its core, this work argues that the standardization of legal translation is inseparable from the project of constructing a coherent, internationally legible Chinese rule-of-law discourse. By integrating perspectives from translation studies, comparative law, corpus linguistics, and digital humanities, the book proposes a multi-dimensional approach to improve translation standardization that balances fidelity to source texts with functional adaptability to target legal cultures. Special emphasis is placed on the role of technology as an enabler of consistency and scalability in large-scale legislative translation.

As China continues to engage actively in global governance, the clarity, precision, and credibility of its translated laws will significantly influence how its legal concepts, institutions, and values are perceived and received abroad. This book is intended not only for translators, legal scholars, and policymakers but also for anyone interested in the intersection of language, law, and governance in a transnational context. It is our hope that the discussions and proposals presented herein will contribute to the development of more robust, systematic, and academically grounded practices in legal translation, practices that uphold the integrity of Chinese law while facilitating meaningful dialogue with the world.

We invite readers to explore these pages with a critical and constructive spirit, recognizing that the journey toward fully standardized legal translation is ongoing, a journey that reflects China's broader commitment to rule-of-law development, open engagement, and the shared advancement of global legal civilization.

Nanjing, China Xiaobo Dong

Contents

About the Authors

Xiaobo Dong is a Distinguished Professor of Jilin International Studies University, a Professor at the School of Foreign Languages and Cultures of Nanjing Normal University, a Deputy Director of the Belt and Road Rule of Law Research Center at the Academy of China's Modernization of Rule of Law, and a Researcher at the Jiangsu Academy of Talent Development Strategy. He is a renowned contemporary Chinese jurist and legal linguist. He is also the Director and Chief Expert of the Jiangsu International Rule of Law Research Center, as well as the Chief Expert on major projects of the National Social Science Fund of China. His research interests include the history of Sino-Western civilization exchanges, legal linguistics, legal translation, language strategy and planning, and cross-cultural communication. In recent years, he has published over 250 interdisciplinary academic papers in prominent journals and more than 80 books, including academic monographs, edited volumes, and translations. He has authored multiple English academic monographs published by internationally leading publishing groups and has dozens of research papers published in high-level journals such as Nature. He enjoys a distinguished academic reputation internationally.

Yafang Zhang is lecturer at the School of Foreign Languages of Southwest University of Political Science and Law and researcher at the Jiangsu International Rule of Law Research Center. Her research interests include Sino-Western cultural exchanges, legal linguistics, translation of Chinese legal classics, and language planning. In recent years, she has published four books in legal linguistics study and multiple interdisciplinary academic papers.

Chapter 1
Introduction

Abstract This chapter introduces the research framework for examining the translation of Chinese laws and regulations from the perspective of national governance. It begins by outlining the core research question, focusing on how translation practices influence the international dissemination of China's legal discourse. The chapter then provides an overview of China's legislative system and the current state of legal translation, highlighting persistent issues such as terminological inconsistency and structural ambiguity. Finally, it underscores the significance of this research in advancing the standardization of legal translation, enhancing cross-jurisdictional legal communication, and strengthening China's role in global governance through linguistically precise and culturally resonant legal texts.

Keywords Legal translation standardization · National governance · Cross-jurisdictional communication

1.1 Research Question

Since the launch of reform and opening-up, China has made remarkable achievements in the construction of the rule of law, culminating in the establishment of a socialist legal system with Chinese characteristics. Particularly since the 18th National Congress of the Communist Party of China (CPC), the comprehensive advancement of law-based governance has become both an essential requirement and a critical safeguard for socialism with Chinese characteristics. In the new era, China's legal development, characterized by logically coherent legal philosophies, well-structured legal institutions, and dynamic legal practices, vividly demonstrates the unique appeal of the Chinese experience, the Chinese approach, and the Chinese path (Gong 2018). As emphasized by President Xi Jinping in the report to the 19th National Congress of the CPC, socialism with Chinese characteristics has evolved into a new era, signifying the continuous evolution of its path, theory, system, and culture. This development "offers a new option for other countries and nations who want to speed up their development

X. Dong, Y. Zhang, *On Translation of Laws and Regulations in China*,
https://doi.org/10.1007/978-981-95-9406-1_1

while preserving their independence; and it contributes Chinese wisdom and a Chinese approach to solving the problems facing mankind" (Dong 2018).

As a significant achievement in global governance, China's rule-of-law development with distinctive Chinese characteristics deserves recognition from the international community. From the perspective of international communication, the discourse system of a nation's legal domain can only foster understanding, support, and resonance among foreign audiences through effective cross-border dissemination. Only in this way can a country establish its intended image as a law-governed state in the international community and contribute China's wisdom and solutions to global governance.

Legal translation is an act of cross-system communication in legal ideologies, legal languages and cultures, as well as legal norms and texts, and also an act of cross-linguistic communication. It serves as a crucial means for China's legal discourse system to engage with the world. Through translation, we can comprehensively summarize the experiences of China's rule of law development, disseminate China's legal discourse on international platforms, and showcase the achievements and direction of its legal system development. This not only helps to further explore the unique connotations of China's legal discourse system, offering Chinese wisdom and solutions to the complex and ever-changing global landscape, but also enables China to occupy the moral high ground for the peaceful coexistence and common development of humanity. By maximizing the mobilization of all forces conducive to China's development and global peace and progress, China can seize the initiative in shaping international public opinion and academic discourse.

The standardization and unification of the translation of China's laws and regulations for international audiences constitute a vital component of enhancing the nation's cultural soft power. A comprehensive review of the history of Chinese legal translation since its modern origins readily reveals that legal translation differs significantly from other forms of practical translation. Whether it be scientific, economic and trade, journalistic, advertising, tourism, or political discourse translation, the fundamental goal of applied translation across these genres is the effective conveyance of information. This is achieved through fluent expression in the target language and the application of specific translation techniques to fulfill the functional purpose of each text type. In contrast, legal translation, as a specialized branch of practical translation, is not merely an act of cross-linguistic and cross-cultural communication but, more importantly, an act of cross-systemic legal exchange. Accuracy in conveying meaning, formal stylistic register, and the inherent complexity and obscurity of terminology are the most distinctive linguistic features of legal translation. These characteristics demand that translators possess not only exceptional language proficiency but also substantial legal knowledge and logical reasoning skills. Currently, the fundamental issue in legal translation in China is the shortage of highly qualified, inter-disciplinary translation talents. Achieving mastery in either a foreign language or law alone is challenging enough; excelling in both fields simultaneously, while also possessing theoretical knowledge and practical experience in translation, is indeed exceptionally difficult.

With China's rapid development and the ever-expanding breadth and depth of its exchanges with the world, there is a growing global demand for information about

China. Various sectors of the nation are now being presented to the international community in an unprecedented and comprehensive manner. Particularly since the 18th National Congress of the Communist Party of China, President Xi Jinping has introduced a series of new concepts, approaches, and requirements, such as "innovating in external communication, striving to create new concepts, categories, and expressions that bridge China and the rest of the world, telling China's stories well, and communicating China's voice effectively". These directives set clear new goals for advancing cultural exchanges and enhancing international communication capabilities in a more effective and profound manner, as well as for improving the quality and capacity of translation, especially in the domain of Chinese-to-foreign language translation. Transparency in policies and regulations is an essential requirement for building an internationalized and rule-of-law-based business environment, as well as a crucial measure for creating a transparent and law-based government. Therefore, enhancing the quality of translation of China's laws and regulations, prioritizing the translation of legal texts, and promoting the global outreach of Chinese legal discourse to contribute Chinese wisdom and solutions to global governance should become an important national strategy.

1.2 Laws and Regulations of China

In China, the term "laws" in the narrow sense specifically refers to legal norms enacted by the National People's Congress (NPC) and its Standing Committee, including basic laws and ordinary laws.

Administrative regulations are an important component of the socialist legal system with Chinese characteristics. The State Council formulates administrative regulations in accordance with the Constitution and laws, which serves as a key means for the State Council to fulfill the responsibilities conferred by the Constitution and laws. Administrative regulations may provide detailed provisions for the implementation of laws and matters related to the State Council's administrative authority, thereby refining and supplementing existing laws. Furthermore, the State Council, properly authorized by the NPC and its Standing Committee, may enact administrative regulations on matters that would otherwise fall under the legislative purview of the NPC and its Standing Committee. Local regulations are also an integral part of the socialist legal system with Chinese characteristics. The people's congresses and their standing committees of provinces, autonomous regions, municipalities directly under the central government, and larger cities may enact local regulations, provided they do not contravene the Constitution, national laws, or administrative regulations. In ethnic autonomous areas, the people's congresses have the authority to formulate autonomous regulations and specific regulations in light of the political, economic, and cultural characteristics of the local ethnic groups. Local regulations may address the implementation of national laws and administrative regulations, as well as matters of local concern. In cases where the state has not yet enacted laws or administrative regulations on certain matters, excluding those exclusively reserved for the NPC and its Standing Committee, local regulations may be formulated first. As such, local regulations serve to refine and supplement national laws and administrative regulations, extend and improve national legislation, and accumulate valuable experience for the national legislative process.

Rules constitute an integral component of the socialist legal system with Chinese characteristics. The ministries and commissions under the State Council, the People's Bank of China, the National Audit Office, and other directly subordinate institutions with administrative functions may formulate departmental rules within their respective jurisdictions in accordance with laws, administrative regulations, decisions, and orders of the State Council. The people's governments of provinces, autonomous regions, municipalities directly under the central government, and larger cities may formulate local government rules in accordance with laws, administrative regulations, and local regulations of their respective administrative regions.

The socialist legal system with Chinese characteristics takes the Constitution as its core and laws as its main body, encompassing multiple legal branches including the Constitution and constitution-related laws, civil and commercial law, administrative law, economic law, social law, criminal law, litigation and non-litigation procedural law, among others. It comprises legal norms at various levels, such as laws, administrative regulations, and local regulations. This system represents a key milestone in the history of the construction of socialist democracy and legal system in China, serving as a significant manifestation of the gradual maturation of the socialist system with Chinese characteristics. It carries profound contemporary relevance and far-reaching historical significance.

Various legislative forms of legal norms with Chinese characteristics exhibit distinct linguistic features due to differences in their issuing authorities, connotations, and legal force. Nevertheless, regardless of the level of legislation, as the carrier of legal norms, their language inevitably shares common characteristics. Legislative language is a crucial and core component of legal language, employed in the process of lawmaking. "The quality of law directly depends on the quality of the language that expresses and communicates it" (He 2008). As the official language of legal activities, legislative language must, on one hand, convey the intent and objectives of the legislators, and on the other, inform citizens and relevant institutions of the scope of the law's application. Therefore, legislative language must be precise, concise, and neutral (Dong 2016: 2).

1.3 Current Status of Translation of Laws and Regulations in China

The translation of China's laws, regulations, and rules was initiated to meet the requirements for its accession to the World Trade Organization (WTO). The principle of transparency served as a central theme throughout China's WTO accession (re-entry into GATT) negotiations. In 1992, China and the United States signed the

Sino-U.S. Memorandum of Understanding on Market Access, which stipulated that China must regularly and promptly publish laws, regulations, judicial decisions, and administrative rulings related to tariffs, trade, and other relevant matters. The United States regarded "full transparency" in China's trade system as one of the conditions for supporting China's re-entry into the General Agreement on Tariffs and Trade (GATT) (Hu and Peng 2012). The establishment of the WTO transparency principle aims to create an open and transparent legal and policy environment for international trade, reduce or even eliminate uncertainties in the operation of the organization and the international trading system, and thereby promote further liberalization of international trade. This, in itself, is one of the objectives of the WTO agreements.

To further promote the reform and opening up, the Chinese government solemnly promised to the WTO as follows:

> Article 2(C) of the Protocol on the Accession of the People's Republic of China stipulates that "China undertakes that only those laws, regulations and other measures pertaining to or affecting trade in goods, services, TRIPS or the control of foreign exchange that are published and readily available to other WTO Members, individuals and enterprises shall be enforced… shall be available no later than the time when they are implemented or enforced"; "China shall establish or designate an official journal for the publication of all laws, regulations and other measures…"; and "China shall establish or designate an enquiry point where… accurate and reliable information shall be provided to individuals and enterprises".
>
> Paragraphs 324 to 336 of the Report of the Working Party on the Accession of China also set forth commitments regarding transparency obligations. Among them, Paragraph 334 requires China to "make available to WTO Members all laws, regulations and other measures pertaining to or affecting trade in goods, services, TRIPS or the control of foreign exchange translated into one or more of the official languages of the WTO… shall be made available to WTO Members no later than 90 days after implementation or enforcement". Procedurally, in accordance with Article 18, Paragraph 4 of the Protocol on the Accession of the People's Republic of China, China is subject to a transitional review mechanism, under which it will undergo a total of nine reviews within the first 10 years after its accession. The first eight reviews are to be conducted annually for the first eight years, with a final review to be undertaken in the 10th year or on an earlier date as decided by the General Council.

In order to fulfill the solemn commitments made upon WTO accession and further deepen reform and opening-up, the translation of China's laws and regulations has been gradually elevated as a key agenda item. In line with the principle that "the issuing body shall organize the translation", the Legislative Affairs Commission of the National People's Congress established a dedicated office responsible for the translation and finalization of laws, while the Legislative Affairs Office of the State Council set up the Department of Translation, Review and Foreign Affairs to oversee the translation and finalization of administrative regulations. Furthermore, various departments under the State Council have established or designated offices responsible for the translation of regulatory rules. To better organize the translation of administrative regulations and promote the translation of regulatory rules, the Legislative Affairs Office of the State Council drafted the *Notice of the General Office of the State Council on Conducting the Translation and Finalization of Authoritative English Versions of Administrative Regulations (Draft)*. With the approval of the State Council, the General Office of the State Council officially issued the circular in February 2003, commonly referred to as the *Notice*. The *Notice* clearly defines the responsibilities and timelines for translation and finalization work, specifies organizational and financial support mechanisms, standardizes operational procedures, and mandates that local governments and departments carry out the translation of regulations issued by them. In addition, the Legislative Affairs Office of the State Council held symposia on the translation and finalization of local regulations and rules in 2004 and 2011, continuously advancing this work. Many local governments have incorporated the translation of regulations and rules into the duties of their legislative affairs bodies through local government regulations or normative documents. Some regions, based on their practical needs, have continually improved internal working systems and standards, ensuring that the translation of regulations and rules is conducted in a well-founded, orderly, and effective manner.

High-quality translation of regulations requires expert support, which has been a successful practice of the Legislative Affairs Office in conducting this work. For instance, the Legislative Affairs Office of the Jiangsu Provincial People's Government has placed great emphasis on collaboration with university scholars and experts, as well as on building a robust team of specialists. It has gradually established a fundamental working model that integrates legal and language experts, general and domain-specific professionals, and translation and review specialists. This has resulted in the formation of a multi-tiered, stratified, and multi-disciplinary team of experts. The Legislative Affairs Office of the State Council has also periodically organized theoretical seminars on regulatory translation, striving to develop a foundational theory for translating laws and regulations. It has compiled the *Research on Several Issues in Regulatory Translation*, exploring basic theoretical questions such as the fundamental principles, working standards, basic methods, and techniques of legal translation review. The research proposes principles and standards for regulatory translation, providing theoretical answers to a series of questions on how to conduct translation and review. Furthermore, based on practical experience in regulatory translation, the Legislative Affairs Office has organized the compilation of the *Handbook of Common Sentence Patterns for Regulatory Translation and Review*. This handbook serves as a practical guide and is continuously refined through application, laying a foundation for standardizing the English versions of administrative regulations.

1.4 Significance of Research

The standardization of legal translation constitutes a foundational project of strategic significance in advancing the modernization of national governance. It is not merely an academic issue of linguistic normalization but a crucial pathway for constructing a discourse system of rule of law with Chinese characteristics and enhancing China's voice in international legal discourse. This research must be approached from the perspective of modernizing national governance, systematically interpreting its institutional value and practical logic through multidimensional lenses such as political science, jurisprudence, and linguistics, thereby establishing a translation theory rooted in China's legal practice while integrating international expressive norms.

The essence of translation lies in cross-civilizational dialogue, and legal translation, in particular, involves the cross-border transmission of national governance will. Research on a three-dimensional legal translation system (linguistic, jurisprudential, and cultural dimensions) based on large-scale Chinese-English parallel corpora can deeply deconstruct the institutional logic and cultural DNA behind legal texts. This promotes precise cross-border transformation of legal concepts with Chinese characteristics while ensuring functional equivalence in legal terms. Such a research paradigm not only provides theoretical support for the international dissemination of "key national legal discourse" but also lays a discursive foundation for China's participation in shaping global legal norms in the new era.

Legal translation is by no means a simple substitution of terminology but a collaborative reconstruction of legal and linguistic systems in cross-cultural contexts. It demands dual equivalence: functional correspondence at the linguistic level and institutional equivalence at the legal level. This dual transformative nature necessitates that legal translation transcend the boundaries of traditional translation studies, evolving into an interdisciplinary field bridging comparative law, legal linguistics, and transnational governance research.

The significance of this research can be articulated in the following three dimensions. First, from the perspective of modernizing national governance, the standardization of legal translation is a key measure to enhance transparency in the rule of law. The establishment of a socialist legal system with Chinese characteristics marks a new phase in China's legislative endeavors (Zhang 1999). Legal transparency is both a formal requirement for building a law-based government and a reflection of the modernization of national governance capabilities. Against the backdrop of deepening globalization, legal translation has become an international extension of government information disclosure, fulfilling China's transparency commitments under the WTO while providing an institutional basis for regulating the conduct of transnational market entities. Second, in terms of constructing international legal discourse power, standardized translation serves as the foundational project for introducing Chinese legal civilization to the world. By accurately conveying the jurisprudential connotation of the rule of law in a socialist market economy, it enhances international understanding and recognition of China's legal path. This not only strengthens the country's institutional discourse power but also contributes Chinese wisdom to the civilization of human rule of law, advancing the dialectical transcendence of socialist rule of law over its capitalist counterpart. Third, in terms of disciplinary development, this research will break down the barriers between law, linguistics, and translation studies, pioneering a new paradigm for legal translation research. By constructing an interdisciplinary methodological system, it will inject new momentum into the innovative development of related disciplines and foster the formation of a theory of legal communication with Chinese autonomous knowledge systems, thereby contributing to the optimization and upgrading of China's philosophy and social sciences disciplines.

References

Dong, X. 2016. *Research on the standardization of legislative language in China*. Beijing: Beijing Jiaotong University Press.

Dong, X. 2018, June 26. Legal translation contributes Chinese wisdom to global governance. *China Social Sciences Today*.

Gong, P. 2018, January 28. Think tanks for the modernization of the rule of law have great potential. *Guangming Daily*.

He, J. 2008, December 28. Legal language should be standardized. *Legal Daily*.

Hu, J. & Peng, D. 2012. Transparency requirements of WTO trade policies: Legal principles and China's practice. *Presentday Law Science*, 1.

Zhang, W. 1999. *Jurisprudence*. Beijing: Higher Education Press.

Chapter 2
Basic Issues of Translation of Laws and Regulations in China

Abstract This chapter systematically examines the fundamental issues in translating Chinese laws and regulations, with a focus on their implications for national governance. It first outlines the core principles guiding legal translation in China, emphasizing accuracy, consistency, and functional equivalence. The chapter then analyzes common translation errors in legislative texts, such as terminological inconsistency, structural ambiguity, and cultural misalignment, and evaluates their impact on the clarity and authority of China's legal discourse in international contexts. Finally, it concludes by underscoring the necessity of standardized translation practices to enhance legal predictability, facilitate cross-border cooperation, and support China's strategic engagement in global governance.

Keywords Translation principles · Analysis · Legal translation and governance efficacy

The translation of China's legislative texts serves as a crucial nexus between domestic legal development and global engagement, fulfilling dual imperatives of inward institutional refinement and outward normative alignment. As China deepens its interactions within global political, economic, and cultural frameworks, the translation of laws and regulations has evolved into an instrumental component of the country's governance strategy, enhancing international legal cooperation, supporting foreign trade mechanisms, and reinforcing policy transparency in response to global expectations. This effort not only facilitates the introduction of international legislative expertise and advanced techniques to enrich China's socialist rule-of-law system, but also projects the achievements of its legal development to the world, cultivating an image of China as a modern rule-of-law state and augmenting its institutional soft power. Simultaneously, as an integral dimension of reform and opening-up, the systematic translation of legislative documents operationalizes China's WTO transparency commitments, demonstrating the government's dedication to open governance and normative predictability. By establishing an accessible, linguistically coherent body of legal texts, China strengthens international confidence in its regulatory environment, attracts sustained foreign investment, and

X. Dong, Y. Zhang, *On Translation of Laws and Regulations in China*,
https://doi.org/10.1007/978-981-95-9406-1_2

fosters a stable framework for high-quality development, thereby embodying the synergy between translational excellence and the modernization of state governance.

As a specialized skill within legal English, legal translation represents a distinct form of purpose-oriented expertise that intersects linguistics, translation studies, and jurisprudence. It transcends mere linguistic conversion, serving as an essential process of decoding and transferring legal cultures across systems. Although China's socialist legal system has largely taken shape (Wu 2011), and considerable achievements have been made in the translation of Chinese legislative texts, the field remains in a developmental stage, lacking a standardized theoretical framework. Existing discussions on legal translation predominantly focus on technical aspects such as terminology and syntax, falling short of forming a comprehensive, systematic theoretical system for legal text translation. The current prevalence of inaccuracies and mistranslations reflects these theoretical and practical limitations. From the perspective of national governance, the absence of a coherent approach to legal translation affects the international readability and normative credibility of China's legal system, thereby influencing the country's capacity for global legal dialogue and regulatory cooperation. This chapter seeks to systematically analyze, categorize, and summarize recurrent translation errors in recent English versions of Chinese legislative texts, with the aim of proposing actionable translation strategies and establishing a foundation for subsequent targeted research in this volume.

2.1 Basic Principles of Translation of Laws and Regulations in China

Translation constitutes a specialized form of linguistic transposition, a hermeneutic process of decoding one language into another, fundamentally anchored in fidelity to the source text. One of the central teleological purposes in studying translation principles and standards has been to uncover the essence of translation and establish universally recognized norms. However, with the progression of eras and rapid economic development, translation principles and standards have themselves undergone historical transformation. The aspiration to discover a single universal principle capable of guiding all translational practices has ultimately proved illusory. Yet, though this dream remains unrealized, it has laid a foundational impetus for the continuous development and vitality of translation studies as an academic discipline. What we now recognize as broadly instructive translation principles and standards have emerged through a dialectical process of sublation, that is, negating and transcending earlier frameworks while incorporating new epochal characteristics and global developmental needs. Within this broader context, legal translation, as a field still in its developmental stage, cannot detach itself from the guidance of these generalized translation principles. Rather, it must build upon them to formulate a self-referential system tailored to the distinctive characteristics of legal language, complete with its own specialized translational norms and criteria.

2.1.1 General Principles and Standards of Translation

Translation, as a form of linguistic re-creation, operates under guiding principles, evaluative standards, and procedural rules. Translation principles serve not only as tools to assist translators in resolving practical challenges but also as externalized manifestations of the translator's subjective decision-making. As Liu (1991: 14) asserts, these principles constitute norms to be observed throughout the translation process, products of millennia of theoretical evolution, refined through cycles of practice and reflection, progressively distilled from rudimentary to sophisticated levels of translational activity and thought. They function as actionable guidelines and behavioral norms that steer both practice and theory, exhibiting broad applicability and universal relevance (Xiong 2011: 97).

Throughout history, translators and theorists from both Eastern and Western traditions have contributed profound insights into these principles. In the West, Cicero's sense-for-sense approach, Horace's dynamic translation, Quintilian's creative imitation, Jerome's complementary use of literal and free translation, Campbell's and Tytler's tripartite principles, Catford's and Nida's functional equivalence, Newmark's text-typology approach, and Fedorov's theory of equivalence all reflect persistent efforts to systematize translation practice. In China, the Tang Dynasty monk Xuanzang, through his journey to the West, established the dual principles of "seeking truth" (求真) and "making it accessible" (喻俗), striving to faithfully introduce sutras and cultures from Central Asia to the Central Plains. In the modern era, Yan Fu's principle of "faithfulness, expressiveness, and elegance" (信达雅) resonated remarkably with Tytler's three laws of translation, both emphasizing the faithful transmission of original content in fluent and comprehensible language (Dong 2016: 156). The development of modern Chinese translation principles gained momentum in the early twentieth century, particularly from the 1930s onward, a prolific period for literary translation theory. Contributions such as Zhu Shenghao's "conveying the spirit" (传神), Lin Yutang's "faithfulness, smoothness, and beauty" (忠实、通顺、美), Lu Xun's "preserving charm" (丰姿), Mao Dun's "artistic conception" (意境), Fu Lei's "spiritual resemblance" (神似), Qian Zhongshu's "sublimation" (入化), Liu Zhongde's "faithfulness, expressiveness, and closeness" (信达切), and Xu Yuanchong's "three beauties" (三美) and "three similarities" (三似) further enriched the discourse. All these principles reflect what Hans-Georg Gadamer (1975: 348) described as the translator's continuous process of negotiation and deliberation in pursuit of optimal solutions, with the ultimate goal of transmitting the linguistic message of the source text as fully and accurately as possible.

The principles of legal translation are fundamentally derived from universal translation theories, representing a specialized manifestation of these general principles within the legal domain and constituting an integral part of the broader theoretical framework of translation. What distinguishes legal translation principles, however, is their subjection to mandatory regulation by the state and government, which imbues general translation norms with legally binding force. Whereas the diversity and continuous evolution of general translation principles stem from their lack of institutional constraints, often emerging as summaries of individual experience and practical insight, legal norms function as components of national governance, designed to standardize social conduct and establish uniform standards.

Owing to this institutional nature of legal texts, their translation principles must rigorously adhere to the specific conventions of legal genres and the normative requirements of legal language. Moreover, the formation of translation principles in legal practice is shaped by a complex array of factors: differences in linguistic systems (e.g., between English and Chinese structures), textual genres, legal domains, translators' cognitive abilities, psychological states, socio-cultural backgrounds, and even their socioeconomic conditions. All these variables may give rise to diverse translational approaches and methodologies. Even state-mandated legal translation principles, despite their authoritative and prescriptive nature, cannot remain immune to such multifaceted influences. In essence, their development represents an ongoing negotiation between institutional requirements and the inherent principles of linguistic transposition.

2.1.2 Basic Principles of Translation of Laws and Regulations

Legal language, as a prescriptive branch of language, is subject in translation to the general criteria applicable to translation as a whole. Principles such as Yan Fu's "faithfulness, expressiveness, and elegance", Eugene Nida's functional equivalence, as well as widely accepted standards like accuracy, coherence, and fluency, all play a guiding role in legal translation. However, compared with other language types, the most distinctive features of legal language are precision and rigor. While legal writing may also value literary quality, when elegance conflicts with accuracy in translation, fidelity must take precedence over stylistic refinement. Furthermore, a competent translation should faithfully convey both the content and the style of the source text, that is, it should achieve linguistic functional equivalence. Nevertheless, in legal translation, greater emphasis must be placed on legal functional equivalence, which refers to the equivalence of legal effect and function between the source and target texts. This principle ensures that translated legal instruments perform the same normative role and produce comparable legal outcomes in their respective jurisdictions. In the context of national governance, adhering to legal functional equivalence in translation reinforces the clarity, authority, and cross-border intelligibility of a state's legal framework, thereby facilitating international legal cooperation and strengthening the rule of law in global governance.

In the domestic academic sphere, early explorations into the principles of legal translation have been undertaken by several scholars, with Qiu (2000) and Du et al. (2004) serving as notable representatives. Qiu (2000) synthesized five core principles for translating legal documents: the use of solemn vocabulary, accuracy, conciseness, terminological consistency, and the employment of specialized terminology. Du et al. (2004) proposed three guiding principles for legal communication: (1) the Principle of Law-Governed Language, positing that language and law mutually constrain each other; (2) the Principle of Seeking Common Ground While Accepting Differences, which asserts that complete equivalence is neither necessary nor feasible in legal exchange, successful communication is achieved when any arising discrepancies are mutually intelligible to the parties involved; and (3) the Principle of Comparison and Compensation. This third principle suggests that gaps caused by differences in legal systems or concepts can be bridged by comparing them to analogous notions within the target legal system or other familiar foreign systems, supplemented by explanatory aids such as annotations, appositives, clarifications, or analogies.

In recent years, domestic scholarship has further refined these foundational principles, resulting in more specialized and concrete guidelines. Zhang (2009) contends that legal translation, distinct from other genres, is poorly served by traditional translation principles due to the inherent precision and concise formulation of legal language. He thus advocates for accuracy and rigor, clarity and conciseness, consistency, and stylistic appropriateness as the fundamental principles for legal translation. Xiong and Xiong (2011) argue that the distinctive principles of legal translation are primarily manifested in four aspects: professionalism, precision, accuracy, and equivalence. Meanwhile, from the perspective of standardizing the translation of Chinese legal terminology, Qu and Shi (2012) proposes that translators should adhere to principles such as "translating a term with a term", following established conventions, maintaining relative consistency in singular translations, and ensuring systematicity in the translation approach. From the perspective of national governance, the ongoing development and refinement of these legal translation principles reflect a strategic alignment with China's engagement in global legal discourse. The emphasis on accuracy, consistency, and functional equivalence directly supports the state's objectives of ensuring the authoritative and unambiguous cross-border communication of its legal norms. This scholarly endeavor contributes to building a transparent, predictable, and internationally intelligible legal framework, which is essential for facilitating international cooperation, attracting foreign investment, and upholding the rule of law within a globalized context.

Based on the principles proposed by scholars both domestically and internationally, the principles of legal translation can be summarized as follows:

(1) The Principle of Accuracy

Accuracy is not merely the essence but the very soul of legal language. When handling legal texts, translators must adhere unwaveringly to this primary principle. For instance, the term *reasonable person* should be translated as "行为能力人" (a person with legal capacity) rather than the literal "通情达理的人" (a person being understanding and reasonable). Similarly, *personal representative* in Hong Kong inheritance law must not be rendered as "个人代表" but correctly as "遗嘱执行人" (executor). This term encompasses *executor* (male), *executrix* (female), or an *estate administrator*, including *administrator* (male) and *administratrix* (female), all of whom are appointed by the court to manage a deceased person's estate.

In Chinese legislation, regulatory documents commonly employ stylistic titles such as "法", "(管理)条例", "(具体/暂行/管理)规定", "(实施/管理)办法", and "(实施/管理)细则". Among these, "法" is uniformly translated as Law in official English versions, as seen in The Contract Law of the People's Republic of China, a convention widely observed in practice. However, from a comparative legal perspective, Law in Anglo-American contexts is a broader concept, encompassing not only statutes enacted by legislative bodies but also jurisprudence, legal principles, case law, and customary law. The term Act typically denotes a statute passed by a legislature, while Code refers to a compiled and systematized body of law. Thus, the consistent translation of Chinese statutory titles as Law of the People's Republic of China reflects a distinctively Chinese approach to legal English.

Furthermore, in Western legal English, key terms are often expressed through synonymous coupling, the use of two or more near-synonyms, to avoid ambiguity arising from polysemy. This practice prevents parties from interpreting contractual clauses subjectively according to their own interests, thereby safeguarding the correct implementation of agreements (Yin 2014: 21). Accordingly, when translating Chinese legal texts, representing a single concept with two or more carefully selected near-synonyms can enhance terminological precision and uphold the authoritative, impartial nature of legal language.

In the context of national governance, such meticulous attention to terminological accuracy and functional equivalence is not merely a technical requirement but a strategic imperative. It ensures that translated legal instruments retain their normative force and interpretive consistency across jurisdictions, thereby reinforcing the state's capacity to engage in transparent and predictable international legal cooperation. This approach ultimately supports the global credibility of China's legal system and facilitates its integration into the world's rule-of-law framework.

(2) The Principle of Consistency

Consistency is paramount in legal language. The accuracy, solemnity, and authority of legal texts necessitate that the same legal term or expression, particularly key legal terminology, names of laws, and legal concepts, be rendered consistently across different legal documents or within the context of the same document. This principle prohibits the pursuit of lexical variety, vividness, or flexibility at the expense of uniformity, as inconsistency risks introducing ambiguity. Once a term is chosen, it must be used consistently throughout. In legal translation, if a term is correctly selected and applied, the translator should not hesitate to reuse it repeatedly. The fear of repetition for stylistic reasons inevitably sacrifices legal precision (Chen 2000: 214). Therefore, the Principle of Consistency and Identity mandates the use of the same legal term to represent the same legal concept throughout the translation process. A lack of consistency and identity in legal translation will undoubtedly confuse legal concepts and compel readers to speculate on distinctions between different terms, thereby impairing the precision and accuracy of legal communication. As Henry Weihofen (1961: 45) emphasized, "Exactness often demands repeating the same term to express the same idea. Where that is true, never be afraid of using the same word over and over again. Many more sentences are spoiled by trying to avoid repetition than by repetition".

For instance, the English language offers two terms for "未成年人": infant and minor. If infant is chosen in translating a document, minor should not be used interchangeably later. Similarly, the term minor offence can denote both a "misdemeanor/petty offense" and an "offense committed by a minor". Without strict terminological consistency, ambiguity is inevitable. Currently, several translations of Chinese legislative texts violate this principle. For example, in the English version of China's General Principles of Civil Law, the verb "规定" (to stipulate) has been variously translated as stipulate (Art. 72), specify (Art. 52), prescribe (Art. 64), require (Art. 65), and provide, among others. Likewise, in the Fishery Law of the People's Republic of China, the Chinese character "禁" is sometimes translated as shall be prohibited and other times as shall be forbidden (Dong 2011: 101).

In a word, adherence to the principle of consistency in legal translation is fundamental to constructing a coherent, stable, and authoritative national legal system. It ensures that laws are communicated without distortion across different languages and jurisdictions, thereby enhancing legal predictability, facilitating international compliance, and reinforcing the state's capacity for effective rule-of-law-based governance in a global context. Terminological consistency minimizes interpretative conflicts, supports the uniform application of laws, and strengthens the credibility of the legal system in transnational interactions.

(3) Principle of Professionalism and Standardization

Legal language differs significantly from everyday language, as well as from literary and business language. It is characterized by two primary features: lexical precision and syntactical rigor. Whether in legislative texts, regulations, contracts, or other legal documents, legal translation must reflect a high degree of integrity and logical stringency in its interplay between language and legal narrative. Throughout the translation of legal texts between English and Chinese, statements are typically rendered as complete declarative sentences, with elliptical sentences generally avoided. These sentences feature explicit referents, direct address, and rigorous logic, embodying the professional nature of law. For instance, the common Chinese term "醉驾" is often translated as drunk driving, a rendering that is ambiguous and potentially misleading. In Western legal statutes, more precise expressions are used, such as driving while intoxicated in the *U.S. Penal Code* or driving in an alcoholic state in the *Canadian Penal Code*. Similarly, the use of "shall" in Chinese legal translations is often excessive. U.S. legal texts frequently achieve greater precision without relying heavily on "shall", which inherently carries subjective intent and is semantically problematic when imposing obligations upon the state itself.

The professionalism and standardization of legal translation are also evident in the syntactical rigor of legal English. This requires strict adherence to the grammatical rules and sentence structures of the target language to accurately convey the discourse structure of the source text. English thinking is linear, emphasizing hypotaxis with clear subject-predicate-object distinctions, where tense, gender, number, and voice are grammatically interconnected. Chinese thinking, by contrast, is nonlinear, prioritizing parataxis and holistic textual cohesion, with less rigid grammatical marking of tense, gender, number, or voice, relying more on shared contextual understanding between writer and reader. In converting between Chinese and legal English sentences, the translator's primary task is to transcend the influence of both languages and restore the idiomatic expressions of the target legal language.

Example 1:

第一百零八条 债务应当清偿。暂时无力偿还的，经债权人同意或者人民法院裁决，可以由债务人分期偿还。有能力偿还拒不偿还的，由人民法院判决强制偿还。

Article 108 Debts shall be cleared. If a debtor is unable to repay his debt immediately, he may repay by installments with the consent of the creditor or a ruling by a people's court. If a debtor is capable of repaying his debt but refuses to do so, repayment shall be compelled by the decision of a people's court. (Translation 1)

Article 108 Debts shall be fully discharged. If a debtor is temporarily unable to repay a debt he may, with the consent of the creditor or as a result of a ruling by the People's Court, repay the debts in installments. If he is capable of repaying the debt but refuses to do so, the People's Court shall issue a verdict to enforce the repayment. (Translation 2)

Article 108 Debts must be repaid. When [the debtor] is temporarily unable to repay, he may repay by installments, with the creditor's consent or a ruling of a people's court. [A debtor] who is able to repay but obstinately refuses to do so may be compelled to repay by a ruling of a people's court. (Translation 3)

These three translations, cited from Zhou's (2008) analysis of syntactic严谨性与专业性 in legal English translation, demonstrate how different interpretations of the source text lead to varied syntactic arrangements, reflecting the critical importance of严谨的句式 in legal translation. The original Chinese article consists of three sentences. In translating the first sentence, Translations 1 and 2 use shall, which conveys greater authority than the must used in Translation 3; replacing must with shall would better reflect the imperative force typical of legal language. Zhou (2008: 13) notes that the term "可以" (may) in the second original sentence indicates legal possibility, which all three translations capture syntactically. Furthermore, "人民法院" (People's Court) is a proper noun unique to China and should be capitalized. The second and third Chinese sentences share a concession-hypothesis structure. Translations 1 and 2 restore this original syntax by using if-clauses. Translations 3, however, uses when to introduce the sentence. While when can imply conditionality, its tone is weaker than if. Using a declarative structure here compromises stringency and dilutes the original legal meaning; a clearer translation would directly employ if or where, as commonly used in legal English.

Standardization constitutes the most fundamental requirement for language. The principle of linguistic standardization in legal English translation mandates the use of officially recognized standardized or formal written language, while avoiding dialect and slang. Although numerous conventions govern the drafting and translation of legal documents (e.g., cautious use of passive voice, foreign words, abbreviations), one rule must be emphasized: the use of official terminology, particularly terms already defined in current law. For instance, target in legal contexts should be translated as "标的" (not "目标"), subject matter as "标的物" (not "主题"), and cause of action as "案由" (not "行为原因"). Standardized translation means that the choice of words, construction of sentences, and organization of the text must conform to the basic paradigms and established conventions of the legal profession (Chen 2007: 120). Legal language is distinctly different from non-legal (ordinary) language in terms of morphology, syntax, and discourse. A standardized legal text employs formal,书面化 vocabulary; its sentence structures are limited to complete declarative patterns; and its discourse is characterized by a highly compact, formulaic style. If a translation uses colloquial vocabulary, or employs other sentence types such as elliptical, exclamatory, or interrogative sentences indiscriminately, the entire text will lack structure, appear disorganized, and fail to meet the standardized requirements of legal genre conventions.

In a word, adherence to the Principles of Professionalism and Standardization in legal translation constitutes a strategic imperative for statecraft in an interconnected world. It is foundational to constructing a legal system that is not only credible and commanding of international respect but also functionally operative across linguistic and jurisdictional boundaries. By ensuring that the translated corpus of national laws communicates with unwavering precision, inherent authority, and rigorous formal integrity, the state safeguards the unambiguous transmission of its sovereign will. This linguistic-legal fidelity is a prerequisite for effective cross-jurisdictional understanding, reliable interpretation, and ultimately, the predictable enforcement of legal norms, that is, the key components for fostering international trade, investment, and judicial cooperation. Furthermore, this principled approach to translation directly enhances the state's institutional capacity to engage as an equal and sophisticated participant in global legal dialogue. It allows for the accurate projection of domestic legal concepts into international forums, enabling meaningful contributions to the development of transnational law and the upholding of the rule of law in global affairs. Consistent and standardized legal translation shapes and sustains a coherent external identity for the national legal order, projecting an image of stability, modernity, and reliability. This, in turn, strengthens the state's soft power and legitimacy on the world stage, facilitating smoother diplomatic negotiations, more effective multilateral engagement, and a more favorable environment for its national interests. Thus, professional and standardized legal translation transcends a mere technical exercise; it becomes an integral instrument of contemporary governance, synchronizing domestic legal sovereignty with the demands of global integration and reinforcing the state's authority in both domestic and international arenas.

(4) The Principle of Conciseness and Simplicity

Linguistic experts posit that the difficulty in comprehending legal English often stems from its deviation from conventional language usage. Reducing the reliance on specialized jargon and avoiding overly complex grammatical structures can significantly enhance the accessibility of legal texts. In the 1970s in the United States, the language used in bank promissory notes was notoriously characterized by excessive length, convoluted structures, and intricate meanings, rendering it incomprehensible not only to customers but also to many lawyers and judges. In response, New York State pioneered the enactment of the Plain Language Law in 1977, which took effect in 1978. President Jimmy Carter subsequently mandated that all federal agencies ensure every promulgated regulation be written in clear and understandable English, accessible to those obligated to comply. This initiative sparked the Plain Language Movement in the U.S., advocating for the use of intelligible language in documents and the elimination of unnecessary verbosity, thereby playing a constructive role in simplifying legal language.

Legal translation should adhere to the principle of conciseness and simplicity, that is, conveying the maximum amount of information with the fewest words possible. Some English translations of Chinese legislative texts suffer from verbosity, redundancy, and unintended ambiguity, which to some extent undermines the image of China as a nation governed by the rule of law.

Example 1:

女职工违反国家有关计划生育规定的，其劳动保护应当按照国家有关计划生育规定办理，不适用本规定。

Labor protection of those women staff and workers that run counter to state stipulations concerning family planning should be treated according to State stipulations concerning family planning. The Regulations are thus inapplicable.

Clearly, this translation is cumbersome and awkward, imposing unnecessary cognitive load on the reader. The original Chinese is a single coherent sentence (with "本规定" as the subject, "不适用" as the predicate, and the scenario as the object), whereas the translation splits it into two sentences, obscuring the logical relationship. A revised translation could be: "These Regulations do not apply to any violation of state family-planning measures by a woman employee whose labor protection is regulated by the said measures".

Therefore, upholding the principle of conciseness and simplicity in legal translation is integral to building a modern, transparent, and user-oriented legal system. Clear and succinct legal language enhances public comprehension and compliance with laws, strengthens the legitimacy of legal institutions, and fosters public trust. In international contexts, precise and streamlined legal translations prevent misinterpretation, facilitate smoother cross-jurisdictional cooperation, and project an image of a competent and accessible legal order. Thus, the pursuit of linguistic clarity is not merely a stylistic preference but a governance imperative that supports both domestic legal efficacy and global legal engagement.

2.2 Analysis of Translation Errors in Chinese Legislative Texts

Guided by the fundamental principles of legal translation outlined above, namely accuracy, consistency, professionalism, and conciseness, this section examines typical issues in the English translation of Chinese legislative texts from the perspective of national governance and international legal communication. The analysis is structured around three key dimensions: lexical, syntactic, and discursive. At the lexical level, the focus lies on the standardization and consistency of terminology. The syntactic level addresses the logical rigor and normative adequacy of sentence structures, while the discursive level considers the coherence of the overall text and its appropriateness to legal genre conventions. By systematically examining these translation errors, this section seeks to elucidate their linguistic features and institutional underpinnings, and proposes preliminary, actionable translation strategies. The aim is to enhance the quality of translating Chinese laws and regulations into English, thereby supporting the modernization of national governance and strengthening the capacity for engagement in rule-of-law exchanges internationally.

2.2.1 Terminology

It is precisely "the existence of a series of numerous legal terms that forms legal language" (Sun 2005: 79). Each legal language possesses its own set of specialized terminology. These terms solidify corresponding legal concepts, and a language's complete set of specialized legal terminology corresponds to its unique system of legal concepts. Research and interpretation of legal terminology are indispensable to various legal sub-disciplines such as jurisprudence, forensic linguistics, and legal translation studies. The paramount challenge in legal translation lies in how the translator interprets, conveys, and formulates legal terms across different legal systems and languages. The ultimate goal is to accurately transform terms rooted in the legal culture of the source language into target-language legal terms that convey equivalent concepts acceptable to readers within the target legal culture (Xiong 2011). Compared to other types of vocabulary, specialized legal terminology most distinctly reflects the characteristic features of a particular legal system or regime. One of the principal difficulties in translating laws and regulations stems from the non-correspondence of terms between legal systems. For instance, Chinese legal terms such as "差额选举" (competitive election), "等额选举" (single-candidate election), and "定罪量刑" (conviction and sentencing) lack direct, one-to-one equivalents in English legal terminology (Du et al. 2004). From the perspective of national governance, the precise and consistent translation of such terminology is not merely a linguistic exercise but a critical component of China's engagement with global legal discourse. It ensures the accurate international transmission of its legal norms, facilitates cross-jurisdictional understanding, and supports the country's role in shaping a transparent and predictable international legal environment.

(1) Legal Terms

The common errors in the English translation of Chinese legal terminology are multifaceted, primarily stemming from: misinterpretation by literal translation, where common terms are mistaken for specialized ones; insufficient understanding of the legal and linguistic cultures of both the source and target countries, leading to mismatched term usage; and violation of the conceptual specificity inherent in legal terms, resulting in inconsistent translations.

(a) Misinterpretation by Literal Translation (Using Common Terms as Specialized Ones)

Legal language is a highly specialized form of communication characterized by strict industry norms, precise semantics, meticulous wording, rigorous logic, and formal style, all reflecting the solemnity and seriousness of legal texts. In translating such texts, the choice of words must be guided by professional considerations, avoiding the pitfall of literal interpretation. For instance, terms like consideration, action, service, negligence, limitation, offer, and acceptance generally mean "考虑", "行动", "服务", "疏忽", "限制", "提供", and "接受" in everyday English. However, in legal English, these words function as technical terms with the specific meanings of "对价" (valuable consideration in a contract), "诉讼" (legal proceedings), "送达" (service of process), "过失" (legal negligence), "时效" (statute of limitations), "要约" (offer in contract law), and "承诺/承兑" (acceptance), respectively.

A prominent example can be found in the *Chinese-English Glossary of Terms in the Laws and Regulations of the People's Republic of China* (1998), jointly compiled by the Legislative Affairs Office of the State Council and its Department of Translation, Review and Foreign Affairs. This glossary translates "物证" as "material evidence". While this rendering appears plausible at first glance, with "物" seemingly corresponding to "material" and "证" to "evidence", it is, in fact, a significant mistranslation. According to *Black's Law Dictionary (seventh Edition),* "material evidence" is defined as "evidence having some logical connection with the consequential facts or the issues", meaning evidence, whether testimonial or physical, that is logically relevant and important to the facts or outcome of a case. The correct English legal terms for the Chinese concept "物证" (physical evidence) are "real evidence" or "physical evidence". Here, "material" does not mean "physical substance" but rather denotes that the evidence is "substantially relevant and important" to the case. Therefore, "material evidence" should be translated as "实质性证据" or "重要证据", not "物证".

Another example is the translation of the term "第三者" from marriage law as "the third party". This is incorrect. In legal English, "the third party" refers to "a person who is not a party to a legal proceeding or agreement but may be affected by it or have rights under it", often corresponding to the Chinese legal concept "第三人" in civil procedure. In contrast, "第三者" in the context of Chinese marriage law specifically refers to a person who interferes with and disrupts a lawful marriage, regardless of gender or marital status. A more accurate translation would be "the other man/woman" or "the outside party (in a marriage)".

(b) Insufficient Understanding of Legal and Linguistic Cultures, Leading to Misplaced Terminology

While translation can overcome linguistic barriers, the profound differences in legal and linguistic cultures across nations remain a major challenge in legal translation. For instance, in the UK and other common law jurisdictions, lawyers are categorized as solicitors and barristers. Hong Kong translates the former as "律师" and the latter as "大律师", which may imply the latter holds a higher status or possesses greater expertise. More descriptive translations, such as "事务律师" or "诉状律师" for solicitor and "出庭律师" or "辩护律师" for barrister, reflect their traditional functional division to some extent, though this distinction is not absolute.

According to Wikipedia,

> Solicitors are lawyers who traditionally deal with any legal matter including conducting proceedings in courts. In the United Kingdom, a few Australian states and the Republic of Ireland, the legal profession is split between solicitors and barristers, and a lawyer will usually only hold one title. However, in Canada, New Zealand and most Australian states, the legal profession is now for practical purposes "fused", allowing lawyers to hold the title of "barrister and solicitor" and practice as both. The distinction between barristers and solicitors is, however, retained. Some legal graduates will start off as one and then decide to become the other.
>
> A barrister is a member of one of the two classes of lawyer found in many common law jurisdictions with split legal professions. Barristers specialize in courtroom advocacy, drafting legal pleadings and giving expert legal opinions. They can be contrasted with solicitors , the other class of lawyer in split professions, who have more direct access with clients and who are in general office based. Barristers are rarely if ever hired by clients directly but instead are retained (or instructed) by solicitors to act on behalf of clients.

Some scholars have attempted an alternative approach, using phonetic transliteration combined with semantic meaning, rendering them as "沙律师" for solicitor and "巴律师" for barrister (Zhou and Hu 2007). However, perhaps because these terms sound like personal names, they have not gained widespread acceptance. It is also worth noting that while the term lawyer is frequently used in American English, it is rarely found on professional business cards in the U.S., where attorney-at-law is the standard designation. In contrast, many Chinese lawyers use lawyer on their cards, which may reflect a lack of familiarity with American legal culture.

Another example is the translation of the Chinese criminal charge "非法侵入住宅罪" (illegally intruding into another person's residence). Some translators have rendered it as "burglary" because the English term contains the element of "the breaking and entering of the dwelling house of another person". However, this is a misunderstanding. The crime of burglary in common law typically requires the intent to commit a felony (like theft) upon entry, resembling the Chinese crime of " 盗窃罪" (theft) under specific circumstances, not simply unlawful entry.

Furthermore, translating "宣判日" (the day a judgment is pronounced) as "Day of Judgment" or "Judgment Day" confuses the legal meaning of judgment with its cultural-religious connotations. In English, "Day of Judgment" or "Judgment Day" does not refer to a court session but to the theological concept of the end of the world or the final divine judgment, which is explained as "The Last Judgment, Final Judgment, Day of Judgment, Judgment Day, or Day of the Lord in Christian theology, is the final and eternal judgment by God of all nations. It will take place after the resurrection of the dead and the Second Coming of Christ" (Revelation 20:12–15). Thus, these terms are entirely unrelated to a court's scheduled judgment pronouncement. The correct translation for "宣判日" should be "date of the pronouncement of judgment" or "the date to pronounce a judgment" (Dong 2011: 234–235).

(c) Violation of the Conceptual Specificity of Legal Terms and Inconsistent Translation

Montesquieu observed in *The Spirit of Laws* that "the language of the law should evoke the same ideas in every person". This underscores the principle that legal concepts or terminology should ideally adhere to a one-term-one-meaning standard to avoid unnecessary ambiguity. Specifically, within a single normative document, the same concept should be expressed with the same term, different concepts should not be expressed with the same term, and different terms should not be used interchangeably (Zhu 2006: 269). This requirement stems from the inherent demand for accuracy and precision in legal language, especially in legislative texts. However, some translators use a single English legal term to represent different legal concepts from the source text. Taking the official translation of Article 28 of the *Criminal Procedure Law* as an example.

> 第二十八条　审判人员、检察人员、侦查人员有下列情形之一的，应当自行回避，当事人及其法定代理人也有权要求他们回避。
>
> Article 28 …a member of the judicial … personnel shall voluntarily withdraw, and the parties … shall have the right to demand his withdrawal…

"回避", a fundamental principle in procedural law, refers to a system where judicial or prosecutorial personnel must recuse themselves from a case under specified circumstances to ensure fair adjudication. This term appears 12 times in the *Criminal Procedure Law*, consistently translated as "withdraw" or "withdrawal" in the official English version. However, the same term "withdraw" is also used five times to translate "撤回" (withdraw, as in withdrawing a complaint or prosecution), as seen in phrases like "the complaint has been withdrawn", and once to translate "退庭" (withdraw from a court session), as in Article 171: "…if he withdraws from a court session without permission of the court, the case may be considered withdrawn by him".

Using "withdraw" to express three distinct legal concepts",回避" (recusal), "退庭" (withdrawal from court), and "撤回" (withdrawal of a legal action), within the same legal text can create confusion and hinder accurate comprehension. Furthermore, the suitability of "withdraw" for "回避" is questionable. According to *Black's Law Dictionary,* "withdraw" as a legal term includes the following definitions: "vt. To refrain from prosecuting or proceeding with (an action) [e.g., withdraw a charge; vt. To remove a juror [e.g., for cause]; vi. (Of a lawyer) to terminate one's representation of a client before a matter is complete".

The first definition corresponds to "撤回" (withdrawal of an action). The second definition relates to "回避", but specifically for jurors, not judges or prosecutors. And the third definition refers to a lawyer's withdrawal from representation, not "撤诉" (withdrawal of a lawsuit). In fact, the appropriate English legal term for the Chinese concept of "回避" (judicial/prosecutorial recusal) is "disqualification", defined as "the act of abstaining from participation in an official action such as a legal proceeding due to a conflict of interest of the presiding court official or administrative officer". This aligns closely with the Chinese concept. Therefore, "回避" should be translated as "disqualification" or "disqualify themselves".

Conversely, it is also common in the translation of Chinese laws and regulations to use multiple different English legal terms to represent the same source-language legal concept. For instance, in the English translation of the *Copyright Law of the People's Republic of China*, the infringement of copyright is translated sometimes as "prejudice" (e.g., Article 12) and other times as "infringe" (e.g., Article 48). An analysis of dictionary definitions and usage reveals a distinction: "infringe" typically emphasizes the violation of a right, especially an intellectual property right, as illustrated by examples like "infringe a rule (an oath, copyright, a patent)" (from the *Oxford Advanced Learner's Dictionary*). On the other hand, "prejudice" has a broader sense, referring to harm or detriment to a person, property, or any existing right or claim. Therefore, "infringe" is more precise and targeted for copyright infringement, while "prejudice" is a more general term. This inconsistency in translation violates the principle of terminological specificity and uniformity, potentially leading to varied interpretations of the legal standard being conveyed.

(d) Strategies for Translating Legal Terminology

The translation of legal terminology is not merely a linguistic or technical exercise, but a critical element of legal system communication and international rule-making. It serves as the foundational pillar for accurately transmitting a nation's legal will, establishing clear international legal expectations, and enhancing the transparency and predictability of its legal environment. Thus, developing and adhering to systematic translation strategies is imperative for aligning China's legal discourse with global governance frameworks, facilitating transnational legal cooperation, and reinforcing the international credibility of its socialist rule of law.

The translation of legal language is, to a large extent, the translation of its terminology (Xiong 2011: 176). When translating legal terms, the first step is to meticulously study the precise meaning of the source-language legal term. After comparing the involved legal systems, the translator must identify a term in the target-language legal system that conveys an equivalent content, a true counterpart to the source term. If, due to irreconcilable differences between legal systems, no acceptable equivalent term can be found, the following strategies may be employed: using the original or a transcribed version of the source term (e.g., transliteration); employing paraphrase (explaining the concept descriptively); creating a neologism, coining a new term in the target language that does not form part of its existing legal vocabulary, supplemented by an explanatory footnote if necessary.

Owing to differences in legal systems and historical-cultural contexts, many Chinese legal terms and norms have no direct equivalents in English, meaning achieving perfect translational equivalence is often impossible. For example, as previously mentioned, the term "第三者" could be rendered into English as "lover", "mistress", "paramour", or "extramarital partner". However, these English terms largely lack the strong pejorative connotation inherent in the Chinese context, where the term often evokes associations with illicit or immoral relationships. Relatedly, the term "插足" (literally, "inserting a foot") implies not merely "participating" but actively intruding upon and usurping another's marital relationship. Common English phrases like "put one's foot in", "participate", or "take part in" fail to capture this nuance. In such cases, a feasible approach is to accurately grasp the term's connotative meaning and then imbue the translation with appropriate semantic shading. Since the consequence of "第三者插足" is the disruption and destruction of a lawful marriage, translating "插足" as "step in" is considered more appropriate, as "step in" carries the dual senses of "participate" (加入) and "intervene" (干扰), while also aptly conveying the physical imagery of the action.

On the other hand, when translating legal terminology, it is crucial to consider the specific contextual environment of the term to accurately understand its meaning within the source text and to translate it faithfully and pragmatically. One must avoid both oversimplification and excessive generalization, as neither approach reveals the essential characteristics of the concept. Legal terms form the core of a legal system, gradually crystallizing and becoming fixed through prolonged use. A term may represent a legal concept (e.g., "物" [object], "法人" [legal person], "无行为能力人" [person without capacity] in civil law), a legal doctrine (e.g., "consideration", "estoppel"), or even link to specific historical contexts (e.g., "sealed contract"). Its meaning cannot be understood solely from the constituent words. Since the nineteenth century, rapid advancements in natural and social sciences have led to the emergence of new products, technologies, and ideas. These developments are inevitably reflected in the legal superstructure, resulting in the continuous creation of new legal terms. Examples include "computer crime", "smuggling of drugs", "securities law", as well as uniquely Chinese terms such as "劳动教养 (reeducation-through-labor)", "承包经营责任制 (contract and responsibility system)", and "人民调解 (people's mediation)" (Xiao 2001).

(2) Non-Terminological Vocabulary

In literary translation, different words are often used to express the same meaning to achieve aesthetic appeal and avoid monotony. However, in legal documents, accuracy is paramount; using synonyms to convey the same meaning is neither necessary nor advisable. Unfortunately, violations of this principle of terminological consistency are common in the English translation of Chinese legislative texts. Take the English translation of the Special Maritime Procedure Law of the People's Republic of China (2003) as an example:

> 第二节 船舶的扣押与拍卖
> 第三节 船载货物的扣押与拍卖
> Section 2 Arrest and Auction of Ships
> Section 3 Attachment and Auction of Cargo Carried by Ships

Both Chinese sections use "扣押", yet the translation employs two different English words, clearly violating the principle of consistency. Which term, "arrest" or "attachment", is more appropriate? According to the *Longman Dictionary of Contemporary English (5th Edition, 2009)*, "arrest" refers to "when the police take someone away and guard them because they may have done something illegal". "Attachment" means "a situation in which part of the money someone earns or money that is owed to them is taken by a court of law and used to pay their debts". The *Oxford Advanced Learner's Dictionary of Current English (5th Edition, 2007)* offers a slightly broader definition of "attachment": "seizing sb's property, etc. with legal authority".

Thus, "arrest" primarily refers to the detention of persons, while "attachment" pertains to the seizure of property by legal authority. Therefore, for consistency and accuracy, Section 2 should also be translated as "Attachment and Auction of Ships" (Liu 2009).

Furthermore, Chinese legislative texts seldom utilize archaic English words such as therein, thereof, thereto, herewith, whereas, and thence. While these archaic terms are no longer widely used in modern English and are gradually fading from common usage, they remain prevalent in legal English. As David and Derek (1969: 222) observed, "It is especially noticeable that any passage of legal English is usually well studded with archaic words and phrases of a kind that could be used by no one else but lawyers". Similarly, the use of Latin terms, a hallmark of legal English, is almost entirely absent in these translations. From the perspective of national governance, this oversight may limit the translations' formal register, international comprehensibility within legal circles, and their ability to seamlessly integrate into established global legal discourse, potentially affecting the perceived sophistication and interoperability of China's legal texts in transnational contexts.

2.2.2 *Stylistic and Syntactic Structure*

The translation of legal texts is not merely a linguistic conversion but a normative representation of a nation's will, governance philosophy, and legal system within a transnational context. Legal English is characterized by its structural rigor, lexical precision, and logical stringency, with a stylistic formality and conservatism surpassing that of other registers, a feature inherent to law's pursuit of certainty, authority, and universal binding force. Therefore, accurately capturing and reconstructing these stylistic and syntactic features in legal translation is of strategic importance for ensuring the accurate transmission, authoritative interpretation, and effective application of China's laws in international exchanges. It constitutes a key component in enhancing the country's image as a rule-of-law state and its capacity to participate in global legal governance.

(1) The Normative Use of Modal Verbs and the Transmission of Legal Authority

In legal English, "shall" is a high-frequency modal verb carrying a distinct mandatory legal connotation, stronger in tone than "will" or "should", and is commonly used to prescribe obligations or indicate compulsory requirements. However, in some Chinese legislative translations, the use of "shall" has been generalized or misapplied, at times undermining legal precision. For example, in the definition of creditor-debtor relationships in the *General Principles of Civil Law*:

> 债是按照合同的约定或者法律的规定，在当事人之间产生的特定的权利义务关系。享有权利的人为债权人，负有义务的人为债务人。

> A debt represents a special relationship of rights and obligations established between the parties concerned, either according to the agreed terms of a contractor legal provisions. The party entitled to the rights shall be the creditor, and the party assuming the obligations shall be the debtor.

Here, "shall be" is used to describe a static legal identity rather than to impose a future obligation. Changing it to the simple present tense "is" more accurately reflects the objectivity and normality of legal definitions, aligning with the stylistic convention of "law stating facts" (The party entitled to the rights is the creditor, and the party assuming the obligations is the debtor). Such refinement helps convey the determinacy of Chinese legal concepts in international legal instruments, avoids interpretive ambiguities arising from modal verb misuse, and thereby reinforces the authority of the legal text.

(2) The Localized Tendency in Syntactic Structures and Alignment with International Norms

Currently, the English translations of most Chinese legislative texts remain heavily influenced by Chinese thinking and source-text structures in terms of syntax, exhibiting a tendency toward "plain English" and failing to fully embody the syntactical rigor characteristic of legal English. For instance, the pattern "Whoever does… shall be…". is frequently used to define conduct and its legal consequences. While grammatically correct, this is not the most typical or idiomatic formulation in the legislative texts of English-speaking jurisdictions. Such structures can appear somewhat rigid and literal.

More critically, the use of highly formulaic syntactic structures common in legal English, such as "subject to…" (in compliance with), "without prejudice to…" (without affecting), "notwithstanding…" (despite), and "save…" (except), remains notably infrequent in Chinese legal translations. These constructions are essential tools for building complex logical relationships within legal texts and ensuring airtight formulation. Their underuse may result in translations that lag behind mainstream international legal style in terms of logical stringency and professional standardization, potentially hindering accurate comprehension and application of the nuanced meanings of Chinese legal provisions by international professionals.

(3) Passive Voice and the Expression of Objectivity

The use of the passive voice is significantly more prevalent in legal English than in general registers, stemming from law's emphasis on the act itself, the responsible entity, and objective outcomes rather than the active agent. While Chinese legal translations do employ the passive voice to some extent, its application requires further systematization and standardization to strengthen the objective, neutral, and impersonal quality of the text, an inherent stylistic requirement of law as a social instrument.

In conclusion, the mastery of stylistic formality, syntactic rigor, and modal verb precision in legal translation is far from a mere linguistic technique; it is a critical dimension of modernizing national governance capacity. By systematically refining the stylistic and syntactic structures of legal English in translations, enabling them to deeply integrate with the international legal discourse at the linguistic level, the clarity, credibility, and operability of China's laws and regulations in international dissemination can be significantly enhanced. This constitutes not only a technical improvement but also a strategic investment, facilitating China's ability to more effectively set agendas, participate in rule-making, and safeguard its rights and interests within the global legal governance landscape. Ultimately, it serves the overarching goal of modernizing the national governance system and governance capacity.

2.2.3 Discourse and Textual Cohesion

The effective conversion of textual forms in Chinese-English legal translation, achieving a precise and effective transition from "translating law linguistically" to "translating the law itself", has long been a subject of inquiry for legal translators, given the differences between the two language systems, stylistic conventions, and syntactic structures. The cohesive patterns inherent to any legal language reflect the legal origins, legal culture, legal system, and legal思维方式 embedded within that language (Xiong 2011: 242). Although the cohesive devices in English and Chinese legislative languages share common roots in general discourse patterns, each is constrained by its own conventional linguistic structures. As Halliday and Hasan (1976) categorize, cohesion can be grammatical (reference, substitution, ellipsis, conjunction), lexical (reiteration, collocation), or logical (conjunction). English discourse coherence is typically achieved through explicit grammatical and logical cohesion, where all necessary elements are overtly present. In contrast, Chinese discourse tends toward lexical cohesion, emphasizing meaning through word collocation, and often exhibits implicitness, allowing certain elements to be omitted when the logical context is clear. This reflects the paratactic nature of Chinese, where inter-sentential relations are primarily built on internal logic, compared to the hypotactic nature of English, which relies more on connective words for sentence linkage (Wang 2003: 108).

Regarding grammatical reference, the English translation of the Preamble to the Constitution of the People's Republic of China demonstrates a conscious adaptation to the target language's cohesive norms.

Example 1:

教育、科学、文化等事业有了很大的发展，社会主义思想教育取得了明显的成效。

Significant advances have been made in educational, scientific and cultural undertakings, while education in socialist ideology has produced noteworthy results.

In terms of lexical cohesion, reiteration is a common strategy.

Example 2:

经济建设取得了重大的成就，独立的、比较完整的社会主义工业体系已经基本形成，农业生产显著提高。

Major successes have been achieved in economic development. An independent and relatively comprehensive socialist system of industry has basically been established. There has been a marked increase in agricultural production.

Furthermore, textual coherence involves not only linguistic form and propositional content but also the expression and comprehension of pragmatic meaning.

Example 3:

1840年以后，封建的中国逐渐变成半殖民地、半封建的国家。

After 1840, feudal China was gradually turned into a semi-colonial and semi-feudal country.

The use of the passive voice here maintains topic consistency and adjusts the positions of given and new information, achieving structural cohesion and semantic coherence with the broader context. This precisely conveys the sense of "being forced into" a particular condition, effectively utilizing the passive voice for textual cohesion while also reflecting the "political" dimensions of translation (Fan 2011).

Compared to the constitutional translation, the textual cohesion in translations of other legislative texts warrants closer scrutiny. Taking the English version of the *Special Maritime Procedure Law of the People's Republic of China (2003)* as an example:

Example 4:

海事法院在发布或者解除扣押船舶命令的同时，可以向有关部门发出协助执行通知书，通知书应当载明协助执行的范围和内容，有关部门有义务协助执行。海事法院认为必要，可以直接派员登轮监护。

While the maritime court issues an order for arresting of a ship, it may send a notice to relevant departments for assistance in execution of the order. In the notice shall be stated the scope and specific tasks of the assistance in execution of the order, and the relevant departments have the obligation to assist in the execution. When the maritime court deems it necessary, it may directly send officers to go aboard for purposes of supervision.

Chinese legislative texts frequently employ noun repetition. To avoid unnecessary redundancy in translation, reference devices such as pronouns are often used to replace recurring nouns, thereby achieving conciseness. However, in this translation, three instances of "it" are used to refer to different antecedents. Readers may need to read carefully to discern that the first and third "it" refer to "the maritime court", while the second "it" anticipates the following action ("directly send officers…"). Translating one or two of these reference points explicitly would enhance clarity. Therefore, a revised translation is suggested: "While issuing an order for arresting a ship, the maritime court may send a notice to relevant departments for assistance in execution of the order. In the notice shall be stated the scope and specific tasks of the assistance in execution, and the relevant departments have the obligation to assist. When deeming it necessary, the maritime court may directly send officers aboard for supervision".

Thus, mastering the nuances of textual cohesion in legal translation is vital for constructing a coherent and internationally intelligible body of legal texts. It ensures that the translated legislation is not only linguistically accurate but also logically consistent and pragmatically clear, thereby supporting effective cross-border legal communication, adjudication, and enforcement. This level of textual refinement strengthens the global credibility and functional utility of China's legal exports, facilitating its active and authoritative participation in the international legal order.

2.3 Conclusion

Fundamentally, legal translation constitutes a dual process of legal and linguistic transmutation. It operates not merely at the linguistic intersection of author, audience, and translator, but within a complex matrix of cross-systemic legal norms, multicultural contexts, divergent jurisprudential concepts, and intricate legal practices. Its paramount significance lies not only in the transposition of legal texts or discourse across languages but, more critically, in the translator's role as a mediator who navigates the inherent lack of perfect equivalence between legal systems. By consciously bridging communicative gaps born of deep-seated legal-cultural disparities, the translator facilitates the core objective of cross-jurisdictional legal communication (Zhu 2011).

From the perspective of national governance, this mediatory function transcends mere technical proficiency. It is a strategic instrument for projecting a nation's legal sovereignty, articulating its governance paradigms, and engaging constructively with the global legal order. High-quality legal translation ensures that a country's laws are accessible, interpretable, and operable in international forums, thereby enhancing the predictability and stability necessary for global economic integration and diplomatic cooperation.

Since the inception of reform and opening-up, propelled by economic globalization and the advancement of the rule of law, China has made notable strides in legal translation, exemplified by the systematic translation of numerous legislative texts into English. Nonetheless, significant challenges persist. On a macro level, the field still suffers from a paucity of systemic theoretical research and a underdeveloped sense of disciplinary autonomy. Legal translation scholarship often remains fragmented, lacking a cohesive framework that integrates jurisprudence, linguistics, and translation studies within the specific context of China's socialist legal system.

The paramount imperative for legal translation is to convey the original intent of the legal text with utmost clarity within the most concise formulation possible. Accuracy is the bedrock of legal translation, while distortion represents its most grave failing. Among the multitude of factors influencing legal translation, several are pivotal for establishing sound principles, methodologies, and evaluative criteria: the specific communicative purpose of the text (e.g., informative, normative, or enforceive); the distinctive stylistic and pragmatic features of legal language, which demand precision, formality, and consistency; and the profound legal-cultural differences embedded within disparate legal systems and institutions (Dong 2011).

Addressing these challenges is not an academic exercise in isolation. It is a governance imperative. By fostering rigorous, theoretically-grounded, and systematically applied legal translation practices, China can more effectively safeguard its legal interests in international affairs, contribute authoritatively to the development of transnational legal norms, and present a coherent and credible image of its evolving legal system to the world. Thus, advancing the quality and standardization of legal translation is integral to modernizing the national governance system and enhancing the country's capacity for global legal engagement.

References

Chen, Z. 2000. *Essays on legal translation*. Beijing: China Legal System Publishing House.

Chen, J. 2007. *Explorations in the Translation of Legal Texts*. Zhejiang: Zhejiang University Press.

Crystal, D., and D. Davy. 1969. *Investigating English style*. Longman Group UK Limited.

Dong, X. 2011. *Legal text translation*. Beijing: University of International Business and Economics Press.

Dong, X. 2016. *Research on the standardization of legislative language in China*. Beijing: Beijing Jiaotong University Press.

Du, J., et al. 2004. Problems and solutions in the English translation of Chinese laws and regulations. *Chinese Translators Journal* 3.

Fan, J. 2011. Strategies for the English translation of the preamble to China's Constitution. *Chinese Science & Technology Translators Journal* 2.

Gadamer, H. G. (ed.), Barden, G. & J. Cumming (trans.). 1975. Truth and method. London: Sheed and Ward.

Halliday, M. A. K., and R. Hasan. 1976. *Cohesion in English*. London: Longman Group Limited.

Liu, C. 1991. *Ten lectures on literary translation*. Beijing: China Translation & Publishing Corporation.

Liu, N. 2009. Analysis of issues in the Chinese-English translation of maritime laws and regulations. *Foreign Languages and Their Teaching* 10.

Qiu, G. 2000. On some principles of legal text translation. *Chinese Science & Technology Translators Journal* 2.

Qu, W., and W. Shi. 2012. *A course in legal English reading and translation*. Shanghai: Shanghai People's Publishing House.

Sun, X. 2005. *The rule of legal professionals*. Beijing: China University of Political Science and Law Press.

Wang, W. 2003. *A contrastive study of English and Chinese languages and translation*. Beijing: Peking University Press.

Weihofen, Henry. 1961. *Legal writing style*. St. Paul: West Publishing Company.

Wu, B. 2011, February 3. The significance and experience of forming the socialist legal system with Chinese characteristics. Central People's Government of the People's Republic of China Website. http://www.gov.cn/ldhd/2011-02/03/content_1798248.htm

Xiao, Y. 2001. Characteristics, etymology and translation of English-Chinese legal terminology. *Chinese Translators Journal* 3.

Xiong, D. 2011. *A comparative and translational study of contemporary English and Chinese legal language*. Changsha: Hunan People's Publishing House.

Xiong, D., and S. Xiong. 2011. Special principles of legal translation. *Journal of Southwest University of Political Science & Law* 2.

Yin, Q. 2014. *A study on the translation of English legal texts*. Master's thesis, Xinyang Normal University.

Zhang, F. 2009. An exploration of the basic principles of legal text translation. *Chinese Translators Journal* 5.

Zhou, H. 2008. *A jurisprudential study of the word 'yingdang' (shall)*. Jinan: Shandong People's Publishing House.

Zhou, Z., and Y. Hu. 2007. A study on countermeasures for mistranslation of legal English terminology. *Journal of Wuhan Maritime Vocational and Technical College* 1.

Zhu, L. 2006. *Legislative science*. Beijing: China Renmin University Press.

Zhu, Y. 2011. Legal translation research: Content and approaches. *Hebei Academic Journal* 3.

Chapter 3
Translation of Titles of Laws and Regulations

Abstract This chapter examines how the seemingly limited task of title translation reflects broader challenges in China's engagement with global legal discourse, exploring how systematic approaches to this foundational element can strengthen the country's capacity for transparent international legal communication and participation in global governance frameworks.

Keywords Title translation · Issue identified · Translation strategies · Standardization

Legal translation operates at the intersection of legal sovereignty and international discourse. At its core, it is a dual process of simultaneous legal and linguistic transformation that extends far beyond mere textual conversion. This complex endeavor involves not only the linguistic competence of authors, readers, and translators, but also navigates between divergent legal systems, cultural frameworks, jurisprudential concepts, and practical legal applications, all characterized by inherent uncertainties. The true significance of legal translation lies not merely in linguistic transposition, but in the translator's critical role as an intercultural mediator who must bridge fundamental legal-cultural divides, particularly in contexts where perfect equivalence proves elusive (Dong 2014: 90).

The translation of legislative titles presents a particularly revealing case study within this broader framework. While superficially involving nominal conversion between languages, this process fundamentally constitutes an act of cultural-legal mediation. Though representing only a fractional component of comprehensive legal translation, the challenges in achieving consistency and standardization in title translation illuminate the vast complexity, systematic difficulties, and cultural-political dimensions inherent in rendering China's legal framework accessible to international audiences.

Achieving uniformity in this domain requires a multi-layered governance approach: domestic legislative titles must exhibit internal consistency; translation practices must adhere to established protocols; and sustainable standardization necessitates consensus-building between academic institutions and governmental

X. Dong, Y. Zhang, *On Translation of Laws and Regulations in China*,
https://doi.org/10.1007/978-981-95-9406-1_3

bodies. In this context, standardized title translation serves as more than a technical exercise, functioning as an instrument of legal diplomacy that enhances the international credibility and operational effectiveness of China's legal system.

3.1 A Comparative Study of Titles of Chinese and Western Laws and Regulations

"A title serves as a highly condensed summary of a law's content and purpose, characterized primarily by conciseness, prominence, and clarity" (Zhang 2017: 28). Translating the titles of Chinese laws and regulations into English thus transcends simple linguistic conversion between Chinese and English; it necessitates careful consideration of the underlying cultures, legal systems, and reader expectations embedded in both languages. Comparative study forms the essential foundation for effective translation practice. By systematically comparing Chinese and Western legislative titles, we can gain deeper insight into the differences in drafting normative texts under distinct legal traditions, clarify the specific characteristics of Western legislative nomenclature, and establish crucial direction and guiding principles for producing titles that align more naturally with the reading habits of Anglophone audiences. As Zhang (2009: 51) emphasizes, "Only by prioritizing the study of the linguistic features of both English and Chinese, the characteristics of Chinese and American legal cultures, and by achieving an accurate grasp of relevant legal knowledge, can one conduct legal English translation accurately and effectively".

Furthermore, this comparative exercise is not merely academic. It represents a strategic step in refining the external presentation of China's legal system. A well-translated legislative title acts as the first point of contact and a conceptual gateway for international stakeholders, such as foreign governments, investors, legal practitioners, and scholars. Titles that are linguistically precise, culturally resonant, and stylistically familiar within the target legal discourse enhance the accessibility, credibility, and authoritative perception of Chinese law abroad. Therefore, a nuanced understanding of Western titling conventions, achieved through comparative analysis, directly supports the broader governance objective of facilitating China's transparent and effective participation in the global legal order, ensuring its laws are not only translated but are also comprehensible and actionable within international frameworks.

3.1.1 Titles of Chinese Laws and Regulations

The title of a Chinese law or regulation serves as a concentrated summation of its substantive content, systematically incorporating three constitutive elements: the scope of application, typically indicated by jurisdictional designations such as "the

People's Republic of China" or a specific province or municipality; the subject matter or content element, which identifies the core object of legal regulation, for instance "teachers" in The Teachers Law of the People's Republic of China; and the indicative or format term that denotes the document's legal force and hierarchical standing within China's legislative system, such as "Law" (法), "Administrative Regulation" (行政法规), "Local Regulation" (地方性法规), "Autonomous Regulation" (自治条例), or "Specific Regulation" (单行条例). Consequently, a structured analysis of these components, namely, scope, subject, and indicative term, provides immediate insight into a statute's jurisdictional reach, normative purpose, and authoritative rank, forming the essential foundation for its accurate translation into the distinct syntactic and terminological conventions of English legislative discourse.

The sources of law in contemporary China are complex, encompassing the Constitution, statutes, administrative regulations, international treaties, local regulations, autonomous regulations, specific regulations, and judicial interpretations. Firstly, the *Constitution* serves as the fundamental law of the state, holding the highest legal authority and symbolic power. It is enacted and amended by the National People's Congress (NPC), the supreme state authority. Secondly, statutes can be understood broadly or narrowly. In a broad sense, the term refers to all normative documents, while in a narrow sense, it denotes normative documents enacted by the NPC and its Standing Committee. These are divided into basic laws, which regulate criminal, civil, state institutional, and other fundamental matters and are enacted and amended by the NPC, and non-basic laws, which include normative resolutions, decisions, provisions, and measures adopted by the NPC and its Standing Committee. Thirdly, administrative regulations are normative documents enacted by the State Council, the highest administrative organ. Their legal status and effect are subordinate only to the Constitution and statutes. They are typically titled as "regulations", "provisions", "measures", or "implementation rules", and occasionally as "decisions" or "orders" (Zhang 2018: 34). Fourthly, local regulations are enacted by the people's congresses and their standing committees of provinces, autonomous regions, municipalities directly under the central government, and cities where provincial governments are located or cities approved by the State Council. They commonly adopt titles such as "regulations", "rules", "provisions", and "measures" (Qin and Dong 2013: 41). Fifthly, judicial interpretations include legal interpretations issued by the NPC and judicial interpretations issued by the Supreme People's Court.

(1) Laws and Regulations

The titles of laws in China uniformly follow the structure of "中华人民共和国" (the People's Republic of China) followed by the specific name of the law, forming a standardized pattern as "《中华人民共和国XX法》", for example, 《中华人民共和国国家情报法》 (*National Intelligence Law of the People's Republic of China*), 《中华人民共和国反恐怖主义法》 (*Counter-Terrorism Law of the People's Republic of China*), and 《中华人民共和国国防教育法》 (*National Defense Education Law of the People's Republic of China*).

Non-basic laws include various forms such as decisions, notices, replies, and measures, as exemplified by 《全国人民代表大会常务委员会关于中国海警局行使海上维权执法职权的决定》 (*Decision of the Standing Committee of the National People's Congress on Authorizing the China Coast Guard to Exercise Law Enforcement Powers in Maritime Rights Protection*), 《全国人大常委会办公厅印发<关于争议较大的重要立法事项引入第三方评估的工作规范>的通知》 (*Notice of the General Office of the Standing Committee of the National People's Congress on Issuing the "Work Standards for Introducing Third-Party Assessment of Important Legislative Matters with Significant Controversy"*), 《全国人大常委会法制工作委员会关于对被告人在罚金刑执行完毕前又犯新罪的罚金应否与未执行完毕的罚金适用数罪并罚问题的答复意见》 (*Reply of the Legislative Affairs Commission of the Standing Committee of the National People's Congress on Whether Fines for New Crimes Committed by a Defendant Before Completion of Fine Enforcement Should Be Combined with Unpaid Fines Under the Principle of Cumulative Punishment for Multiple Crimes*), and 《中华人民共和国香港特别行政区选举第十三届全国人民代表大会代表的办法》 (*Measures for the Election of Deputies to the Thirteenth National People's Congress by the Hong Kong Special Administrative Region of the People's Republic of China*).

(2) Local Regulations and Rules

Local regulations in China commonly adopt four drafting formats: "条例" (Regulations), "规定" (Provisions), "实施办法" (Implementation Measures), and"规则"(Rules). Their respective title structures are as follows: 《XX (Region) XX (Subject Matter) Regulations》, 《XX (Authority) Provisions on XX (Matter)》, 《XX (Region) Implementation Measures of the <XX Law>》, and 《XX (Region or Authority) Rules on XX (Matter)》 (Tian 2004: 191–193).

Regulations are legal documents formulated and approved by local legislative authorities to govern specific matters, such as the *Regulations of Jiangsu Province on Air Pollution Prevention and Control*. Measures refer to regulatory instruments that either govern specific matters administratively or provide detailed, operable provisions for implementing higher-level laws. An example is the *Measures of Jiangsu Province for Air Particulate Matter Pollution Prevention and Control*. Provisions generally address specific aspects of a matter with partial or specialized determinations, such as the P*rovisions of Jiangsu Province on High-Rise Building Fire Safety*. Rules or detailed implementation rules establish systems or charters for collective adherence, as seen in the *Work Rules of People's Government of Jiangsu Province*. Decisions made by local people's congress standing committees are also included, such as the *Decision of the Standing Committee of the Jiangsu Provincial People's Congress on Prohibiting the Use of Unauthorized Drugs in Livestock and Poultry Production*. Additionally, normative documents issued by local governments include opinions, public notices, announcements, notifications, guidance opinions, implementation plans, and work standards.

(3) Judicial Interpretations

Judicial interpretations refer to normative documents formulated by the Supreme People's Court and the Supreme People's Procuratorate in accordance with the law, concerning the specific application of laws. Judicial interpretations are primarily categorized into abstract interpretative documents and specific interpretations provided to lower judicial organs on matters of legal application. For example, the *Interpretation of the Supreme People's Court on Several Issues Concerning the Application of the Insurance Law of the People's Republic of China*.

In general, the diversity of legal sources in China has led to a wide variety of standardized terms and structural formats in laws and regulations. These include: "法" (Law); "条例" (Regulation), which may be "暂行条例" (Provisional Regulation), "管理条例" (Administrative Regulation), or "工作条例" (Work Regulation); "办法" (Measure), such as "管理办法" (Administrative Measure), "试行办法" (Trial Measure), "实施办法" (Implementation Measure), or "暂行办法" (Provisional Measure); "规定" (Provision), including "暂行规定" (Provisional Provision), "管理规定" (Administrative Provision), or "若干规定" (Several Provisions); "决定" (Decision); "决议" (Resolution); "通知" (Notice), such as "通知" (Notice) or "补充通知" (Supplementary Notice); "意见" (Opinion), including "实施意见" (Implementation Opinion), "指导意见" (Guiding Opinion), or "若干意见" (Several Opinions); "公告" (Announcement); "则" (Rule), which encompasses "规则" (Rule), "工作规则" (Work Rule), "实施细则" (Implementation Rule), or "通则" (General Rule); "规范" (Standard); and "函件类" (Correspondence Documents), such as "批复" (Official Reply), "函" (Letter), or "复函" (Reply Letter) (Chen and Qiang 2012: 97).

3.1.2 Titles of Laws and Regulations in Common Law Systems

In common law jurisdictions such as the United Kingdom and the United States, legislative titles reflect distinct historical traditions and drafting conventions, characterized by relatively flexible grammatical structures yet precise hierarchical indications. The *Compact English-Chinese Dictionary of Anglo-American Law* (Xie 2013: 1345) defines the seventh meaning of "title" as: "the heading, subject, or name of a statute, legal document, book, article, etc.". The *Black's Law Dictionary (Ninth Edition)* (Garner 2009: 1623) offers three variations under the third definition of "title", detailing different forms and functions of titles within legal contexts: *general title*. A statute's name that broadly and comprehensively identifies the subject matter addressed by the legislature. Cf. restrictive title; *long title*. The full, formal title of a statute, usu. Containing a brief statement of legislative purpose; *short title*. The abbreviated title of a statute by which it is popularly known; a statutory nickname.

According to the annotations in *Black's Law Dictionary*, a title refers to the name of a statute or other legal document. Unlike the naming conventions for Chinese laws, legislative titles in common law systems are divided into three types: the general title, the long title, and the short title. The general title refers to the official name of a statute, the long title provides a detailed description of the legislative purpose and scope, and the short title serves as an abbreviated form of the statute's name. Among these, the short title represents the commonly used abbreviated form of a statute's title in legal practice and citations.

According to Gifford and Salter (1996), "The first Acts of Parliament did not have titles. The first time that an Act of Parliament was given a title was about 1495. Even when the long title came to be added to each Act of Parliament as a matter of course, as it did from about 1513, the long title was not regarded as part of the Act of Parliament itself. Today, however, the position is different: the long title is part of the Act of Parliament". In the legislative traditions of common law systems, the relationship between statutory titles and textual interpretation has undergone significant evolution. Historically, since the titles of parliamentary acts were assigned by parliamentary clerks rather than by Parliament itself, there existed a long-standing rule that titles could not be used as aids in statutory interpretation. However, this practice has been largely abandoned in most contemporary English-speaking jurisdictions. Today, both the long title and, frequently, a short title are integral components of legislative bills from their initial drafting stages, and they are routinely considered in the interpretive process. In the United States, this principle is further reinforced by constitutional requirements in most states, which mandate that legislative enactments must carry a title that provides clear and accurate notice of the law's substantive content.

(1) General Title

U.S. laws typically follows a naming structure of "Subject Matter + Act/Law" to clearly and directly reflect the law's central content and regulatory scope, as exemplified by the *Americans with Disabilities Act*, the *Civil Rights Act,* the *Copyright Act,* and the *Semiconductor Chip Protection Act*. The naming conventions exhibit certain parallels with the structural patterns observed in Chinese legislative titles. Whether in China or in the U.S., the majority of statutes employ "Law" as the indicative term, following a format where the subject matter is directly combined with "Law". It not only embodies the practical characteristic of Anglo-American legislative language, which emphasizes "content correspondence", but also reflects its high regard for the "identifiability" and "citation convenience" of legal texts. From the perspective of legal translation and cross-jurisdictional communication, understanding this naming logic holds significant reference value for translating the titles of Chinese laws and regulations. It aids in achieving "functional equivalence" rather than mechanical "literal correspondence" within an English-language context, thereby enhancing the standardization, recognizability, and acceptability of China's legal texts in international exchanges.

British legislative nomenclature typically adheres to the structural pattern of "Subject Matter + Act + Year", which serves to clearly indicate the core content and enactment date of the law, as exemplified by the *Childcare Act 2016*. This naming convention reflects the emphasis within the British legislative system on the temporal validity and historical context of laws, while also facilitating the rapid identification and citation of legislation from specific periods in legal literature. Understanding and drawing upon this naming logic can assist in more accurately conveying the temporal relevance and legislative background of Chinese laws and regulations in translation, thereby enhancing the standardization, systematicity, and traceability of legal texts in international exchanges.

(2) Long Title

The Long Title serves as a structural component of legislative texts, fulfilling the dual functions of delineating the scope of the law and articulating its legislative purpose. Its language exhibits a highly formalized character: it typically begins with the fixed phrase "An Act…", followed by performative expressions such as "to amend…", "to make provision for…", "for codifying…", or "for the purpose of…". Through this grammatical system of intentional markers, it constructs a logical bridge from legislative motivation to normative content. This design not only aligns with the common law tradition of textualizing legislative intent but has also evolved into a significant auxiliary tool in judicial practice for interpreting legal ambiguities. In the context of increasingly deepened transnational legal dialogue, understanding the construction logic of the Long Title holds methodological significance for achieving functional equivalence in the foreign-language translation of Chinese legislative texts. It reminds us that when translating expressions of legislative purpose such as "旨在" (with a view to) or "为了" (for the purpose of), we must move beyond literal correspondence and reconstruct a normative discourse framework that aligns with the cognitive conventions of the target legal system.

Long titles vary significantly in length, ranging from relatively concise formulations such as: "*An Act to authorize the making of collective agreements with a term of more than three years in the public and parapublic sectors*", to more structurally complex and detailed titles, such as: "*An Act for further promoting the Revision of the Statute Law by repealing Enactments which have ceased to be in force or have become unnecessary and for facilitating the publication of Revised Editions of the Statutes*".

Among these, the most typical extended titles are found in Anglo-American legislative practice, which follows strict formatting conventions: the title must begin with "An Act" or "A Bill" and be written entirely in capital letters. For example, the full title of the Uniform Commercial Code reads: *AN ACT TO BE KNOWN AS THE UNIFORM COMMERCIAL CODE, RELATING TO CERTAIN COMMERCIAL TRANSACTIONS IN OR REGARDING PERSONAL PROPERTY AND CONTRACTS AND OTHER DOCUMENTS CONCERNING THEM, INCLUDING SALES, COMMERCIAL PAPER, BANK DEPOSITS AND COLLECTIONS, LETTERS OF CREDIT, BULK TRANSFERS, WAREHOUSE RECEIPTS, BILLS OF LADING, OTHER DOCUMENTS OF TITLE, INVESTMENT SECURITIES, AND SECURED TRANSACTIONS, INCLUDING CERTAIN SALES OF ACCOUNTS, CHATTEL PAPER, AND CONTRACT RIGHTS; PROVIDING FOR PUBLIC NOTICE TO THIRD PARTIES IN CERTAIN CIRCUMSTANCES; REGULATING PROCEDURE, EVIDENCE AND DAMAGES IN CERTAIN COURT ACTIONS INVOLVING SUCH TRANSACTIONS, CONTRACTS OR DOCUMENTS; TO MAKE UNIFORM THE*

LAW WITH RESPECT THERETO; AND REPEALING INCONSISTENT LEGISLATION.

This long title comprises three distinct layers of content: the first layer specifies the common name of the statute, namely THE UNIFORM COMMERCIAL CODE; the second layer delineates the regulatory scope and substantive content of the statute through three parallel participial structures, "RELATING TO…", "PROVIDING FOR…", and "REGULATING…"; the third layer articulates the legislative purpose of the statute and includes supplementary provisions introduced by participial phrases (Teng and Kong 2008: 126). This structured approach not only systematically defines the law's scope and core content but also, through its clearly organized linguistic framework, provides explicit textual guidance for legal interpretation and application.

This highly formalized approach to title construction not only reflects the common law tradition's pursuit of rigor and completeness in legislative drafting but also functionally achieves a multi-layered definition of the law's scope, legislative intent, and systemic positioning. For the practice of translating Chinese legal texts, understanding the underlying logic of such title construction holds significant instructive value: when translating Chinese legislative texts into foreign languages, emphasis should be placed on developing title formulations that accurately convey the substantive content of the law while adhering to international conventions for legal texts, thereby enhancing the cross-border acceptability and interpretative consistency of Chinese legal texts.

(3) Short Titles

In the common law system, the titles of statutes are often notably lengthy, primarily to meet various formal requirements. However, such titles prove highly inconvenient for reference in practical legal activities. Consequently, many significant statutes include dedicated short title provisions. For instance, Article 1–101 of the Uniform Commercial Code stipulates:

§ 1–101. Short Titles.
(a) This [Act] may be cited as the Uniform Commercial Code.
(b) This article may be cited as Uniform Commercial Code—General Provisions.

Short title provisions emerged precisely to address the practical limitations of lengthy statutory titles and are thus unique to common law jurisdictions. They consistently follow formulations such as "This Act may be cited as…" (Teng and Kong 2008: 129). This mechanism not only enhances the efficiency of legal citation but also reflects the pragmatic adaptation of legislative drafting to the needs of judicial and professional practice.

(4) Multi-line Titles

In addition to the aforementioned title formats, regulations, notices, rules, and similar documents issued by U.S. government agencies often adopt a multi-line heading structure. For example:

NOTICES
ENVIRONMENTAL PROTECTION AGENCY
[EPA-HQ-OW-2012-0217; FRL-9955-27-OW]
Drinking Water Contaminant Candidate List 4—Final
Thursday, November 17, 2016

This multi-line format organizes complex heading information into distinct lines for greater clarity. Typically, the first line states the document type in uppercase (e.g., "NOTICES"), followed by the issuing agency, the regulatory docket or index number, the specific title of the regulation or notice, and finally the publication date (Zhang 2018: 38). It should be noted that the arrangement of elements across lines may vary between countries and jurisdictions. Other variations exist, such as:

Ministry of National Planning and Economic Development
Directorate of Investment and Company Registration
Announcement No. 1/2013

In general, the number of formal indicative terms used in the titles of laws and regulations in common law jurisdictions like the United Kingdom and the United States is relatively limited. According to the "Table of Statutes" and "Table of Statutory Instruments" appended in the *Modern English Legal System,* only four primary formal terms are consistently used for naming legislative instruments: Act, Regulation, Order, and Rule (Chen and Qiang 2012: 97).

3.2 Key Issues Identified in Translating Titles of Chinese Laws and Regulations and Corresponding Strategies

Given that laws and regulations constitute a highly specialized genre imbued with ideological connotations, they inevitably contain numerous expressions reflective of distinct national institutional characteristics and cultural traits. These unique formulations often lack fully equivalent concepts in other legal systems, rendering the English translation of legislative titles (including the names of specific provisions) particularly challenging (Wang 2013: 230). Under China's current framework, the translation of laws and regulations follows the principle of "the enacting body organizes the translation": laws promulgated by the National People's Congress (NPC) and its Standing Committee are translated under the auspices of the Legislative Affairs Commission of the NPC Standing Committee; administrative regulations issued by the State Council are coordinated and reviewed by the Ministry of Justice (formerly the Legislative Affairs Office of the State Council); and local regulations and rules are translated by the judicial or legislative affairs departments of respective local governments. While this division of responsibility clarifies accountability, the multiplicity of involved entities and the lack of a robust coordination mechanism have led to insufficient systemic integration of translation principles and standards. Although the translation of legislative titles represents only one facet of the overall translation endeavor, it serves as a revealing "microcosm", the issues emerging in title translation reflect broader, systemic challenges in China's legal translation practice, including cross-system conceptual transfer, terminological consistency, and the effective communication of institutional discourse.

3.2.1 Current Status and Disputes over Translation of the "Format terms" in Titles of Chinese Laws and Regulations

(1) Current Status

Chen and Qiang (2012: 97) conducted a systematic investigation into the prevalent translation practices for Chinese laws and regulations. The survey data were sourced from the PKU Law Database, covering 7926 translations of names of national and local laws and regulations, with findings synthesized into tabular form. Building upon their foundational work, we have further expanded and refined this analysis. Such empirical research provides critical insights for standardizing the external communication of China's legal system. It highlights not only the current inconsistencies in translation but also underscores the necessity of establishing a coherent, system-aware framework for legal translation, which aligns with China's legislative hierarchy and facilitates accurate cross-jurisdictional understanding. This endeavor is integral to enhancing the global credibility and operational clarity of Chinese law in international contexts.

Chinese Format Terms		Translation
法		Law of …
条例	暂行条例	Interim Regulation of …
	管理条例	Regulation on the Administration of …
	工作条例	Administrative Regulation of … Working Regulation on …
办法	管理办法	Administrative Measures Measures for the Administration of …
	试行办法	Trail Measures Pilot Measures Trial Procedures
	实施办法	Implementation Measures Measures for the Implementation of …
	暂行办法	Interim Measures Tentative Measures
规定	暂行规定	Interim Provisions Tentative Provisions
	管理规定	Provisions for the Administration of … Standards
	若干规定	Several Provisions
决定		Decisions
决议		Resolutions

Chinese Format Terms		Translation
通知	通知/通报	Notice/ Circular
	补充通知	Supplementary Notice/Circular
意见	实施意见	Implementation Opinions Opinions on the Implementation of … Suggestions
	指导意见	Guiding Opinions
	若干意见	Several Opinions
通告/公告		Announcements
公报		Bulletin
规则	规则	Rules
	工作规则	Working Rules
	实施细则	Rules for the Implementation of …
	通则	General Rules
规范	规范	Norms
	工作规范	Norms Work Norm
实施方案		Implementation Program
函件	批复	Reply Official Reply
	函	Reply Letter
	复函	Letter of Reply
政府令		Decree Order
印发		Print and Issue Print and Distribute
转发		Transmit
发布		Promulgate

Analysis of the table reveals that the "format terms" in Chinese laws and regulations (such as 通知, 暂行, 印发, 规定, 办法, 条例, etc.) are not only diverse in type but also lack uniformity in their English translations. Scholars have pointed out that translating "通知" as "Notice" is insufficient in terms of formality, with "Circular" (referring to a printed notice intended for mass distribution) being a more standardized equivalent; translating "暂行" as "Tentative" is inappropriate, whereas "Interim" more accurately conveys its provisional and transitional nature; for "印发", the translations "Print and Promulgate" or "Print and Issue" carry a more official documentary tone than "Print and Distribute" (Wang 2015: 138).

Further observation indicates that the same Chinese format term is often rendered differently across texts, while the same English term may correspond to multiple Chinese format terms. For example, the term "规定" might be translated as "rule", "provision", or "measure"; "办法" may correspond to "rule", "regulation", or "procedures"; and "条例" is commonly translated as "regulation". Conversely, the English term "rule" can refer to either "办法" or "规定", and "regulation" may correspond to either "办法" or "条例" (Wen 2003: 28). This交叉and混乱of terminological correspondence not only compromises the accuracy and authority of legal texts but also creates comprehension barriers in international legal exchange and practice. In addition, Liu Fagong examined Chinese-English versions of regulatory document titles from official publications and government portals at various levels. His research identified six primary English renderings for the term "管理办法" (Liu 2012: 102).

Titles	Translation
《精神药品管理办法》	Measures for the Control of Psychotropic Drugs
《汽车金融公司管理办法》	Administrative Rules Governing the Auto Financing Company
《上海市出口加工区管理办法》	Rules of Shanghai Municipality for Administration of Export Processing Zones
《海上救捞潜水员管理办法管理办法》	Regulations on Management for Divers to Drag under the Sea
《陕西省组织机构代码管理办法》	Procedures of Shanxi Province for Managing Organization Code
《新化学物质环境管理办法》	Provisions on the Environmental Administration of New Chemical Substances

It can be observed that the term "管理办法" corresponds to six different English translations: Measures, Administrative Rules, Rules, Regulations, Procedures, and Provisions. The fact that a single concept is rendered in six distinct ways sufficiently illustrates the complexity inherent in translating the titles of laws and regulations, as well as the considerable challenge involved in achieving standardization and uniformity in this endeavor.

Such phenomena underscore the urgency of establishing terminology standardization in the foreign-language translation of Chinese laws and regulations. It is recommended that authoritative national bodies take the lead in integrating academic research and practical experience to formulate and issue a binding Guidelines for Standardized Terminology in Legal Translation. These guidelines should specify preferred translations for core format terms and common legal concepts, establish a dynamically updated terminology database, and promote the implementation of norms through training and review mechanisms. This would enhance the accuracy, consistency, and international receptivity of China's legal texts in global dissemination.

(2) Disputes over the Application of "Law" and "Act"

The nomenclature of Chinese laws predominantly follows the pattern of "The People's Republic of China XX Law". In English translations, the term "Law" is commonly used, for instance, *Law of the People's Republic of China on Work Safety*. However, scholarly opinions on the translation of "法" diverge, forming two distinct perspectives.

Scholars skeptical of the prevailing use of "Law" in Chinese translation practice argue that "law" encompasses a broad semantic range, extending beyond statutory legislation to include decrees, regulations, rules, resolutions, decisions, orders, case law, customs, principles, the rule of law, and the judicial sphere. They emphasize that in common law jurisdictions, "law" is rarely employed in the titles of specific statutes. Instead, "Act" is the preferred term, as seen in examples such as the *Trading with the Enemy Act of 1917*, the *Soldiers' and Sailors' Civil Relief Act of 1918*, the *Selective Draft Act of 1917*, and the *Selective Training and Service Act of 1940* (Song and Zhu 1998: 129; Wang 2012: 129; Wang 2015: 137). From the perspective of legal hierarchy, scholars contend that despite systemic differences, Chinese and English legal hierarchies are broadly comparable. Therefore, "法" in Chinese legislative titles should correspond to "Act" or "Code" (Chen and Qiang 2012: 98).

In contrast, scholars who find the use of "Law" acceptable argue that "law" can indeed denote specific statutes, and its meaning is contextualized within the legislative framework. They note that in common law systems, "Act" is reserved for laws passed by parliaments or congresses. China's legislative process is based on the people's congress system, with no equivalent to a "Congress". Given the distinct legal traditions and legislative procedures, it is neither necessary nor appropriate to rigidly adopt the common law convention of "Act" (Qi 2012: 16). Supporting this view, Zhang (2018: 38) observes that in New York State's Consolidated Laws of New York, the term "Law" is extensively used in statutory titles, akin to Chinese practice. For example, the *Racing, Pari-Mutuel Wagering and Breeding Law*, the *Railroad Law*, the *Rapid Transit Law*, the *Real Property Law*, and the *Real Property Actions and Proceedings Law*. This demonstrates that "Law" is not inherently unsuitable for legislative nomenclature.

This terminological debate reflects deeper questions about how China's legal identity is projected internationally. The choice between "Law" and "Act" is not merely linguistic but involves considerations of legal tradition, systemic representation, and cross-jurisdictional clarity. A principled approach, whether aligning with international conventions or asserting distinctiveness, must ultimately serve the goals of accurate communication, legal predictability, and the effective integration of China's legal framework into global discourse.

(3) Debates over the Legitimacy of "Measure" and "Provision"

Disputes over the English translation of format terms in the titles of local regulations highlight the terminological standardization challenges inherent in cross-system legal translation. In current practice, "办法" is often translated as "Measures", while "规定" is frequently rendered as "Provisions". Examples include the translation of 《江苏省电信设施建设与保护办法》 as *Measures of Jiangsu Province on the Construction and Protection of Telecommunication Facilities*, and 《江苏省行政程序规定》 as *Provisions of Jiangsu Province on Administrative Procedures*.

However, scholars have questioned the "legal appropriateness" of these translations, noting that in the Anglo-American legal tradition, "provision" is rarely used in the titles of statutory instruments, and "measure" is not a specialized legal term (Song and Zhu 1998: 129). Some emphasize that "measure" lacks the semantic weight of a legal text, while "provision" typically refers to specific clauses within agreements. Neither is considered suitable as a formal format term for legislative titles, leading to suggestions that "regulation" or "act" should be used instead (Gu and Zhang 2007: 22). Other scholars advocate for a systematic correspondence approach, proposing that terms such as "条例", "规定", and "办法" in local regulations be uniformly translated as "Ordinances". They further distinguish between "State Ordinances" for administrative regulations issued by the State Council and "Local Ordinances" for local regulations (Chen and Qiang 2012: 99). Such disagreements reflect the current "terminological competition" stage in the English translation of format terms in Chinese laws and regulations, where a cross-tier, cross-regional consensus has yet to emerge.

From the perspective of legal communication, terminological inconsistency may undermine the authority and predictability of Chinese legal texts in international exchanges. It is recommended that judicial and administrative authorities take the lead, collaborating with legislative bodies, academic institutions, and translation practitioners to develop Guidelines for Translating Legal Terminology. These guidelines should clarify preferred translations for format terms across different legal hierarchies and text types, grounded in functional equivalence and comparative legal research. An authoritative database could further solidify these norms, enhancing the systematicity, professionalism, and international acceptability of Chinese legal translations.

3.2.2 Issues Identified in the Translation of Titles of Laws and Regulations

In academic discussions on the English translation of Chinese legislative titles, several scholars have highlighted notable grammatical irregularities in existing translations, including improper omission of articles, inconsistent use of singular and plural forms, and misuse of prepositions (Wang 2012; Qi 2012; Hu 2018). While these issues may appear linguistically minor, they directly impact the professionalism and international acceptance of the translated texts, potentially undermining the authority and interpretive consistency of China's legal documents in transnational governance dialogues. This book focuses specifically on the widespread and systematic problem of nonstandard preposition usage. Through comparative analysis, mistranslation attribution, and functional reconstruction, it explores how such issues reflect deeper challenges in cross-system legal translation and offers linguistically grounded solutions to enhance the effectiveness of China's legal communication in global contexts.

(1) Literal Translation in Title Translation: Overly Chinese-Style Rendering

Whether translating national laws or local regulations, there exists a prevalent tendency toward "literal-translation", a rigid, word-for-word rendering that strictly adheres to the syntactic structure of the Chinese title without necessary adaptation or innovation. This approach neglects the principle of "domestication" in translation, resulting in English titles that mirror the length and complexity of their Chinese counterparts. Such translations are often visually cumbersome, syntactically awkward, and difficult to parse, with convoluted grammatical relationships and subordinate structures that obscure clarity.

For example, the title《全国人民代表大会常务委员会关于国务院机构改革涉及法律规定的行政机关职责调整问题的决定》is translated as *Decision of the Standing Committee of the National People's Congress on Issues concerning Adjustments to Functions of Administrative Organs Prescribed by Laws as Involved in the Institutional Reform of the State Council*. This translation retains the extended prepositional chains and embedded clauses characteristic of Chinese legislative drafting, failing to reorganize the information hierarchy in a manner natural to English legal discourse.

However, titles are crucial for legal texts and government documents, as readers typically engage with content by first scanning the title. An effective translation must therefore be concise, accessible, and capable of capturing the reader's attention. The excessive length of many translated titles stems from the inherent verbosity of Chinese administrative language, which often includes issuing authorities, forwarding bodies, and multiple layers of procedural references. In today's digital age, where readers skim content for key information, titles spanning three to four lines hinder comprehension and reduce engagement. Since English translations of Chinese documents are primarily intended for international audiences, it is essential to reformat these lengthy titles by adopting conventions common in common law jurisdictions and international documents. This involves restructuring titles to highlight core content, simplify institutional references, and align with global expectations for clarity and functionality, ensuring that Chinese legal texts are not only accurately translated but also effectively communicated across linguistic and cultural boundaries.

From the perspective of national governance, comparing with such translations that would hinder the international readability and functional utility of China's legal texts, potentially affecting their reception and application in cross-jurisdictional contexts, a more functionally oriented approach, one that prioritizes logical clarity, terminological precision, and syntactic fluency in the target language, would better serve the communicative and normative aims of China's legal system in global engagement.

(2) Inconsistent Use of Pre-modifiers Before Format Terms

Generally, the translation of Chinese legislative titles predominantly follows the pattern of "Law of the People's Republic of China on…", where the format term "Law" appears without a pre-modifier. For example, 《中华人民共和国人民陪审员法》 is translated as *Law of the People's Republic of China on People's Assessors*. However, in some translations, a modifier is placed before "Law", as seen in 《中华人民共和国国家情报法》, which is rendered as *National Intelligence Law of the People's Republic of China*.

In the translation of local regulations and rules, titles commonly begin with the structure "Format Term + of…", with pre-modifiers used less frequently, regardless of the length of the original title. For instance, 《江苏省高速公路条例》 is translated as *Regulations of Jiangsu Province on Expressways*. Nevertheless, there are exceptions where a modifier precedes the format term, such as 《北京市审计条例》, translated as *Audit Regulation of Beijing Municipality*.

The use of pre-modifiers before format terms, while a matter of detail, may not impede basic comprehension when translating legislative titles that are relatively concise in Chinese. However, from the perspective of systemic external communication of China's legal framework, such details constitute an essential aspect of building a standardized, consistent, and predictable legal translation system. Although considerable achievements have been made over years of translating Chinese laws and regulations into English, there remains a notable lack of systematic regulation at the micro level, encompassing terminology structure, syntactic arrangement, and formatting consistency. These inconsistencies in detail may affect how the international community perceives the rigor and authority of China's legal texts and could hinder the formation of a stable and coherent discourse on Chinese rule of law within global governance.

(3) Diverse Prepositional Collocations

Zhang Qing's (2018: 36) analysis of title translations in the *Compilation of Laws of the People's Republic of China (Chinese-English)* and the *Compilation of Laws and Regulations of the People's Republic of China (Chinese-English)* reveals that the format term "Regulations" is followed by three prepositions: "on", "of", and "for"; while "Provisions" is followed by four: "to", "of", "on", and "concerning". Examples from national laws, administrative regulations, and local regulations illustrate this diversity:

Example 1:
《中华人民共和国中小企业促进法》
Law of the People's Republic of China on Promotion of Small and Medium-sized Enterprises

Example 2:
《国务院关于进一步做好新形势下就业创业工作的意见》
Opinions of the State Council on Further Efforts Relating to Employment and Business Startup under the New Conditions

Example 3:
《中华人民共和国香港特别行政区选举第十三届全国人民代表大会代表的办法》
Measures for the Election of Deputies to the Thirteenth National People's Congress from the Hong Kong Special Administrative Region of the People's Republic of China

These examples demonstrate the variability in prepositional usage following format terms: "of", "for", and "concerning" are used to denote content or scope, while "on" and "concerning" both serve to express "about" or "regarding". In local regulations, prepositions such as "on" and "of" directly follow format terms, while "on" and "for" are employed to convey the sense of "concerning".

Chen (2000: 182) categorizes two approaches to prepositional usage: "Approach A: Reflects the social relations regulated by the law without using prepositions or quasi-prepositions, relying instead on noun phrases or adjective phrases; Approach B: Uses prepositions or quasi-prepositions (e.g., concerning) to reflect the regulated social relations". There is no insurmountable right-or-wrong divide between Approach A and Approach B; rather, the difference lies in the level of appropriateness. Grammatically speaking, the use of prepositions in translating legislative titles is not inherently correct or incorrect. However, the wide variation in translation practices underscores a lack of rigor and standardization in the English translation of Chinese legal titles. This inconsistency not only affects the coherence and professionalism of translated texts but also undermines the clarity and authority of China's legal discourse in international contexts.

3.2.3 Analysis of Causes Behind Problems Identified in Title Translation

(1) Inherent Characteristics of Title Formulation of Chinese Laws and Regulations

The official names of the country and the highest legislative body in China are inherently lengthy. Moreover, all laws, regulations, or decisions of the Standing Committee of the National People's Congress must be prefixed with "中华人民共和国" (the People's Republic of China) or "中华人民共和国全国人民代表大会常务委员会" (the Standing Committee of the National People's Congress of the People's Republic of China). In local regulations and rules, numerous normative documents are centered on terms such as "转发" (transmit), "印发" (issue), "实施" (implement), and "通知" (notice), aiming to convey or implement higher-level laws and national normative documents. Since the titles of these higher-level documents are often already lengthy, local regulations inevitably reference them when formulating implementation rules, resulting in even longer titles at the local level.

(2) Translators' Reliance on Literal Translation

"Translators overemphasize 'foreignization' and 'faithfulness,' and coupled with the inherently lengthy nature of Chinese legal documents, the translated titles often appear lengthy" (Gu and Zhang 2007: 22). The literal translation approach aligns with Nida's formal equivalence and Yan Fu's principle of "faithfulness", reflecting the convergence of legal language carriers of similar information amid growing cross-cultural exchanges. While this method ensures specificity and formal closeness to the source text, effectively conveying Chinese characteristics, it often leads to wordiness and complexity in syntactic subordination, obscuring the social relations regulated by the law. Key questions arise: Is direct translation always necessary? Can certain elements be omitted? "Must words such as '管理' (management) be translated verbatim? Must the full names of the country and legislative bodies always be rendered in their complete forms?" (Gu and Zhang 2007: 23). Whether translators can further simplify translations remains an area requiring standardization.

(3) Fragmented Approach to Title Translation without Unified Translation Norms and Mechanisms

In China, the translation of laws and regulations generally follows the principle of "the enacting body organizes the translation". However, the numerous bodies involved in legislation, including the National People's Congress and its Standing Committee, the State Council, local people's congresses, and local legislative affairs offices, result in a decentralized translation process. Translation is inherently subjective, and differences in translators' understanding of legal texts, as well as variations in lexical choices, syntax, and structural decisions, inevitably lead to diverse translated versions. Standardization in legal translation involves both vertical and horizontal dimensions: vertically, consistency between higher-level and subordinate laws; horizontally, uniformity across different regions. Local approaches to organizing translation work vary, some legislative offices hire full-time translators, others collaborate with university scholars, and some outsource to translation agencies. These differences in management contribute to inconsistencies across local translations. Furthermore, local translations of government regulations may not reference the translated versions of higher-level laws, leading to discrepancies between translations of superior and subordinate legal instruments.

In a word, the underlying causes of issues in the English translation of Chinese legal titles are systemic in nature. First, the formulation of Chinese legislative titles inherently carries distinct institutional identifiers and hierarchical transmission characteristics: the statutory integrity of the country's name and the highest legislative body, coupled with the dependency of local normative documents on central documents, collectively shape a tradition of lengthy titles with Chinese characteristics. Second, translation practices, influenced by traditional translation theories, often prioritize formal equivalence at the expense of cognitive efficiency for target-language audiences, failing to advance from "linguistic conversion" to "effective governance communication". Third, the current decentralized mechanism of "the enacting body organizes the translation", while reflecting accountability, lacks cross-departmental and cross-level coordination, resulting in inconsistencies in terminology, syntactic structures, and stylistic conventions. At their core, these issues reveal gaps in the specialization, standardization, and internationalization of China's legal communication system. To enhance the country's rule-of-law image and its influence in international rule-making, it is imperative to develop a strategic translation framework that balances jurisprudential accuracy, cross-cultural readability, and compatibility with international norms. Legal translation must thus evolve into a pillar of modernized national governance rather than remain a technical weakness.

3.2.4 Concrete Strategies for Standardization of Title Translation of Chinese Laws and Regulations

(1) Standardizing Modifiers Preceding Format Terms and Appropriately Adopt the "Subject Term + Law/Act" Model

Although China and common law countries belong to different legal traditions, and common law does not directly guide civil law systems, it is both feasible and advisable to draw upon foreign expression conventions in translating Chinese legislative titles. This consideration is rooted in the target readership of China's legal translations, the reading habits of international audiences, and the effectiveness of cross-cultural communication. As Zhang (2017: 170) argues, "In translating legislative titles, we should adopt the naming patterns of statutes from common law jurisdictions and regions. The purpose of translating legal texts is to meet the reading needs of audiences in English-speaking countries and regions. Translating and naming according to their conventions caters to the reading and comprehension habits of the target audience".

Depending on the length of the Chinese title and the social relations it regulates, we can move beyond the rigid "Format Term + of" structure and appropriately adopt the "Subject Term + Law/Act" model.

Example 1:
《中华人民共和国进出口商品检验法》 could be translated as:
Import and Export Commodity Inspection Law of the People's Republic of China.

(2) Adopting a Multi-Line Heading Format for Lengthy Chinese Titles

Lengthy Chinese legislative titles differ from common law long titles, which typically state legislative purpose, a function often fulfilled in Chinese laws by dedicated "purpose" clauses. For translating lengthy Chinese titles, the multi-line heading format, as illustrated earlier, can be applied. This involves restructuring characteristically long Chinese titles: the first line states the format term, the second the issuing authority, the third the substantive content, and the fourth the issuance date. This layout enhances clarity.

Example 1:
《全国人民代表大会常务委员会关于中国海警局行使海上维权执法职权的决定》
Decision
Standing Committee of the National People's Congress
Exercising of the Marine Right Safeguarding and Law Enforcement Functions and Powers by the China Coast Guard
[Month] [Date], [Year]

(3) Encouraging Appropriate Creative Translation

"Legal translators should, based on their assessment of the uniqueness of the target language and culture and the expectations of the target readers, fully leverage their linguistic creativity. The translation should not be a mere replica of the original but a product of both science and art, one that respects the legal conventions of the source text while demonstrating a degree of creativity" (Li and Zhang 2006: 18). Although legal translation demands authority, accuracy, and consistency, translators can exercise agency beyond achieving absolute precision in terminology. This agency may involve "appropriately adjusting linguistic issues in the source text and striving for reasonable structural reorganization" (Hu 2017: 74).

We contend that translators can appropriately employ creativity in translating laws and regulations, primarily in two aspects: First, when the source text exhibits drafting shortcomings, such as excessive verbosity or redundancy, translators need not be bound rigidly by the original and may make adjustments. Second, considering the varying writing and reading conventions across nations, translators may adapt the structure of the source text to align with target readers' habits. As Zhang (2017: 170) suggests, "By integrating English expression patterns with the characteristics of Chinese legal culture, we can identify corresponding English names for Chinese laws and regulations", thereby better serving the needs of the target audience.

As previously discussed, the verbosity and complexity in translating Chinese laws and regulations stem largely from the inherent lengthiness of the Chinese legislative texts themselves, where titles invariably include "中华人民共和国" or "全国人民代表大会及其常委会". In translation, it is permissible to omit the rendering of "of the People's Republic of China" from the titles of laws enacted by the National People's Congress and its Standing Committee, retaining only the translation of the core content, such as "…Law". However, in specific contexts where it is necessary to clarify that the law is Chinese, "(PRC)" may be appended, for example, *Marriage Law (PRC)*, *Adoption Law (PRC)*, *Law of Succession (PRC)*, *Labor Law (PRC)* (Zhang 2018: 38).

Furthermore, certain issues in legislative drafting also contribute to translation challenges. For instance, penalty clauses in laws and regulations often include the phrase "依法" (according to law). Chen (2008: 11) argues that rights and obligations are defined by law, as are the means of exercising or fulfilling them. Acting outside the law is inherently impossible. Therefore, "依法" is self-evident and redundant. He describes it as "the most common superfluous phrase in legislative drafting" and insists that it must be entirely eliminated to refine legislative style. Legal translators, he contends, have a duty not to translate such redundant terms. In other words, translators may omit obviously extraneous words in legislative texts. Overemphasis on "faithfulness" to the source text may only magnify its verbosity.

Another example is 《中华人民共和国香港特别行政区基本法》 (*The Basic Law of the Hong Kong Special Administrative Region of the People's Republic of China*). The term "基本" (basic) is not a standard legal term but a purely political expression. Translators, disregarding established conventions for translating legal titles, rendered it as "The Basic Law…", causing confusion among both English-speaking and non-English-speaking international audiences. In reality, it could simply be translated as Act of Hong Kong, omitting the perplexing word "Basic" while maintaining precision and accuracy (Gu and Zhang 2007: 24). The tendency to mechanically replicate the source text reflects the lingering influence of traditional translation principles centered on "faithfulness", which discourages deviation.

Translator creativity also extends to the structural organization of laws and regulations. Translators may adjust the structure to align with the reading habits of the target audience. "Sometimes, translators may find the original title too broad or lengthy, and a literal translation may not suit the reading habits of the target audience. In such cases, translators should employ necessary techniques to enhance the readability of the translated title. This approach is particularly applicable to translating long titles, while adhering to the principles of preserving and highlighting the core elements of the original title and striving for conciseness and clarity" (Zhang 2017: 170).

3.3 Standardization of Translation of Titles of Chinese Laws and Regulations

The translation of laws and regulations appears on the surface to be a matter of linguistic conversion, yet at its core, it involves disparities in legal culture and systems. Moreover, the entire translation process encompasses organizational, managerial, and coordinative aspects of translation work. Standardizing the English translation of legislative titles must not only focus on analyzing and discussing specific translation strategies the micro level, but also taking into account the entire translation process on the macro level, from "source text—translator—translation" to the underlying legal environment and workflow.

The law constitutes a multi-tiered system with varying levels of authority, efficacy, and scope of regulation. Such a system requires different legislative bodies to produce multi-layered and diverse legal texts. Consequently, the standardization of legal translation is a systematic endeavor that must become a routine undertaking. At the operational level, it involves both drafters of legal and governmental normative texts and translators. In terms of legal hierarchy, it entails the standardization of both superior and subordinate laws, as well as coherence between them. In the realm of legislative domains and scopes, it encompasses the standardization of national, central, and ministerial legislation, as well as local regulations and rules. While the translation of national, central, and ministerial laws may achieve a degree of normative, guiding, and referential consistency, greater attention is currently needed to standardize the translation of local regulations and rules. The translation practices of provinces, municipalities, autonomous regions, and special economic zones often operate independently. Some regulatory documents are translated by translation agencies, where speed may compromise quality. As Wang (2015: 139) notes, "Resolving this issue requires the long-term collaborative efforts of legal professionals, translators, and relevant government departments".

3.3.1 Improving Understanding of Competent Departments and Prioritizing Standardization in Title Translation

Currently, efforts to standardize the translation of Chinese laws and regulations are driven by two main forces: the practical initiatives of governmental bodies such as the Legislative Affairs Office of the State Council and local legislative offices, and the theoretical contributions of academia. In 1998, the Legislative Affairs Office of the State Council published the *Chinese-English Glossary of Terms in the Laws and Regulations of the People's Republic of China* (hereafter referred to as the "Glossary"), which provided standardized English translations for common terms in administrative regulation titles. Additionally, in 2005, the same office compiled the *Handbook of Common Sentence Patterns for Legal Translation (for internal use)*. At the local level, the Shanghai Legislative Affairs Office's Translation and Foreign Affairs Division pioneered standardization efforts through its internal journal *Legal Translation* (launched in 2002), whose influence extended nationally, with content regularly republished on the State Council Legislative Affairs Office website.

However, these initiatives have not been sustained or fully implemented. As Li and Dong (2015: 229) noted, "These standards have not been updated in a timely manner. With rapid societal development, new terms and sentence structures constantly emerge in local regulations, rendering existing translation standards inadequate. Translators still lack comprehensive, authoritative, and specific guidelines, which has contributed to persistent issues in translating local regulations". In recent years, the scope of translating local regulations has expanded significantly. In Jiangsu Province alone, four cities, Nanjing, Suzhou, Wuxi, and Xuzhou, have initiated translation projects for local regulations. However, as social and economic development introduces new concepts and terminology, corresponding translation standards have lagged. For instance, updates to Shanghai's Legal Translation ceased after 2013 on the State Council Legislative Affairs Office website, and the English version of the Shanghai Government Legal Information Network stopped updating its translations of regulations after 2014 (Hu 2018: 143).

These efforts reveal several underlying issues:

(1) Accountability and Fragmentation

While translation responsibility lies with the enacting bodies, standardization efforts remain fragmented and lack cohesive influence. The Legislative Affairs Office of the State Council and local legislative offices must take greater responsibility for sustaining and expanding standardization work.

(2) Central-Local Coordination

Effective standardization requires both top-down guidance and bottom-up innovation. Authoritative references such as the *Compilation of Laws of the People's Republic of China (Chinese-English)* by the NPC Standing Committee and the *Compilation of Laws and Regulations of the People's Republic of China (Chinese-English)* by the State Council Legislative Affairs Office provide valuable models. Local offices should proactively develop and implement standardized translation guidelines tailored to regional needs.

(3) Bridging Theory and Practice

As Du et al. (2004: 75) observe, "For a long time, translation practice and research in China have been disconnected, preventing translation theory from effectively supporting practice and hindering the development of systematic theoretical frameworks". Academic research on legal translation has advanced, but its findings often remain isolated from governmental practice. To address this, it is essential to: establish collaborative mechanisms between translation practitioners and academic researchers; form dedicated teams to develop and update standardization guidelines; and ensure timely application of academic insights to translation practice.

The translation of laws and regulations is a critical tool for international exchange and communication. As Liu (2012: 102) emphasizes, "Inconsistent translation of legal document titles inevitably confuses legal concepts, undermines the seriousness of the law, and affects the accuracy of legal content". However, "achievements in standardizing Chinese legal terminology lag far behind the progress made in translating laws and regulations. Relevant departments have not accorded sufficient importance or clarity to the standardization of legal terminology translation" (Qu 2012: 71). To advance the standardization of legal translation, governmental bodies must prioritize this work and collaborate with academia to create a unified, systematic, and sustainable framework.

3.3.2 Enhancing the Quality of Chinese Legislation and Strengthening Its Uniformity and Standardization

"The function of the source text is a primary factor determining legal translation strategies" (Qu 2013: 237). Translation that disregards the source text can hardly be called translation, it may even amount to creation. In other words, translation is constrained by the source text; it is "dancing in chains". The standards of translation, faithfulness, expressiveness, and elegance, require fidelity to the original. Guided by the principle of faithfulness, translators often treat the source text as an absolute authority, adhering to it meticulously, lest they be criticized as "defying all norms". If the source text itself lacks standardization or conciseness, the translation will inevitably inherit these flaws. The verbosity and lack of conciseness in Chinese legislative drafting directly contribute to lengthy and cumbersome translations. As Gu and Zhang (2007: 23) noted, "Some of China's laws are inherently lengthy, lacking the brevity and rigor expected of legal language. For example, laws concerning land ownership, development, utilization, and protection are titled 《中华人民共和国土地管理法》 (*Land Administration Law of the People's Republic of China*), when simply 《土地法》 (*Land Law*) would suffice. The addition of '管理' (administration) is unnecessary".

Given the mutual influence between the source text and its translation, the standardization of English translations for Chinese laws and regulations is not merely a matter of English proficiency. Translation is an interactive dialogue involving the "author—source text—translator—translation". Thus, it is essential to elevate the discussion to the level of Chinese legislative drafting itself. Improving the quality, uniformity, and standardization of Chinese legislative language is the foundational prerequisite for achieving consistent and standardized English translations of legal titles.

Legislative language must strive for conciseness and accuracy, which are both the most basic and the highest standards. Conciseness operates on two levels: first, the expression must be succinct, where every necessary word is included and every unnecessary word is omitted, neither over-adorned nor understated, to avoid redundancy and repetition and use the fewest words to convey the fullest and most complete meaning; second, the language must be clear and comprehensible, avoiding ambiguity or fuzziness. As Dong (2015: 167) states, "The purpose of law is to 'resolve disputes and clarify boundaries.' As the external form of law, the fundamental principle of legal language is accuracy". Accuracy means using precise and unambiguous language to express the content of laws and regulations. The quality and authority of laws derive from the accuracy, scientific rigor, and standardization of their language. However, "at present, irregularities in China's legislative language are widespread and significant. Due to violations of linguistic norms and rules, legislative texts often suffer from grammatical errors, semantic ambiguity, logical inconsistencies, chaotic classifications, stylistic imbalances, and overlapping provisions" (Dong 2016: 9).

The lengthiness of many translations is largely a reflection of the Chinese legislative titles. For instance, 《中华人民共和国法官法》 is translated as *Judges Law of the People's Republic of China*. Without the country name, it could simply be rendered as *Judges Law*. In common law jurisdictions, laws are generally not prefixed with the country name, making their titles more concise. Some scholars argue that "the inclusion or omission of the country name in the titles of administrative regulations and government rules has led to inconsistency in China's legal nomenclature and contributed to excessively long titles, undermining the conciseness and clarity required of legal language" (Shen and Han 2006: 32). In practice, omitting the country name from legal titles may not have adverse effects. Whether to include it warrants further discussion and consensus among legislative bodies.

Additionally, irregularities persist in China's legislative drafting process, as seen in the use of ambiguous and contentious terms such as "试行" (trial), "暂行" (provisional), and "若干" (several) in legal titles. As Tian (2004: 193–194) noted, "In China's legislative practice, some laws, regulations, and rules include the terms '试行' or '暂行.' 'Trial' indicates that the legislature is uncertain about the social relations regulated or the measures prescribed and intends to revise the law at an appropriate time. 'Provisional' suggests that the issues addressed or measures prescribed are temporary, and the law will lose relevance after a period. However, many 'trial regulations' have been in effect for over two decades, and many 'provisional provisions' remain in force years later. This undermines the authority of the law, conflicts with the principle of legal stability, and even casts doubt on the dignity of the law. Such terminology is a product of a specific historical context. In the late 20th century, China's legal system was underdeveloped, yet rapid social development demanded the swift enactment of laws. Given immature legislative techniques, 'trial' and 'provisional' laws served a purpose. Today, with an emphasis on legislative quality, their continued use is less justified … Some regulations include the term '若干' in their titles. This term should not appear in either the title or the content of a law. First, '若干' has two meanings: a question ('how many') or an indefinite quantity. Precision is a hallmark of law, and '若干' contradicts this requirement. Second, its use in a title offers no help in understanding the content or the number of provisions. Third, the number of provisions and the content of a regulation are definite, not vague, rendering '若干' unnecessary in the title".

Translation, as a cross-linguistic communicative act, is fundamentally an extension and representation of a nation's governance system in the international arena. The non-standard phenomena observed in the English translation of Chinese laws and regulations, such as inconsistent terminology and verbose sentence structures, stem not only from choices in translation strategy but also reflect deeper issues in the standardization, conciseness, and systematization of Chinese legislative texts. Addressing these challenges requires moving beyond mere linguistic conversion and engaging in systematic reflection from the strategic perspective of modernizing national governance and enhancing the international dissemination of China's legal system. This demands shared governance responsibility between legislators and translators: legislative bodies must further refine legislative language by eliminating ambiguous expressions and redundant structures, thereby providing a clear and rigorous textual foundation for translation. Translators, while respecting the original legal intent, should actively explore expressions that align with international conventions of legal drafting. Only through synchronized optimization of both legislative and translational practices, and through mutual enrichment of theory and application, can a legal discourse system be constructed that embodies Chinese characteristics while maintaining international readability. This, in turn, will enable the effective communication of China's rule-of-law narrative in global governance and strengthen its institutional voice on the world stage.

3.3.3 *Establishing Collaborative Mechanisms: Translators Require Professional Support from Legislative Bodies*

The complexity of legal translation necessitates the establishment of collaborative mechanisms. On one hand, language and culture are inseparable. Traditional views of legal translation position the translator as a mere "message carrier" between the "text producer" and the "text recipient", effectively isolating the translator from cultural and contextual considerations. In reality, the translation of laws and regulations, while superficially a matter of word and text processing, fundamentally involves the conversion of language across legal cultures and systems. The complexity of the translation process inevitably requires consideration of different translation contexts and target audiences. As Wang (1989: 125) noted, "Translators deal with individual words but face two vast cultural landscapes". Legal texts and normative documents are produced within different countries and legal systems, apply to different subjects and scopes, and exhibit distinct cultural characteristics. "Legal translation is not merely an act of translation but, more importantly, a bridge for communication between the source and target legal environments" (Pan 2017: 301).

On the other hand, legal translation is interdisciplinary and cross-cutting in nature. "Legal translation spans three major disciplines: linguistics, translation studies, and jurisprudence" (Dong 2016: 203). Ideally, legal translators should possess knowledge in both law and translation studies, getting an in-depth understanding of Chinese laws and regulations while also having practical translation experience and skills. However, in reality, there are very few specialized professionals capable of undertaking legal translation, particularly for translating Chinese laws and regulations into English. Legal translation is a highly demanding and specialized activity, and relying solely on translators working in isolation may not meet the high standards of accuracy and standardization required.

In some Western countries, the role of legal translators has gradually evolved beyond a passive position since the twentieth century. "Some Western legal translation theories argue that legal translators should be 'text producers' with a certain authority and responsibility. Susan Šarčević further suggests that since the 1970s, with Canada's legislative reforms and the introduction of a new bilingual drafting model, the status of legal translators underwent a revolutionary change, shifting towards 'co-drafters' with broad decision-making authority" (Qu 2013: 235–236). This shift in the translator's role has significant implications for legal translation, not only elevating the translator's agency but also establishing a dynamic relationship between legal translators and text producers. Legal translation thus becomes an open communicative activity involving both text producers and translators in dialogue with the reader.

In China's current legal and social context, the leap to translators as "co-drafters" remains considerable. In China, laws and regulations are drafted first and translated afterward, typically by the departments responsible for their enactment or administration. The translated versions do not carry the same legal force as the Chinese originals. Legal translators come from diverse backgrounds: some legislative offices employ dedicated translators, others commission translations from university professors, and still others outsource to professional translation agencies or companies. Translation is generally a relatively independent activity compared to the drafting of legal texts, and translators' involvement lacks the "bidirectional negotiation" characteristic of "co-drafters" (Šarčević 1997: 77). However, given the specialized nature of legal translation, not all translators are equally equipped for the task. Translators lacking expertise and background knowledge require assistance from the drafters of legal texts, particularly in interpreting terms and concepts. This underscores the need to establish communication mechanisms between translators and legislative bodies, ensuring translators receive professional support from authoritative legislative institutions.

3.3.4 Building Consensus and Developing Systematic Standards

In recent years, numerous scholars have conducted research on standardizing the translation of legal titles. However, significant disagreement persists regarding the translation of titles, especially “format terms”. On one hand, there are differing views on whether standardization and uniformity are necessary. Most scholars advocate for further standardization and provide supporting arguments. For instance, Liu (2012: 104) states that “the translation of legal titles must adhere to the principles of seriousness and consistency in legal translation, and the ‘pluralism’ of translated titles is not permissible”. On the other hand, some scholars argue that “the terminology and format of Chinese statutory titles have gradually gained acceptance in the international community and contain no critical flaws. Retaining their current form without imitating foreign models better reflects China’s unique characteristics, close to the civil law tradition yet distinctively socialist” (Qi 2012: 16).

On the other hand, studies supporting standardization often focus on case analyses and lack systematic depth. Many studies select specific translation examples or samples to highlight existing issues. For example, in his article Translation of Legal Titles, Chen Zhongcheng summarizes five principles for translating legal titles: firstly, legal translations must be concise and precise, which is particularly important for title translation; secondly, the greatest challenge in translating legal titles lies in accurately expressing the social relations they regulate; thirdly, the strict rule for addressing this challenge is to avoid unnecessary prepositions whenever possible, absolutely prohibiting redundant “-ing” forms that render translations cumbersome; fourthly, when prepositions are unavoidable, the shortest possible prepositions, especially “on”, should be used; fifthly, the preposition “about” is rarely, if ever, used in English legal titles and should be avoided in translations (Chen 2000: 184–185).

Xin Gu (2003: 25) analyzes inconsistencies in the two Chinese versions of the Report of the Working Party on the Accession of China, arguing that “when translating Chinese laws and regulations or their provisions, efforts should be made to restore the original meaning; when translating treaties, agreements, or foreign laws, complete fidelity to the source text or alignment with official national versions is essential”. Chen and Qiang (2012) review the current state of English translations of Chinese legal titles from the perspective of legal hierarchy and offer recommendations. Zhang (2018) identifies three major issues in the English translation of Chinese legal titles.

Overall, consensus has yet to be reached on many of the issues discussed, and standards for standardization and uniformity urgently require clear definition. Furthermore, the problems to be standardized are not systematically organized. We believe that consensus must be reached in the following areas to develop systematic outcomes.

(1) Standardization for Translation of Format Terms

Currently, scholars have conducted extensive academic discussions and summaries on the unification and standardization of format terms. For instance, Chen and Qiang (2012: 100), from the perspective of legal hierarchy, proposed recommendations for translating the names of Chinese laws and regulations as follows.

Legislative Bodies	Title	Suggested Translation
National People's Congress and its Standing Committee	宪法	Constitution
	法	Acts/Codes
	通则、条例、规则	Acts
	各种规定、决定、办法等	NPC Rules
	解释	NPC Legislative Interpretations
State Council and Ministries thereunder	条例、实施细则、规定、办法……	Regulations, Orders, Rules
Provincial (Local) People's Congress and its Standing Committee	地方性法规；条例，办法……	Local Bylaws
Local Governments	规章；政府令，规定，办法……	Regulations, Orders, Rules
The Supreme People's Court/ The Supreme People's Procuratorate	意见	Opinions
	解释	Judicial Interpretations
	决定	Decisions
/	通知	Notices

Wang (2013: 233) argues that the selection of terminology denoting the hierarchical authority of laws and regulations should be based on their legal effect and the enacting bodies, providing standardized references as follows:

Type	Translation
基本法	Act
国务院条例或地方条例	Regulations Ordinance By-law
司法解释的意见；批复；办法、决定	Opinion Approval Rule Decree Decision
通知、转发、批转、印发、发布	Notice Transit Approve and Transmit Print and Distribute Promulgate

The diversity of sources of China's laws and regulations directly determines the variety of "format terms" in their titles, and correspondingly, there are multiple possible approaches to translating them. Scholars have yet to reach a consensus on these methods. We believe that the unification and standardization of legal translation do not depend on how many different viewpoints scholars propose, but rather on whether a practical, operable common standard can be established. Relying solely on individual scholarly efforts often leads to a "contention of a hundred schools of thought" without forming a cohesive system. Therefore, it is essential for authoritative institutions to take the lead in organizing experts and scholars from various fields to systematically review and discuss "format terms" based on existing translation achievements. Particular attention should be paid to "carefully comparing the different meanings of 'format terms' in English legislative document titles, such as: Law, Act, Code, Ordinance, Regulation, Rule, Interpretation, Decision, etc" (Zhang 2017: 170). On this basis, professional consultation should be conducted to clarify the corresponding translations for various "format terms", establish authoritative and unified normative standards, and develop systematic translation guidelines. These should be compiled into manuals and made publicly available. Only through such institutionalized and systematic efforts can true consistency and standardization in terminology, structure, and style be achieved in legal translation. This, in turn, will enhance the effectiveness of international communication of China's legal texts and ensure a unified representation of the country's rule-of-law image.

(2) Standardization of Pre-modifiers Before the Format Terms

Whether to include pre-modifiers in the English translation of "format terms" remains inconsistent in current translation practice. While the inclusion or omission of such modifiers does not inherently affect the accuracy or comprehensibility of the translated meaning, such details often reflect the translator's commitment to rigor and normative principles throughout the translation process. As Chen (1984: 27) aptly noted, "Striving for excellence and continuously improving translation quality aligns with the natural progression of professional development". Therefore, while flexibility may exist in stylistic choices, the pursuit of precision and consistency in structuring format terms, whether with or without pre-modifiers, should be guided by systematically established norms to enhance the overall coherence and professionalism of legal translations.

(3) Standardization of Prepositional Usage Following the Format Terms

Analysis of English translations of Chinese legislative titles reveals that prepositions such as "on", "of", and "for" are most commonly used, with occasional appearances of "concerning" and "relating to". While there is considerable flexibility in prepositional choice, it is essential to categorize and clarify which prepositions are appropriate in specific contexts. As Zhang (2018: 39) notes, "If consistent structural standards are established for regulations with different format terms, the chaotic use of prepositions following format terms can be avoided". Therefore, developing clear guidelines for prepositional collocation based on the semantic and syntactic functions of format terms will enhance the uniformity and professionalism of translated titles.

(4) Developing Systematic Normative Standards

In 1998, the Department of Translation, Review, and Foreign Affairs under the Legislative Affairs Office of the State Council of China formally published the *Chinese-English Glossary of Terms in the Laws and Regulations of the People's Republic of China*. This Glossary provides standardized English translations for commonly used terms in the titles of administrative regulations, as illustrated in the accompanying table.

Format Terms	Translation
条例	Regulations
实施条例	Regulations for the Implementation of …
暂行条例	Interim Regulations
令(命令)	Decree
通令	Circular Decree
施行(实施)细则	Rules for the Implementation of …
规则	Rules
规定	Provisions
暂行规定	Interim Provisions
办法	Measures
暂行办法	Interim Measures
实施办法	Measures for the Implementation of …
国务院关于批转……的通知	Circular of the State Council on Its Approval and Transmission of …
国务院办公厅关于转发……的通知	Circular of the General Office of the State Council on Its Transmission of …
通告	Announcement
通则	General Rules
暂行通则	Interim General Rules
批复	Official Reply
简则	Basic Rules

The leading role of the Legislative Affairs Office of the State Council in standardizing title translation inherently carries authority. However, the "format terms" listed in the Glossary are not exhaustive. With the continuous expansion of China's legal translation efforts and the growing translation of local regulations and rules, the range of "format terms" in legislative titles extends far beyond those included. As discussed earlier in the section on the current state of translation, numerous "format terms" and their English equivalents have been identified. The Glossary must evolve with the times, gradually incorporating norms for format terms, premodifiers, and prepositional usage following format terms, thereby forming a systematic set of standards to guide the translation of laws and regulations. On the other hand, compiling standardized translation outcomes does not signify the end of the standardization process, nor should these results be shelved. It is essential to promptly publish and promote these standards, advocating for their adoption in the translation of local regulations and rules nationwide. Furthermore, establishing mechanisms for translation review and strict supervision will ensure that translation activities align with these normative benchmarks, fostering consistency and quality across all legal translations.

(5) Enhancing Translator Competence to Ensure Translation Quality

Translator competence is an indispensable factor in ensuring the quality of translations. The translation of laws and regulations falls under the category of applied translation, distinct from literary translation. Legal translation is highly specialized, and without a thorough understanding of relevant legal knowledge, it is impossible to undertake such work competently. As Šarčević (1997: 90) noted, "Generally speaking, all translations of language for specific purposes (LSP) are interdisciplinary in nature. Therefore, in addition to translation skills, professional translators must possess specialized knowledge in specific fields. If translators are to make decisions regarding language and law, they must be proficient in both translation and legal expertise".

Dong (2016: 202) argues that legal translation must first adhere to the principle of elitism. The intended readers of Chinese legal translations include foreign government departments, lawyers, multinational corporations, import-export companies, legal researchers, and scholars. These elite groups demand extremely high accuracy in translation, and the precision inherent in legal language itself adds to the technical difficulty of translating laws and regulations. In a sense, legal translators are also part of the social elite.

The differences between Chinese and foreign legal systems mean that there is often no exact correspondence between legal terms in the two traditions. Effective legal translation requires more than mechanically copying dictionary definitions. Translators must be familiar with the cultural, institutional, and contextual factors underlying both legal languages, proficient in both law and the languages involved. Those who understand foreign languages but lack legal expertise, or those with legal knowledge but insufficient translation skills, will struggle to produce high-quality translations. The specialized nature of legal translation necessitates professional competence in translators. When translating legal titles, translator professionalism manifests in three key aspects.

Firstly, translation involves the conversion between two languages, requiring a profound grasp of their fundamental characteristics. As Chen (1992: 210) states, "Sino-English translation inevitably involves comparisons between Chinese and English (whether consciously or unconsciously)". Professional and experienced translators must have a conscious awareness of these comparisons. Only through comparative analysis can they identify the fundamental differences between languages and cultures, enabling them to use expressions that align with the reading habits of the target audience.

Secondly, due to significant differences in Chinese and English legal cultures and the specialized nature of law, free translation should be employed when literal translation is not feasible. As Dong (2016: 204) explains, "Sometimes, to better align with the conventions of the target language, translators may need to supplement information in the translation when it is lacking in the source text". Translator professionalism lies not in mechanically replicating the source text but in demonstrating creativity in translation choices. The translation must transition from the context of the source text to that of the target language, achieving effective conversion between different contexts.

Thirdly, translators should make diligent use of legal English reference materials and tools. "A craftsman must sharpen his tools to do his work well". Adequate preparation is essential before undertaking legal translation, including linguistic and legal knowledge. However, no one can master all knowledge completely, making the use of reference materials crucial for in-depth understanding and interpretation of specialized vocabulary. As Xia (2014: 44–47) emphasizes, "Experienced and senior translators attach great importance to preparatory work, including basic reference books, various maps and English-Chinese name manuals, legal professional books and reference materials, large-scale reference works, and series". Zhang (2017: 170) adds a critical note: "It is particularly important to rely primarily on English-language legal dictionaries, legal works, and documents for specific research, rather than depending solely on ordinary English-Chinese dictionaries, English-Chinese legal dictionaries, or other indirect reference materials".

If legal translation is regarded as a bridge for the international dissemination of a nation's rule-of-law discourse, then the professional competence of translators serves as the cornerstone supporting this bridge. The three dimensions outlined above, conscious awareness of linguistic comparison, creative balance in translation choices, and systematic use of professional tools, collectively form the core of the competency matrix for legal translators. However, the cultivation of such professional competence should not remain at the level of individual practice but must be integrated into the strategic framework of national talent development for foreign-related legal affairs. In the context of global governance, legal translation is not merely a technical conversion but a critical medium for dialogue between China's institutional discourse and the world's legal civilizations. The professional judgment of translators is reflected not only in their precise capture of "legal language" but also in their sensitive mediation of cultural differences. It requires both adherence to the normative authority of legal texts and the cross-cultural interpretive ability to transform Chinese-specific expressions into internationally recognized jurisprudential discourse. Therefore, enhancing translator competence is not only a technical safeguard for translation quality but also a strategic investment in China's participation in international rule-making and the enhancement of its soft power in rule of law. Only through systematic training, the establishment of practical platforms, and the integration of academic resources can we cultivate interdisciplinary translators who are deeply versed in the spirit of Chinese rule of law and proficient in international legal discourse. In doing so, every legal translation can become a professional envoy conveying the civilization of Chinese rule of law to the world.

(6) Strengthening Project-Based Management of Translation Review

A project is defined as "a temporary endeavor undertaken to create a unique product, service, or result. The 'temporary' nature of a project means that it has a definite beginning and end" (Project Management Institute 2013: 3). The translation of laws and regulations is such a temporary endeavor, often requiring translators to complete their work within specified deadlines. With the continuous development of modern society, the translation industry faces significant challenges, including a wide range of translation needs, large volumes of work, and diverse language requirements. In response, large-scale and professional translation agencies have gradually established comprehensive workflows to ensure translation quality when meeting the demands of clients and enterprises.

As Wang and Wang (2012: 5) note, "Traditional translation services, often resembling artisanal workshops, rely on individual experience, capability, and reputation to ensure quality. When faced with large-scale tasks, they typically resort to simplistic 'human-wave' tactics. Due to a lack of effective organization, coordination, and management, as well as the absence of corresponding quality assurance systems and measures, it is difficult to fully leverage each individual's potential. This approach increasingly fails to meet the strict demands of modern business for both quality and efficiency".

While the clients of translation agencies differ from the government entities commissioning legal translation, the need for rigorous monitoring of the translation process remains the same. As Hu (2017: 73) emphasizes, "Project management is a mindset, a standardized approach to work that requires the application of a reasonable set of project management steps".

In the context of legal translation, adopting project-based management can help streamline workflows, ensure consistency, and enhance the overall quality of translations. This involves clearly defining project scopes, setting measurable milestones, allocating resources efficiently, and implementing systematic review mechanisms. By integrating project management principles, translation teams can better coordinate tasks, mitigate risks, and deliver accurate, timely, and consistent translations that meet the high standards required for legal and governmental texts. Furthermore, such an approach fosters accountability, facilitates collaboration among linguists, legal experts, and reviewers, and ultimately strengthens the credibility and usability of translated legal documents in international and domestic contexts.

(7) Standardization as a Continuous and Ongoing Process

The standardization and unification of English translations of laws and regulations constitute a continuous and ongoing process, primarily for three reasons. First, the diversity of departments organizing legal translation work presents significant challenges to standardization. As Zhang (2018: 34) explains, "The translation of Chinese laws and regulations follows the principle of 'the enacting body organizes the translation.' Laws enacted by the National People's Congress and its Standing Committee are translated under the responsibility of the Legislative Affairs Commission of the NPC Standing Committee, while administrative regulations issued by the State Council are translated under the authority of the Legislative Affairs Office of the State Council". With the increasing translation of local regulations and rules, standardization must address both vertical alignment, ensuring consistency between translations of national and central ministerial laws and those of local regulations, and horizontal coordination, harmonizing translations across different regions. This is a massive undertaking that requires unified communication mechanisms and departments to coordinate efforts among various translation bodies.

Second, the unification of legal translation is not a one-time task. Laws and regulations reflect the characteristics of their time, and as society evolves, so do the social relations they govern. Over time, existing laws may require adjustments, revisions, or even repeal, while new phenomena and social relations demand new legal frameworks. Both at the national and local levels, the continuous issuance of normative documents necessitates ongoing translation efforts, making standardization a perpetual endeavor to safeguard translation quality.

Third, the standardization of legal translation is itself a pursuit that demands relentless effort and refinement. Resolving disputes and reaching consensus is not an instantaneous process but requires continuous discussion and negotiation. As Qu (2012: 75) cautions, "Low-level, repetitive compilation of dictionaries and databases is futile; they cannot solve major problems. They may partially facilitate translation convenience but hardly achieve the standardization and unification of legal terminology. Clearly, standardized English translations of legal terms require further refinement. The fundamental solution lies in organizing experts to update and supplement existing standardized outcomes". For example, the Chinese-English Glossary of Terms in the Laws and Regulations of the People's Republic of China translates "物证" as "material evidence", a rendering that appears correct but is semantically distant from the intended meaning. The accurate meaning is "substantive evidence", while the proper legal term for "物证" is "real evidence" or "physical evidence" (Dong 2014: 86).

3.4 Conclusion

As a seemingly minor yet crucial component of legal translation, the translation of titles profoundly reveals the professional complexity and systemic challenges inherent in this work. Legal translation is far from a mere conversion of linguistic symbols; it requires a deep understanding of different legal systems, precise grasp of textual characteristics, and scientific anticipation of readers' cognitive habits, aiming to construct a dynamic equilibrium amid linguistic differences, cultural barriers, and institutional tensions, a practice of cross-civilizational communication. Uniformity and standardization are the lifelines for ensuring translation quality and preserving legal authority. The path to standardization must be illuminated by a "permanent beacon", continuously guiding the way forward. Although China has achieved phased accomplishments in legal translation, the standardization of title translation still faces systematic challenges due to the involvement of numerous departments, intertwined procedures, and interdisciplinary intersections, indicating a long and arduous journey ahead.

The effective advancement of legal translation requires not only translators' professional competence but also the establishment of institutional dialogue mechanisms across systems. As scholars have pointed out, "Beyond traditional interpersonal communication, it is essential to effectively communicate with other institutions, enabling judicial practice departments such as the police, courts, and procuratorates to understand, recognize, accept, and embrace legal translation work" (Pan 2017: 301). This necessitates breaking down professional barriers and integrating translation into the entire chain of legal operations. The standardization of legal translation is a systematic project that demands serious attention and proactive leadership from relevant authorities to consolidate resources. Simultaneously, it requires collaborative efforts from legislators, translators, scholars, legal departments, and communication agencies to form a synergy of theoretical development, practical advancement, and institutional safeguards, collectively contributing wisdom and strength to building a legal translation standardization system with Chinese characteristics and international recognition.

References

Chen, Z. 1984. Striving for excellence in the English translation of the Constitution. *Chinese Translators Journal* 5.

Chen, Z. 1992. *Talks on legal translation*. Beijing: China Translation & Publishing Corporation.

Chen, Z. 2000. *Essays on legal translation*. Beijing: China Legal System Publishing House.

Chen, Z. 2008. *A critical analysis of the English translation of the general principles of civil law*. Beijing: Law Press.

Chen, X., and F. Qiang. 2012. Legal hierarchy and the English translation of Chinese legal names. *Chinese Translators Journal* 5.

Dong, X. 2014. An analysis of several issues in the standardized English translation of China's legislative texts. *Foreign Language Learning Theory and Practice* 3.

Dong, X. 2015. On the "equivalent" translation of English-Chinese legal terminology. *Journal of Xi'an International Studies University* 3.

Dong, X. 2016. *Research on the standardization of legislative language in China*. Beijing: Beijing Jiaotong University Press.

Du, J., F. Zhang, and L. Yuan. 2004. Problems and solutions in the English translation of Chinese laws and regulations. *Chinese Translators Journal* 3.

Garner, B. A. 2009. *Black's law dictionary*. 9th ed. St. Paul: West Publishing Co.

Gifford, D. J., and J. Salter. 1996. *How to understand an Act of Parliament*. 19th ed.

Gu, W., and J. Zhang. 2007. Domesticated English translation of Chinese legal names and their terms. *Journal of Hebei University (Philosophy and Social Science)* 2.

Hu, B. 2017. Translator's subjectivity in legal translation. *Journal of Zhejiang Shuren University* 4.

Hu, B. 2018. Problems and countermeasures in the English translation of local regulations and rules: Based on translation practice in Jiangsu Province and Shanghai. *Journal of Chongqing Jiaotong University (Social Sciences Edition)* 1.

Li, J., and X. Dong. 2015. Standardization and countermeasures in the translation of local regulations and rules: A study based on translation practice in Jiangsu Province. *Southeast Academic Research* 4.

Li, K., and X. Zhang. 2006. *Legal texts and legal translation*. Beijing: China Translation & Publishing Corporation.

Liu, F. 2012. On the English translation of "administrative measures" in regulatory document titles. *Chinese Translators Journal* 5.

Pan, Q. 2017. *Forensic Linguistics*. Beijing: China University of Political Science and Law Press.

Project Management Institute. 2013. *A guide to the project management body of knowledge*. 5th ed. Beijing: Publishing House of Electronics Industry.

Qi, Y. 2012. Reflections on the English translation of names of Chinese statutory laws. *Overseas English* 9.
Qin, S., and X. Dong. 2013. *Sixteen lectures on legal basics*. Beijing: University of International Business and Economics Press.
Qu, W. 2012. Problems and causes in the translation of Chinese legal terminology for foreign audiences: With remarks on the standardization of Chinese legal term translation in recent years. *Chinese Translators Journal* 6.
Qu, W. 2013. *Starting from dictionaries: A translation history study on the unification and standardization of legal term translation*. Shanghai: Shanghai People's Publishing House.
Šarčević, S. 1997. *New approach to legal translation*. The Hague: Kluwer Law International.
Shen, H., and B. Han. 2006. China's legal names should not be prefixed with the country's name. *People's Congress Studies* 8.
Song, L., and L. Zhu. 1998. Translation of English-Chinese legal names. *Modern Law Science* 3.
Teng, C., and F. Kong. 2008. *English-Chinese legal translation: Theory and practice*. Hangzhou: Zhejiang University Press.
Tian, C. 2004. *Theory and practice of local legislation*. Beijing: China Legal System Publishing House.
Wang, Z. 1989. *Translation: Reflections and attempts*. Beijing: Foreign Language Teaching and Research Press.
Wang, J. 2012. A study on the English translation of legal names. *Journal of Southwest University of Political Science & Law* 6.
Wang, J. 2013. *Research on legal translation*. Chengdu: Sichuan University Press.
Wang, W. 2015. An analysis of inconsistencies in the English translation of legal norms. *Journal of Jiangxi Normal University (Philosophy and Social Sciences Edition)* 5.
Wang, H., and H. Wang. 2012. *Practical translation project management*. Beijing: China Translation & Publishing Corporation Ltd.
Wen, X. 2003. Translation of legal names. *Chinese Science & Technology Translators Journal* 3.
Xia, D. 2014. *English-Chinese translation skills for legal English*. Beijing: Law Press.
Xie, B. 2013. *The compact dictionary of Anglo-American Law (Abridged edition)*. Beijing: Peking University Press.
Xin, G. 2003. Translation of titles of laws and regualtions. *Chinese Science & Technology Translators Journal* 3: 21–27.
Zhang, F. 2009. An analysis of cultural factors in legal English translation. *Chinese Translators Journal* 4.
Zhang, F. 2017. *A contrastive study of Chinese and Western legal language and culture*. Beijing: Peking University Press.
Zhang, Q. 2018. A study on problems in the English translation of Chinese laws and regulations. *Journal of Zhejiang Gongshang University* 1.

Chapter 4
Translation of Terminology in Laws and Regulations

Abstract This chapter systematically examines the translation of terminology in Chinese laws and regulations. It begins by defining the core concepts, classifications, and linguistic characteristics of legal terminology, emphasizing its role in maintaining the precision and authority of legal texts. The chapter then identifies common issues in terminology translation, such as conceptual mismatches, inconsistent renderings, and cultural overgeneralization, proposing strategic solutions grounded in functional equivalence and comparative legal analysis. Furthermore, it explores pathways toward standardizing terminology translation, advocating for a coordinated framework that integrates legislative intent, target-language conventions, and corpus-based validation. The conclusion underscores that terminology translation is not merely a linguistic task but a crucial mechanism for aligning China's legal discourse with global governance norms.

Keywords Terminology translation · Issues identified · Translation strategies · Standardization

Legal language serves as the vehicle for judicial justice, and its distinction from ordinary language lies precisely in its specialized terminology. Legal terminology comprises "the unique lexical members of legal language, and it is their presence that endows legal language with a professional character distinct from general language" (Yang, 2003: 37). In recent years, with the deepening implementation of the "going global" strategy for culture, legal culture has played an increasingly significant role in international exchanges. Legal translation has built a communicative bridge for legal and cultural interactions, gradually moving to the forefront and center of translation studies. The translation of terminology in laws and regulations has consistently been a focal point in terminology translation research.

The translation community and academia have placed great emphasis on the study of legal terminology for two primary reasons. On one hand, in the process of translating laws and regulations for international audiences, irregularities in the translation of specialized terminology persist, making the standardization of terminology translation a perennial topic of discussion. Without resolving the practical

X. Dong, Y. Zhang, *On Translation of Laws and Regulations in China*,
https://doi.org/10.1007/978-981-95-9406-1_4

challenges of terminology translation standardization, academic debates and exchanges will naturally continue. On the other hand, with the in-depth expansion of comparative linguistics and comparative studies of Chinese and Western legal language and culture, understanding of legal language and specialized terminology has deepened. Scholars' differing opinions on terminology translation remain prevalent, and for some specialized terms, due to differences in legal systems, national conditions, institutions, and socio-cultural contexts, a definitive consensus in translation has yet to be reached. The translation of legal terminology is the core content of legal translation. "The essential competency of a legal translator lies in their ability to establish terminological correspondences" (Qu, 2017: 206). In-depth research into the translation of legal terminology holds significant importance for enhancing the expressive effectiveness and communicative functions across different legal cultures, warranting more thorough and systematic investigation.

4.1 Concept, Classification, and Characteristics of Terminology in Laws and Regulations

With the advent of the twenty-first century, terminology studies have garnered increasing attention across multiple disciplines. Terminology is closely related to linguistics, logic, taxonomy, ontology, informatics, and other fields. Experts from nearly all disciplines find it necessary to engage with terminology science, and among the branches of applied linguistics, few have attracted as much attention and concern from experts in other fields as terminology science. Whether in natural sciences or social sciences, terminology provides a window into the overall characteristics of a discipline and serves as a distinctive marker of disciplinary differentiation. Legal terminology is no exception.

4.1.1 The Concept of Terminology in Laws and Regulations

The *Contemporary Chinese Dictionary (7th edition)* defines "术语" simply as "the specialized vocabulary of a particular discipline" (Dictionary Editing Office, Institute of Linguistics, Chinese Academy of Social Sciences, 2016: 1216). By extension, the terminology of laws and regulations can thus be defined as the specialized vocabulary of legal science. However, this definition remains somewhat broad and lacks the specificity required to capture the core essence of legal terminology. In contrast to the dictionary's definition, scholars have provided more detailed and nuanced explanations. For example, "术语" refers to a set of designations used in a specific disciplinary field to represent concepts. They are conventional linguistic symbols expressed through speech or writing to define scientific concepts and serve as tools for the exchange of ideas and knowledge. Terminology can take the form of words or phrases used to accurately label objects, phenomena, characteristics, relationships, and processes in specialized fields such as production technology, science, art, and social life" (Wang & Wang, 2012: 119).

As a scientific discipline, law, like other sciences, possesses its own specialized terminology. These terms represent the unique phenomena and corresponding legal concepts within legal science. According to the Dictionary of Legal Science, "legal specialized terminology" refers to the precise technical vocabulary used by legal professionals in theory, legislation, judicial practice, and other contexts, formed in accordance with the intentions of jurists. This vocabulary facilitates clear thinking and reasoning, thereby enhancing the efficacy of the law (Zou & Gu, 1991: 1039). The *Chinese Encyclopedia of Law* further elaborates: "Legal specialized terminology refers to the words or phrases in legal texts that express specific concepts. They serve as the foundational material for creating norms and normative documents. Specialized legal terminology belongs to legal technique, carries specific meanings, and functions as a technical means to articulate the content of the law. In legal technique, legal terminology holds universal, fundamental, and indispensable significance, serving as the initial link in reflecting the legislative will within the law" (Sun, 1997: 118). Defining legal specialized terminology must emphasize the professional nature of law and address the essential attributes of legal language.

4.1.2 Classification of Terminology in Laws and Regulations

In the early stages of academic research, the classification of legal terminology was relatively simplistic. For example, Jiang (1994: 35) focused on the internal structure and external function of terms, categorizing legal terminology into two broad types: "words" and "phrases". With the continuous development of linguistics and comparative linguistics, academic research on legal terminology has expanded to encompass broader and more profound dimensions. Studies now include both macro-level, general theoretical research and micro-level, detailed analyses of individual terms, leading to a rich and diverse body of research on the classification of legal terminology.

Pan (1997: 190) posited that the vocabulary used in legislative language falls into two categories: legal vocabulary and ordinary vocabulary. Legal vocabulary carries specific meanings and defined scopes of application, and should not be arbitrarily extended or replaced by other terms.

Li (1998: 22) classified legal vocabulary into legal terminology and non-legal terminology. Legal terminology is further divided into full legal terms and quasi-legal terms, while non-legal terminology includes idiomatic expressions and classical Chinese words. Legal vocabulary thus comprises specialized legal terms, legal expressions borrowed from ordinary vocabulary, and idiomatic expressions that characterize legal discourse.

Liu (1999: 39) categorized legal terminology into two types: specialized legal terms, which are used exclusively in legal matters and related contexts and rarely appear elsewhere; and general legal terms, which are applicable both in legal matters and other contexts.

Liu (2003: 13–14) divided legal English terminology into four categories: (1) general terms, these terms have permeated daily life and gradually merged with general vocabulary; (2) exclusive terms, also known as "sub-terms", which exclude ordinary meanings unrelated to legal concepts while retaining specific legal connotations; (3) specialized terms, also referred to as "pure terms", which denote singular legal concepts, exhibit the highest level of specialization, and adhere to the three fundamental characteristics of terminology: monosemy, accuracy, and strict conceptual differentiation; and (4) borrowed terms, which are specialized terms from related fields that have been incorporated into legal terminology, many of which have become firmly established and occupy fixed positions.

Wang (2004: 19–20) proposed that legal vocabulary can generally be classified into four categories: (1) strict terms, which are terms used exclusively within legal science, characterized by precise meanings and singular usage. They form the core vocabulary of legal documents; (2) assigned-meaning terms, which are terms from other disciplines that have been endowed with legal meanings; (3) restricted terms, which are terms conditionally adopted into legal documents to enrich their expressive quality, add vividness, or convey the nuanced emotions of the law; and (4) dual-use terms, which are terms that are applicable both in the legal field and other social domains.

4.1.3 Characteristics of Terminology in Laws and Regulations

(1) Systematicity

The legal language system serves as the symbolic system of legal culture, while legal culture provides the contextual backdrop for the development of legal language. The contemporary world is primarily dominated by two major legal systems: the civil law system and the common law system. China's legal system is a socialist legal system with Chinese characteristics, built upon the foundation of statutory law. It is rooted in the cultural traditions of the Chinese legal system while fully integrating elements from both civil law and common law traditions, embodying a spirit of inclusivity and synthesis.

As noted by Du et al. (2004: 73), "Each legal language possesses a series of specialized terms that solidify corresponding concepts. The set of specialized terms in a legal language corresponds to a system of legal concepts. Compared to other types of vocabulary, specialized legal terminology more distinctly reflects the typical features of a particular legal system or regime". Legal terminology embodies the culture, institutions, and modes of thinking inherent to an entire legal system and cannot exist in isolation from it. China's legal sources include the Constitution, laws, administrative regulations, local regulations, autonomous regulations of ethnic regions, normative documents of special economic zones, rules, laws of special administrative regions, international treaties, and international customs. These involve fundamental legal forms and contents such as "法" (law), "条例" (regulations), "办法" (measures), "规定" (provisions), and "决定" (decisions), categories not similarly subdivided in Western legal systems.

As Du (2004: 87) explains, "Legal terminology represents complete legal concepts, which are formed through the long-term accumulation, evolution, and refinement of a series of elements. Legal concepts, in turn, are fundamental components of the legal system, with each concept organically linked to others, interdependent and mutually constraining. Therefore, understanding and using legal terminology must be grounded in the entire legal system and supported by legal concepts". This systematic nature underscores that legal terminology is not merely a collection of isolated terms but an interconnected framework reflecting the structure, principles, and cultural nuances of a legal system. Translating such terminology requires not only linguistic precision but also a deep understanding of the systemic relationships and conceptual foundations that underpin the source and target legal systems.

(2) Specialization

The specialization of legal language refers to the state in which the law is articulated through a professional lexicon (Song, 2012: 171). Legal language is partially composed of words with specific legal meanings and partially of everyday vocabulary. Words with specific legal meanings, such as "预谋" (premeditation), "过失" (negligence), and "非法侵害" (unlawful infringement), are rarely used in everyday contexts. Beyond these specifically legal terms, many words commonly used in daily life take on distinct legal meanings when they appear in legal texts, reflecting what we often refer to as the "specialization" of legal vocabulary (Dong, 2015a: 146).

As a set of social rules with mandatory functions, the law requires a language that represents its characteristics, this is legal professional language. Without such a specialized language, the legal attributes cannot be delineated, legal language would be indistinguishable from other forms of social language, and the law would cease to be what it is. Although the specialization of legal language is an inherent requirement for the establishment of law, it does not mean that the more specialized, the better. Over-specialization can be counterproductive, creating a growing distance from the general public. Legal language must maintain a balance between specialization and accessibility. As Song (2012: 174) noted, "If expressed in numerical proportions, specialized language should be controlled between 10% and 20%, no less than 10% and no more than 20%. If it falls below 10%, the language becomes largely popularized, and the characteristics of legal language would essentially disappear. If it exceeds 20%, the public would find the law difficult to understand, hindering the realization of its value".

(3) Precision

Legal terminology is neutral and free from subjective emotional connotations. Accuracy or precision can be considered the lifeblood and soul of legal language (Zhang, 2017: 70). Accuracy refers to the ability of a legal term to express the legal concept it reflects as precisely and concisely as possible, while aligning with the essential characteristics of the legal matter or phenomenon it represents. Legal language must be clear and unambiguous to clarify the rights and obligations of all parties involved. For example, Article 92 of the *Criminal Law of the People's Republic of China* stipulates: "*The term 'property owned privately by citizens' as used in this Law refers to the following property: (1) lawful income, savings, houses, and other means of subsistence of citizens; (2) means of production lawfully owned by individuals or families; (3) lawful property of individual businesses and private enterprises; (4) shares, stocks, bonds, and other property lawfully owned by individuals*".

The precision of legal terminology lies in its clear conceptual expression and well-defined semantic boundaries. Law is a science, and scientific rigor and accuracy are prerequisites for objectivity. This determines that legal terminology must also embody objectivity, employing accurate and rigorous scientific language to reflect the characteristics of matters within the field of legal science.

(4) Monosemy

"Monosemy is the most important characteristic of legal vocabulary. As legal terms, they must be understood in only one way everywhere, with no variation in meaning across contexts" (Li, 1998: 18). As the core component of legal vocabulary, legal terminology exhibits an even stronger tendency toward monosemy. Generally, once legal terms are established, they acquire a specific user base, a relatively fixed meaning, and a formal determinacy. Even if some terms were not entirely precise at the time of their formation, if their connotations have become widely recognized, they should not be arbitrarily altered. The meaning of legal terminology must be singular and fixed, with everyone interpreting it consistently under any circumstances. Not only must specialized legal terms have a single meaning, but vocabulary derived from the common language of the nation must also express a singular legal concept (Dong, 2015b: 108). In legal language, especially in legislation, it is essential to emphasize that a term should have only one sense rather than two or multiple meanings. The meaning must be fixed and not subject to multiple interpretations. For instance, terms such as "缓刑" (probation), "假释" (parole), and "正当防卫" (justifiable defense) have fixed meanings in criminal law.

In summary, the above-mentioned four characteristics of legal terminology, systematicity, specialization, precision, and monosemy, collectively form the foundational support for the discourse system of a country's rule of law. These features not only reflect the inherent principles of legal language but also directly serve the strategic needs of modernizing the national governance system.

First of all, systematicity ensures the internal coherence and hierarchical coordination of the legal system. China's legal terminology system integrates the traditions of the Chinese legal system, the structure of the civil law tradition, and the features of socialist rule of law, forming a conceptual network with Chinese characteristics. This systematicity provides a terminological foundation for cross-departmental and cross-level legal coordination, ensuring logical consistency from the Constitution to local regulations and avoiding governance fragmentation caused by terminological confusion.

Secondly, specialization reflects the refined requirements of national governance. While maintaining the necessary professional threshold (with specialized vocabulary accounting for 10%–20% of the total), legal terminology also considers public comprehensibility. This balance embodies the linguistic practice of the concept of "integrated development of rule of law in the country, the government, and society". The appropriate use of specialized terminology not only preserves the authority of legal norms but also enhances the penetration of legal communication through the transformation and application of everyday vocabulary.

Thirdly, precision serves as a technical guarantee for the effectiveness of governance. The accurate definition of legal terminology directly relates to the clear delineation of rights and obligations. For instance, the itemized enumeration of "private property" in the Criminal Law essentially institutionalizes property rights protection through terminological precision. This precision not only improves the predictability of judicial rulings but also provides a stable institutional environment for market entities, aligning with the governance objective of "optimizing the business environment".

Lastly, monosemy maintains the uniformity and authority of the rule of law. The nationally unified meaning of terminology prevents governance disparities that may arise from localized interpretations, ensuring the implementation of the governance concept of "coordinated national planning" at the linguistic level. This rigidity of monosemy naturally reflects the unitary state system in the language of the rule of law, providing linguistic assurance for the smooth implementation of central government directives.

These four characteristics are interconnected, collectively shaping the discourse system of socialist rule of law with Chinese characteristics: systematicity constructs the conceptual framework, specialization establishes normative authority, precision ensures implementation effectiveness, and monosemy maintains the uniformity of directives. In the process of advancing the modernization of national governance capabilities, continuously optimizing the development of legal terminology holds fundamental significance for enhancing institutional discourse power and improving the capacity for foreign-related rule of law. In the future, mechanisms for terminology standardization should be further refined to enable the legal terminology system to better serve as a linguistic bridge connecting legislative wisdom with governance practice.

4.2 Issues Identified in Translation of Terminology in Laws and Regulations and Corresponding Strategies

Although legal terminology does not constitute the entirety of legal language, its role within laws and regulations is pivotal. The translation of legal terminology directly impacts the quality of legal document translation. If errors occur in the translation of legal terms, they may lead to misinterpretation of entire legal provisions and, on a broader scale, result in serious legal disputes, undermining the effectiveness and quality of legal and cultural exchanges. At present, the translation of terminology in Chinese laws and regulations still faces several issues, which can be summarized as follows: incorrect translation of terms, stemming from misunderstandings of source-language concepts or inappropriate choices of target-language equivalents; lack of precision in term translation, where the general meaning is preserved but nuances are lost, leading to blurred boundaries of legal concepts; inconsistency in term translation, where the same concept is rendered differently across texts or even within the same text, compromising the internal coherence of the legal system.

These three issues often coexist, reflecting both a shortage of interdisciplinary talent in legal translation and the lag in establishing terminology standardization mechanisms. To enhance the international communication efficacy of China's rule-of-law discourse, it is imperative to prioritize the standardization of terminology translation and build a systematic, dynamic, and authoritative system for translating and writing legal terminology.

4.2.1 Issues Identified

(1) Incorrect Translation of Terminology

Incorrect translation of terminology represent one of the most direct and detrimental problems in legal translation. They primarily stem from misinterpretations of source-language legal concepts or incorrect selections of equivalent terms within the target legal system. Such errors often arise due to translators' insufficient grasp of legal expertise, contextual misunderstandings, or a lack of sensitivity to legal-cultural differences, which can lead to disruptions in legal logic or even substantial misalignments in rights and obligations. In cross-border judicial cooperation or international commercial contracts, such errors may trigger interpretive conflicts, enforcement obstacles, or even contradictory judicial rulings, directly undermining the authority and enforceability of legal texts.

In the English translation of the *Property Law of the People's Republic of China* published by the Legislative Affairs Office of the State Council, the term "物权法" is rendered as "property law".

Example 1:

第二条　本法所称<u>物权</u>，是指权利人依法对特定的物象有直接支配和排他的权利，包括所有权、用益物权和担保物权。

Article 2 The <u>property right</u> mentioned in this Law means the exclusive right enjoyed by the obligee to directly dominate a given thing according to law, which consists of the right of ownership, the usufruct and the security interest on property.

However, according to the *Compact English-Chinese Dictionary of Anglo-American Law*, "property" is defined as "(1)所有权，一个人对某项财产享有的独占性支配权，由对财产的占有、使用和以出租、出借、设定担保、转让、赠与、交

换等方式予以处分等'一束权利'。(2)财产，即所有权的客体，包括一切有金钱价值的物与权利，大体上可以分为有形财产与无形财产两类，前者指一切以物理形态存在的物体，如土地、房屋、家具、粮食等有形物；后者为各项财产性权利——如继承权、知识产权、损害求偿权等——及其他不以物理形态存在的事物。" (Xue, 2003: 1107).

Thus, the meaning of property extends beyond the scope of "物" (thing). Therefore, "物权法" and property law are not equivalent. Then, how should "物权法" be accurately translated? It is essential to first clarify the meaning of "物权" (real right). According to the *Concise Dictionary of Jurisprudence* (Zeng, 2000: 672), "物权" is defined as: "The right to directly control, utilize, and dominate an object while excluding interference by others".

In addition, "物权"possesses the following characteristics: the content thereof is exclusively prescribed and created by law; the object is a tangible thing; the object must be a specific thing, generic goods, before being specified, can only serve as the subject of creditor's rights and cannot be the object of real rights; it is a right of domination, allowing the right holder to directly exercise control over the object, hence also called a 'right in rem'; it is an absolute right or a right against the world, with obligations binding on unspecified persons; it possesses exclusivity, two complete ownership rights or two incompatible real rights cannot coexist over the same object; it has a right of pursuit, meaning the right holder may claim the object from any possessor, regardless of how it was transferred (e.g., through loss or theft); the object is property that already exists and has been specified.

In contrast, the *Concise Dictionary of Jurisprudence* (Zeng, 2000: 480) defines "财产权" (property rights) as "rights that encompass tangible material content or directly reflect material interests". "财产权" can be divided into two major categories: tangible property rights and intangible property rights. The former are rights with objects that occupy physical space in nature and can be controlled or utilized by humans, specifically including real rights, creditor's rights, and inheritance rights. The latter are property rights with intangible intellectual products as their objects, i.e., intellectual property rights.

Such rights generally lack strict personal attachment and can be freely transferred; they possess direct economic content and can be measured monetarily; when unlawfully infringed, compensation is typically provided through property liability. Property rights exist not only in civil relations but also in legal relationships such as marriage and labor, for example, claims for support, maintenance, or alimony among family members, or claims for wages and pensions arising from labor relations. Property rights reflect the legal embodiment of the specific distribution of material resources, and their nature varies across different societies.

From these definitions, it is evident that "物权" is a subset of "财产权", specifically referring to rights over tangible objects, whereas "财产权" encompasses a broader range of rights, including intangible assets. Therefore, translating "物权法" as Property Law risks conflating the specific concept of real rights with the general concept of property rights. A more precise translation could be "Law of Real Rights" or "Real Rights Law", which more accurately reflects the legal doctrine of rights over tangible objects as distinct from broader property rights. This approach aligns with the civil law tradition and avoids the ambiguity inherent in the term property law, which in common law jurisdictions often encompasses both tangible and intangible property rights.

Incorrect translation of legal terminology transcends mere linguistic inaccuracy to become a critical issue impacting national governance and international legal discourse. Such errors not only compromise the precision and enforceability of individual legal instruments but also undermine the integrity and authority of China's legal framework in cross-border interactions. When key concepts are misrepresented, it creates interpretive ambiguities that can lead to diplomatic misunderstandings, impede international judicial cooperation, and weaken the persuasive power of China's legal positions in multilateral forums.

From the perspective of global legal dialogue, terminology mistranslations may inadvertently distort the distinctive features of China's socialist rule-of-law system, hindering the accurate transmission of its conceptual foundations and practical innovations. This linguistic imprecision becomes particularly consequential as China increasingly participates in shaping international norms and standards, where precise communication of legal concepts is essential for meaningful engagement and leadership. Ultimately, terminology accuracy represents more than technical precision, it embodies China's commitment to legal clarity, international transparency, and the authentic global presentation of its legal philosophy. By elevating terminology translation to a strategic priority in legal system development, China can more effectively communicate its legal innovations, facilitate international legal cooperation, and contribute meaningfully to the evolution of global legal discourse while maintaining the integrity of its distinctive legal tradition.

(2) Lack of Precision in Terminology Translation

The lack of precision in terminology translation not only compromises the professional communication of legal texts but also undermines the authority of China's legal system in international exchanges. Specifically, this issue manifests in the following four dimensions. First, the substitution of specialized legal terms with ordinary vocabulary remains prevalent. Many translators fail to thoroughly examine existing equivalent or closely corresponding terms in common law systems when dealing with specialized legal concepts, resulting in translations that lack precision within legal professional contexts. Second, terminology selection tends to be ambiguous, either opting for near-synonyms with differing connotations and denotations or failing to choose the most professionally precise legal terms, thereby hindering the accurate transmission of core legal concepts. Third, translations often suffer from redundancy. Concepts that could be expressed through one or two precise words are instead conveyed through circumlocution or over-explanation, which not only disrupts the conciseness expected of legal texts but may also introduce unnecessary semantic ambiguity. Fourth, unfamiliarity with and avoidance of Latin legal terms lead to difficulties in accurately translating concepts rooted in Roman law traditions. This impedes effective cross-system correspondence through concise and precise Latin terminology, thereby affecting the accurate positioning of legal concepts within global legal discourse. The persistence of these issues reflects systemic shortcomings in current legal translation practices, particularly in terms of professional depth, comparative studies across legal systems, and the development of terminology standardization.

(a) Substituting Specialized Legal Terms with Ordinary Vocabulary

Language serves as the vehicle of law, and the expression of legal content is constrained by linguistic form. At the same time, law constitutes the substantive essence of legal language, requiring legal language to faithfully serve legal content. Legal communication must adhere to the "principle of language subordination to law", which should be reflected across all levels of language, including word choice, sentence structure, textual organization, definition, interpretation, and description (Du, 2004: 209). However, in practice, many translators frequently replace specialized legal terminology with common vocabulary, failing to recognize that even within common law systems, precise or closely equivalent legal terms exist for many concepts. This substitution not only diminishes the professional rigor of legal texts but also compromises the accuracy of legal communication. Taking "停留"in the Article 2 of the *Exit and Entry Administration Law of the People's Republic of China* as an example.

Example 1:

第二条　中国公民出境入境、外国人入境出境、外国人在中国境内停留居留的管理，以及交通运输工具出境入境的边防检查，适用本法。

Article 2 This Law is applicable to the administration of exit and entry of Chinese citizens, entry and exit of foreigners, stay and residence of foreigners in China, and the exit/entry border inspection of transport vehicles.

In the English Translation, the term "停留" is rendered as "stay", a common vocabulary term. According to Black's Law Dictionary (Garner, 2009: 1548), "stay" in legal English means: "*1. The postponement or halting of a proceeding, judgment, or the like. 2. An order to suspend all or part of a judicial proceeding or a judgment resulting from that proceeding, Also termed stay of execution; suspension of judgment*". What's more, the Compact English-Chinese Dictionary of Anglo-American Law (Xue, 2003: 1293) defines "stay" as "v. 中止，延迟，暂缓。n. 停留；中止；诉讼中止，可以是中止整个诉讼的进行，也可以只是中止诉讼的某一阶段，如中止对判决的执行。如stay of action诉讼中止，stay of execution 执行中止".

"'Stay' in this translation adopts its everyday meaning while being elevated to the status of a legal term, yet in common law systems, it clearly carries other legal interpretations. This choice of terminology violates the monosemy characteristic of legal terms and may generate ambiguity in legal-cultural exchange and reference" (Zhao, 2017:46). In legal English, there exists another specialized term, "sojourn", which can better denote "停留". According to *Black's Law Dictionary* (Garner, 2009:1519), "sojourn" means "*A temporary stay by someone who is not just passing through a place but is also not a permanent resident<she set up a three-month sojourn in France>*". Thus, the use of "stay" to translate "停留" introduces ambiguity, as it conflates the everyday meaning of temporary residence with the distinct legal meaning of suspending proceedings. For greater precision and alignment with legal terminology conventions, "sojourn" may serve as a more appropriate translation in this context.

Such practices often stem from two interrelated challenges: insufficient comparative legal knowledge and an over-reliance on superficial semantic correspondence. Insufficient comparative legal knowledge manifests as a limited understanding of the structural, historical, and cultural contexts of both the source and target legal systems. This gap prevents translators from discerning the deeper jurisprudential logic behind terminology, leading to the mechanical substitution of common words for specialized legal concepts. Over-reliance on surface-level semantic correspondence, meanwhile, encourages a form of linguistic literalism that prioritizes apparent meaning over functional and doctrinal equivalence, risking the distortion of legal intent.

To address these issues, translators must transcend basic linguistic conversion and immerse themselves in the jurisprudential foundations of both systems. This involves not only studying statutory texts and judicial interpretations but also engaging with legal scholarship, case law, and the systemic principles underpinning each legal tradition. Such a deeper understanding enables translators to identify terminology that aligns not only at the lexical level but also in terms of legal function, conceptual scope, and doctrinal implications. By rigorously adhering to the "principle of language subordination to law", translators can better navigate the complexities of legal discourse. This principle demands that linguistic choices be guided by legal substance rather than mere verbal resemblance. When applied consistently, it ensures that translations preserve the precision and authority inherent in legal texts, avoiding ambiguities that could undermine their enforceability or interpretive clarity.

Ultimately, such an approach facilitates clearer cross-jurisdictional understanding, supporting more effective international legal cooperation, fostering trust in transnational legal interactions, and contributing to the accurate global dissemination of a nation's legal norms. In an era of deepening legal globalization, the role of the legally-informed translator thus becomes not merely technical but profoundly constitutive of the very possibility of meaningful dialogue across legal systems.

(b) Ambiguous Terminology Selection

Ambiguity in terminology selection manifests primarily in two forms: the use of near-synonyms that differ in connotation and denotation, or the failure to employ the most precise legal terms available. Both tendencies hinder the accurate transmission of core legal concepts and compromise the integrity of legal communication.

For instance, in translating Chinese legal terms into English, the choice between "obligation" and "duty" may seem interchangeable in everyday language, but in legal contexts, they carry distinct nuances. "Obligation" often refers to a specific legal or contractual requirement, while "duty" may imply a broader moral or legal responsibility. Similarly, translating "侵权行为" as "tortious act" rather than the more precise "tort" may obscure the specific legal framework governing civil wrongs in common law systems.

This ambiguity often stems from a lack of deep engagement with comparative legal systems. Translators may rely on superficial semantic equivalents without considering the doctrinal, historical, or contextual dimensions of the terms. For example, rendering "法人" as "legal person" aligns with civil law traditions, but in common law contexts, "corporation" or "juridical person" might offer greater precision depending on the specific legal framework being referenced.

To address this issue, translators must adopt a functional equivalence approach, which prioritizes the legal effect and conceptual alignment of terms over literal correspondence. This requires: first, contextual analysis, that is, understanding how a term operates within its source legal system and identifying its functional counterpart in the target system; second, doctrinal mapping, that is, tracing the jurisprudential foundations of terms to ensure alignment in legal reasoning and application; and third, dynamic validation, that ism testing terminology in practical legal scenarios, such as contractual drafting or judicial interpretation, to verify its precision and clarity. By refining terminology selection through these strategies, translators can enhance the accuracy and authority of legal translations, ensuring that core legal concepts are transmitted with the clarity and precision demanded by both domestic and international legal discourse.

(c) Redundancy in Translation

Redundancy in legal translation constitutes a significant impediment to textual clarity and professional rigor. This phenomenon often manifests in two primary forms: circumlocution (the use of excessive words to express concepts that could be conveyed concisely) and over-explanation (the elaboration of self-evident or implicit content), both of which contravene the principle of linguistic economy essential to legal drafting. For example, translating "医疗费用"as "expenses for medical care", though attempting to capture nuances, introduces syntactic complexity that obscures the well-established translation "medical expenses".

Taking "起诉状"in Article 113 of the *Civil Procedural Law of the People's Republic of China* as another example.

Example 1:

第一百一十三条　人民法院应当在立案之日起五日内将起诉状副本发送被告，被告在收到之日起十五日内提出答辩状。

Article 113 The people's court shall send a copy of the statement of complaint to the defendant within five days from the date of docketing the case, and the defendant shall file a statement of defense within 15 days from the date of receipt of the copy of the statement of complaint.

According to *the Compact English-Chinese Dictionary of Anglo-American Law* (Xue, 2003:270), "Complaint" refers to "1.<美 > 民事起诉状，根据民事诉讼规则或法律开始一项民事诉讼的文书，起诉人应在其中简要说明法院具有管辖权的根据并阐明要求获得法律救济的请求。2. <英 > 民事起诉状，在治安法院开始一项要求被告付款的民事诉讼的文书，原告在诉状中述明案件事实，原告也可以口头起诉。". Therefore, in Article 113, "起诉状" is translated as "the statement of complaint", which is somewhat redundant, simply "complaint" would suffice.

Such redundancy often arises from: defensive translation, that is, over-clarifying terms due to anxiety about audience comprehension or cross-system differences; source-text adherence, that is, mirroring verbose or repetitive source-text structures without adapting to target-language conventions; lack of terminological confidence, that is, avoiding established legal terms in favor of descriptive paraphrases. The consequences extend beyond stylistic inelegance. Redundant phrasing can dilute legal precision, introduce interpretive ambiguity, and undermine the normative authority of texts. In international contracts or treaties, verbose formulations may even generate unintended loopholes or conflicting interpretations.

To counteract redundancy, translators should prioritize lexical precision, utilizing authoritative legal dictionaries and parallel texts to identify concise, widely recognized equivalents, embrace functional equivalence, focusing on conveying legal effect rather than replicating source-text syntax, and applying critical editing, revisiting drafts with a focus on eliminating superfluous modifiers, redundant pairs (e.g., "null and void"), and explanatory asides that add no legal value. By cultivating conciseness as a core translational virtue, legal translators not only enhance textual clarity but also fortify the juridical integrity of the documents they produce.

(d) Unfamiliarity with Latin Terminology

Contemporary legal English is rooted in the common law tradition, which itself traces its foundations to Roman law as administered by the medieval Roman Church. Since Roman law was both written and implemented in Latin, it is unsurprising that modern legal English retains a significant number of Latin terms. Latin holds an authoritative position in legal language, characterized by its conciseness, conventional usage, and standardized expression (Zhang, 2016: 58). Here are some examples of common Latin terms.

ab hoc	专案，特定	actus reus	犯罪行为
ad litem	诉讼期间	alibi	不在犯罪现场
arguendo	为争论起见	bona fide	善意，诚实信用
de novo	重新	ex parte	偏袒一方的
force majeure	不可抗力	habeas corpus	人身保护令状
inter alia	在其他事物中	nil	(什么都)没有
prima facie	初步的，表面的	stare decisis	遵循先例
ultra vires	越权行为	versus	诉，对

However, these Latin terms are rarely employed in the translation of Chinese laws and regulations. This omission stems from two primary factors: first, many translators lack familiarity with Latin terminology; second, the translation of Chinese laws and regulations is primarily conducted in English, with little established practice of incorporating Latin expressions. As a result, the occurrence of Latin terms in translated legal texts remains minimal. Taking "自始；从……开始"as an example.

Example 1:

第五十八条 无效的民事行为，从行为开始起就没有法律约束力。

Article 58 Civil acts that are null and void shall not be legally binding from the very beginning.

In this article, "从......开始" is rendered as "from the very beginning", without utilizing the Latin legal term "ab initio" commonly employed in legal English. According to *Black's Law Dictionary* (Garner, 2009:5), "ab initio" is defined as "*[Latin] From the beginning < the injunction was valid ab initio >* ". Thus, it is suggested that the translation be revised as: A void civil activity is void ab initio.

This revision not only aligns with the concise and authoritative style of legal English but also enhances the precision and doctrinal clarity of legal expression through the use of a recognized Latin term. The Latin term "ab initio" carries the full jurisprudential connotation of "void from the outset" within the common law tradition. Its application avoids the potential semantic fuzziness of the ordinary English phrase "from the very beginning", while also reflecting the professional continuity of legal language across time and space. Such terminological choice exemplifies the principle in legal translation that "conceptual equivalence" takes precedence over "literal correspondence", thereby allowing Chinese civil law concepts to be more precisely positioned within the context of international comparative law.

Moreover, the English translations of Chinese legislative texts demonstrate a notable underutilization of archaic English vocabulary, such as "therein" (在其中), "thereof" (其), "thereto" (附随), "herewith" (与此一道), "whereas" (鉴于), and "thence" (从那里). While these archaic terms have gradually faded from widespread use in modern general English, they remain highly prevalent in legal English, serving as essential linguistic features that preserve its solemnity, precision, and historical continuity. The persistence of archaic language in legal texts not only reflects the historical depth of the common law tradition but also enhances the logical rigor and interpretive stability of legal documents through their highly formulaic expressions. The current tendency to avoid such vocabulary in translations reveals limitations in translators' grasp of the stylistic conventions of legal English and, to some extent, diminishes the professional recognition of these translations within international legal discourse. This phenomenon reminds us that legal translation is not merely a linguistic conversion but also a cross-temporal and cross-cultural dialogue between legal traditions and stylistic norms.

(3) Inconsistent Translation of Terminology

Inconsistency in terminology translation is not merely a superficial issue of linguistic norms but strikes at the core of the authority and interpretive certainty of legal texts. As emphasized by Reed Dickerson, the father of American legal drafting, the foremost principle in legal drafting is "consistency of expression". A competent legal drafter must ensure that the same term maintains a consistent meaning whenever it recurs, while also avoiding the use of a single word to convey multiple meanings... In short, the same meaning must be expressed in the same way, and different meanings must be distinguished through different expressions" (Dickerson,

1986: 15–16). This principle holds fundamental significance in legal translation as well, where adherence to the "law of identity" in translating terminology has become an inviolable "golden rule" in the translation of legal texts (Zhong & Wu, 1994: 13). However, in the official English translations of China's current laws and regulations, it remains common for the same term to be rendered differently across provisions, or even within the same text.

For example, in the English translation of the *General Principles of the Civil Law of the People's Republic of China*, the term "法定代理人" appears eight times. The first seven occurrences, found in Articles 12, 13, and 14, are all translated as "agent ad litem". The eighth occurrence, in Article 64, is translated as "statutory agent". Across these four different articles, the meaning of "法定代理人" remains entirely consistent. The unnecessary variation in translation terminology clearly violates the "principle of terminological consistency" and should be standardized using the same term (Fan, 2014: 88).

Such inconsistencies not only undermine the internal logical rigor of legal texts but may also lead to interpretive conflicts in international judicial cooperation or cross-border commercial activities, thereby damaging the external credibility of China's legal system. The confusion in terminology translation fundamentally reflects a lack of systematic norms in the translation process and inadequacies in the mechanisms for conceptual alignment across legal traditions.

4.2.2 Principles of Terminology Translation

Translation principles have long been a subject of scholarly discussion. While general principles such as "faithfulness, expressiveness, and elegance" can broadly guide the translation of texts, legal texts possess distinct characteristics, systematicity, specialization, accuracy, rigor, and consistency, necessitating the development of specialized translation principles tailored to legal practice. The principles of legal translation have consistently been a focal point in academic discourse. We have compiled and summarized the relevant translation principles as follows:

Year	Scholar	Principles or Standards of Legal Translation
1998	Wang Qing, Feng Wei	Accuracy Standardization Fluency
2000	Qiu Guixi	Principle of using solemn language Principle of accuracy Principle of conciseness Principle of terminological consistency Principle of using professional terminology
2004	Du Jinbang, Zhang Fu, Yuan Liang	Treating legal expression as the primary objective Adhering to the norms of legal English as much as possible Active involvement of translators Emphasizing translation factors and their interactions (Standards: translation aligns with the spirit of the source text, meets legal objectives, and fully reflects the original)

Year	Scholar	Principles or Standards of Legal Translation
2005	Du Jinbang	Principle of language subordinating to law Principle of preserving differences while seeking common ground Principle of comparison and supplementation
2005	Li Kexing, Zhang Xinhong	Accuracy and precision Consistency and uniformity Clarity and conciseness Specialization Linguistic standardization Collaborative work
2008	Xiong Demi	Accuracy Equivalence Appropriateness Professionalism
2009	Zhang Falian	Accuracy and rigor Clarity and conciseness Consistency Stylistic standardization
2011	Xiong Demi, Xiong Shudan	Professionalism Rigor Accuracy Equivalence
2012	Song Beiping	Principle of explaining cultural background differences Principle of interpreting legal system differences Principle of presuming identical textual context Principle of localizing vocabulary and discourse
2014	Dong Xiaobo	Accuracy and equivalence Consistency and uniformity Professionalism and standardization Conciseness and simplicity
2017	Pan Qingyun	Principle of legal equivalence Principle of pragmatic equivalence, Principles of legal communication Principle of static equivalence Principle of aligning with source text type

Due to the prevalence of specialized legal terminology in legal translation, as well as industry-specific vocabulary in laws and regulations, scholars have proposed dedicated translation principles for terminology.

Year	Scholar	Principles or Standards of Terminology Translation
2002	Zhu Dingchu	Correctly understand the precise meaning of the source term in context Strive to find equivalent or near-equivalent specialized terminology in the domestic legal system When no equivalent exists, translate ambiguity with ambiguity and clarity with clarity.
2005	Jiang Dan	Accuracy (the translation must align with the characteristics of legal language and the linguistic conventions of the target text, maintaining consistency in legal connotation with the source text).

Year	Scholar	Principles or Standards of Terminology Translation
2011	Zheng Yanan	Accuracy Rigor Consistency Linguistic standardization.
2012	Qu Wensheng	Adhere to the principle of "translating terms with terms" Follow the principle of "established usage" or "precedent" Observe the relative principle of "one term, one translation" Comply with the principle of systematic translation.

By comparing the content in the tables above, we can identify several frequently recurring keywords, such as equivalence, accuracy, conciseness, and consistency. The summarization of translation principles reflects scholars' understanding of legal language and the distillation of experience gained through legal translation practice, representing personalized interpretations. Although the principles proposed by scholars vary in form, their core essence remains largely unified, with no significant divergence among them.

It must also be noted that proposing translation principles does not guarantee their complete adherence in practice. Even Yan Fu, who articulated the principles of "faithfulness, expressiveness, and elegance", may not have fully adhered to or achieved these goals himself. After all, translation is a complex intellectual activity, and the translation of legal terminology transcends the linguistic level, ascending to the realm of communication and exchange between legal cultures and national systems. As Song (2012: 320) aptly remarked, "It seems that people are eager to set standards, rules, and norms for others to follow, while they themselves may lack the ability to practice what they preach". Ultimately, translation principles represent idealized conventions, guidelines, and norms that we should strive to achieve, even if their full realization may remain elusive.

4.2.3 *Strategies and Methods for Terminology Translation*

In recent years, concepts such as "equivalence" and "equivalency" have served as important guiding principles in the study of legal terminology translation. Susan Šarčević, who long served as the head of legal translation for the European Union, combined practical translation experience with translation theory to propose a functional perspective on legal translation, viewing it as a communicative act within legal mechanisms. In her early work, she defined functional equivalence as "terms for concepts or institutions in the target legal system that perform the same functions as specific concepts in the source legal system" (Šarčević, 1997: 205), and categorized terminology translation into approximate equivalence, partial equivalence, and non-equivalence (Šarčević, 1997: 206). Šarčević's theory has had a significant impact on domestic legal translation studies and has become a frequently cited resource among scholars in the field.

Under the framework of "equivalence" as a guiding translation philosophy, scholars have also focused on discussing different translation methods. Bao (2011), analyzing the non-equivalence between English and Chinese legal terms, proposed strategies such as literal translation, explanatory translation, borrowing/substitution, neologism, non-translation, and free translation. Dong (2015a), based on Šarčević's equivalence theory, addressed the degree of equivalence between source language terms and their target language counterparts in terms of linguistic and legal functions. He suggested using exact equivalents when concepts are fully equivalent; functional equivalents when they are nearly or partially equivalent; and paraphrasing, neutral terms, borrowed terms, or neologisms when they are completely non-equivalent. Dong (2016: 177) further emphasized that the translation of legal terminology requires not only basic correspondence at the linguistic level but also fundamental equivalence in legal function between the translated term and the original. In other words, the translation of legal terms involves not only linguistic conversion but also the adaptation and coordination of different legal thinking and concepts. Wu (2016), from the perspective of equivalence construction in legal terminology translation, revisited the issue of standardization in translated terms, arguing that the formation of translated legal terminology is a translation issue but also extends beyond translation itself, involving the adaptation and reconstruction of legal culture. Zhao (2018) proposed that "equivalence" in legal terminology translation should be a dual model combining form and semantics, achieving an "equivalency" effect through the organic integration of both.

Discussing the translation of Chinese legal terminology for international audiences essentially revolves around two scenarios: "equivalence" and "non-equivalence". On one hand. if the source legal term has a conceptually equivalent term in the target legal culture, every effort should be made to identify and use this equivalent to ensure the accuracy of the terminology translation. On the other hand, if the source legal term lacks a conceptually equivalent term in the target legal culture, compensatory methods such as explanatory translation, borrowing, or creative translation should be employed to achieve effective transmission of legal function.

(1) Accuracy as the Paramount Principle

Accuracy is the lifeblood of legal language (Pan, 2004: 22). Similarly, accuracy serves as the foremost principle in legal terminology translation, a consensus widely acknowledged among scholars. As Liu (2010: 125) stated, "Accuracy and precision are the life and soul of legal terminology translation". Qu and Shi (2012: 162) emphasize that "the accurate transformation of terminology in legal translation forms the foundation for preserving the seriousness and authority of legal texts". Fan (2017: 103) further noted that "the quality of translating laws and regulations into foreign languages affects the effectiveness of China's legal exchanges with the international community and shapes the international image of China's rule of law. It is imperative to ensure translation accuracy to avoid unnecessary misunderstandings or even disputes abroad". Based on the case analyses of inaccurate terminology translations in current legal and regulatory translations, most issues arise from an insufficient understanding of the concepts and connotations of the "terms" themselves, coupled with an inadequate grasp of equivalent legal vocabulary in English. To achieve accuracy in legal terminology translation, the following four aspects must be diligently addressed.

(a) Consulting Specialized Legal Dictionaries

Translation involves the conversion between two languages. To translate laws and regulations, it is essential to consult both English and Chinese legal dictionaries. Chinese dictionaries are the prerequisite for understanding Chinese professional terminology, while English dictionaries provide the foundation for finding English equivalents. The use of dictionaries should be comprehensive and diverse, drawing from multiple sources whenever possible, as the explanations for the same term may vary between general dictionaries and specialized legal dictionaries. For example, the term "扶养" (support) is annotated in the *Contemporary Chinese Dictionary (7th edition)* (2016: 399) as "养活:把孩子~成人 *(to raise: to raise a child to adulthood)*", whereas the *Concise Dictionary of Jurisprudence* (Zeng, 2000: 463)offers a more detailed annotation: "通常由广狭两义。广义指一定亲属间一方基于身份关系，对无生活呢你的另一方在物质上和生活上的帮助好照顾。包括平辈之间的扶养、长辈对晚辈的抚养以及晚辈对长辈的赡养。狭义专指夫妻之间在物质上和生活上的帮助和照顾。非亲属关系间也能产生'扶养'，如公民可以与扶养人或集体所有制组织签订遗赠扶养协议。(*Generally has broad and narrow meanings. Broadly, it refers to the material and living assistance and care provided by one party to another who is incapable of supporting themselves, based on kinship. This includes support between peers, upbringing by elders to juniors, and support by juniors to elders. Narrowly, it specifically refers to material and living assistance and care between spouses. 'Support' can also arise in non-kinship relationships, such as when citizens enter into legacy-support agreements with supporters or collectively-owned organizations*)".

Another example is "采信" (admissibility of evidence), which is not included in the Concise Dictionary of Jurisprudence. The *Contemporary Chinese Dictionary (7th edition)* (2016: 120) annotates it as "相信(某种事实)并用来作为处置的依据:被告的陈述证据不足，法庭不予~/这组数据不准确，不宜~" (to believe (a fact) and use it as a basis for disposal: the defendant's statement lacks sufficient evidence, and the court does not admit it~/ this set of data is inaccurate and should not be admitted).

The same applies to English terminology. For instance, the term "identification" lacks a specialized annotation in *Black's Law Dictionary (9th edition)*, whereas the *Compact English-Chinese Dictionary of Anglo-American Law* (Xue, 2003: 657) provides the following annotation: "n. 鉴定；识别；认定同一；辨认；验明。证明某个被指控犯有某项罪行的人确是该罪犯或某项被提交到法庭之物正是该存在争议之物或诉讼所涉之物，或认定两种笔迹同一，以及查明诉讼中涉及的某人的身份等的过程。(*Identification; recognition; establishing identity; verification. The process of proving that a person accused of a crime is indeed the perpetrator, that an item submitted to the court is the disputed or relevant item in the litigation, establishing the identity of handwriting, or determining the identity of a person involved in the litigation*)".

Some terms may not be found in one dictionary but could be explained in great detail in another. Using different dictionaries allows for complementary resources, and specialized legal dictionaries offer greater professional advantages over general dictionaries. When translating legal terminology, it is crucial to clarify the core meaning of each term and strive to find equivalent vocabulary between the two language systems based on this core meaning.

(b) Reading Specialized English Legal Newspapers and Journals

The purpose of reading English legal newspapers or journals is to move beyond the limitations of dictionary definitions and accumulate richer legal language materials. After all, language use is dynamic, fluid, and evolving, while dictionary compilation is fixed and often lags behind the latest developments in language. Moreover, the usage of vocabulary changes depending on the context.

Reading contemporary newspapers or journals serves two main purposes: First, it helps pay attention to the use of terminology in specific contexts. Matching isolated units of meaning across cultures is merely the prelude to translation, as translators always encounter concepts within contexts. Only by considering the context can appropriate linguistic expressions be selected (Baker, 2004: 251). Second, to ensure better acceptance by the target readers of the translation, "determining functional equivalents is only the first step in a cumbersome process. Although functional equivalents perform the same function as the source concept, this does not necessarily mean they are acceptable in translation" (Šarčević, 1997: 205). The target audience for English translations of Chinese laws and regulations includes readers from both English-speaking and non-English-speaking countries. The translation of legal texts must ultimately consider the acceptability to the target audience. Contemporary English newspapers and magazines in the target language environment serve as the most suitable texts for target readers and are also the language models that translators need to read carefully, study, summarize, and emulate.

(c) Considering the Translation of Terminology Across Related Texts Systematically

To standardize the translation of legal terminology, a systematic approach is essential. This systematic thinking is reflected in two main aspects. On one hand, it is necessary to adhere to the principle of "established usage". For example, the English translation of Chinese legal titles consistently uses "Law", as seen in the translation of 《中华人民共和国刑法》 as *Criminal Law of the People's Republic of China*. Although there is considerable academic opposition, with arguments that "法" should be translated as "Act", the existing translations have been in use for a long time and have gradually gained acceptance among translators and readers. While theoretical discussions may allow for differing opinions, practical translation should generally follow established conventions.

On the other hand, the translation of terminology must be systematically considered across related texts. As Šarčević (1997: 94) notes, "For legal texts to be effective, the principle of linguistic consistency applies not only to the text being translated but also to all related texts. Therefore, when selecting equivalents, translators must consider terms used in other documents that have already acquired legal force. Since the authoritative text is considered definitive, its language serves as a precedent". For instance, Article 1 of the *Jiangsu Province Regulations on the Development of New Wall Materials* references its superior law, namely the《中华人民共和国循环经济促进法》. If the translator, during the initial translation, fails to locate the official translation of the superior law and renders it as "the *Law of the People's Republic of China on Circular Economy Promotion*", this would conflict with the officially promulgated translation "the *Circular Economy Promotion Law of the People's Republic of China*". Such inconsistency inevitably causes confusion among readers and undermines the authority of the law and the coherence of the entire legal system.

(d) Seeking Assistance from Relevant Experts

Legal translation in the new era operates against a backdrop of information explosion and unprecedented frequency of international exchanges. With the deepening of comparative linguistics and studies on Chinese and Western legal language and culture, academic demands for accuracy in legal translation have grown increasingly stringent. The specialization and complexity of legal translation have become more pronounced, necessitating greater professional support for translators to ensure the quality and effectiveness of translations.

For the translation of Chinese laws and regulations, the primary source of assistance should come from professional support provided by legislative authorities. However, as Li and Dong (2015: 228) observe, "Most regions have not yet established communication mechanisms between translators and legislative authorities when translating local regulations and rules. The translation quality of local regulations and rules is influenced by the legislative intent of the local regulations, the legislative intent of superior laws, and the tradition of official translations. With the increasing specialization in modern society, legislative work is highly professional, and the meanings and legislative intent of legal provisions (including translations) are often complex and profound. Sometimes, legislative authorities even issue specialized judicial interpretations. However, in translation work, translators are usually unable to participate in the legislative process (or the official translation process of superior laws), and many translators lack sufficient legal expertise. Therefore, to fully understand the legislative intent of regulations and rules and produce accurate translations, it is necessary to establish communication channels with the legislative authorities of local and superior laws, as well as with institutions responsible for translating relevant legal provisions, such as the Legislative Affairs Office of the State Council".

(2) Explanatory Translation

For terms that cannot find direct equivalents in the target language, or for terminology with distinct Chinese characteristics that lack corresponding terms with identical connotations in English, explanatory translation methods become necessary. "From a legal perspective, the most effective way to compensate for terminological inconsistencies may be to clarify the intended meaning in neutral language understandable to lawyers worldwide" (Šarčević, 1997: 218). For example, the term

"宅基地" (homestead) that appears in the *Property Law of the People's Republic of China* is a typical example of vocabulary with Chinese characteristics.

Example 1:

第一百五十三条　宅基地使用权的取得、行使和转让，适用土地管理法等法律和国家有关规定。

Article 153 Such laws as the Land Administration Law and the relevant State regulations shall be applicable to the obtaining, exercising and transferring of the right to the use of house sites.

Here, "宅基地" is translated as "house site", which literally means "land for building houses". The Chinese-English Dictionary defines "宅基" as "the foundation of a house; the site of a house" (English Department Dictionary Group, Beijing Foreign Studies University, 1997: 1580). This dictionary also adopts an explanatory translation approach, as there is no exact equivalent concept in the common law system. However, does this translation fully convey the connotations of "宅基地"?

According to the *Contemporary Chinese Dictionary (7th edition)* (2016: 1643), "宅基地" refers to "我国公民个人依法取得农村集体所有的用于建造房屋并有居住使用权的土地 (*land collectively owned by rural communities in China, legally obtained by individual citizens for building houses and possessing residential use rights*)". The core connotations of this term lie in its "rural" nature and "collective ownership". In contrast, the United States has one of the highest rates of private home ownership in the world, with approximately 65% of households owning their homes (Zhang, 2001: 31). Such differences in national contexts make it difficult to achieve complete equivalence at the lexical level, and "house site" does not convey these institutional distinctions. To enable English-speaking readers to accurately understand the collective ownership nature of China's rural housing land, an explanatory translation method should be adopted, such as translating it as "house site on collectively-owned rural land". This approach supplements the concept of "collective ownership" and specifies the "rural area" limitation, thereby more fully conveying the legal and social implications of the term.

(3) Borrowed Translation

The process of legal translation is one of legal exchange, transplantation, and development. Chinese legal terminology has been continuously enriched through translation, and borrowed translation has played a significant role in this regard. Some terms unique to China or traditional legal terms have established usage in Chinese legal texts and corresponding authoritative translations. Translators may directly borrow these existing translations, provided they correctly understand the source term's meaning, without the need to "create new translations" (Liu, 2013: 87).Taking "行政复议"as an example.

Example 1:

第二条　公民、法人或者其他组织认为具体行政行为侵犯其合法权益，向行政机关提出行政复议申请，行政机关受理行政复议申请、作出行政复议决定，适用本法。

Article 2 This Law is applicable to a citizen, legal person or any other organization who considers that his or its lawful rights and interests have been infringed upon by a specific administrative act, and applies for administrative reconsideration to an administrative organ which accepts the application for administrative reconsideration, and makes a decision of administrative reconsideration.

Although common law countries have their own systems for resolving administrative disputes, the terminology, rules, and procedures differ significantly. In the absence of an exact equivalent concept, translators should prioritize using legal language that expresses a similar concept. Translators familiar with common law culture will likely associate the term with "reconsideration" as used in parliamentary law. Black's Law Dictionary defines "reconsider" as: "To discuss or take up (a matter) again. Under parliamentary law, a motion to reconsider sets aside a certain vote already taken and restores the motion on which the vote is being reconsidered to its status immediately before the vote occurred. Making a motion to reconsider suspends a vote already taken until the assembly decides whether to reconsider it" (Garner, 2009: 1387).

According to legal scholars, the term "行政复议" is composed of "复" (meaning "again" or "re-") and "议" (meaning "deliberation and decision"), prefixed by "行政" to indicate that the administrative organ reviews and re-examines administrative disputes (Ying & Liu, 1999: 1). Therefore, translating "行政复议" as "administrative reconsideration" is not only straightforward and comprehensible but also aligns with the conventions of the target legal language (Teng & Kong, 2008: 63).

(4) Creative Translation

Creative translation of terminology is not as straightforward as one might imagine. Although Šarčević (1997: 92) advocated that legal translation should "break free from constraints and exercise creativity" this "creativity" is subject to limitations. Legal translation is "more constrained than other types of translation". Translators' creativity is limited to the parts of legal texts he refers to as "free", that is, the portions of the text not governed by specialized terminology or standardized formats. Translators are encouraged to select words, expressions, and grammatical structures in the target language that best convey the meaning of the source text.

In the process of "learning and adoption of Western law in the East", particularly in English-to-Chinese legal translation, numerous creative translations have emerged. For example, common law systems place great emphasis on litigation procedures, leading to the introduction of concepts previously absent in China's judicial system, such as "plea bargain" and "plea agreement" (辩诉交易, 辩诉协议). Similarly, terms like "pension warrants" (年金支付通知), "share warrants" (认股权证书), and "fidelity insurance" (职工忠诚保险) have been adopted into China's legal practice. However, the situation differs for Chinese-to-English legal translation.

It is believed that creative translation must withstand the scrutiny of target-language readers. Unlike English-to-Chinese translation, where the Chinese context is familiar and the acceptance of newly coined terms can be gauged relatively easily, translating Chinese laws and regulations into English requires entering an

English-language context and gaining acceptance from English-speaking readers. Assessing and measuring this acceptance is no simple task.

With the acceleration of internationalization, collaborative international translation has gained increasing attention in fields such as classical literature and philosophy. International sinologists, researchers, and translators are increasingly favored in translation activities, as native English speakers are often the best practitioners and gatekeepers for translating Chinese into English. Notably, creative translation of Chinese legal terminology may require the support and collaboration of legal scholars and linguists from target-language countries. In other words, the localization and creative translation of Chinese legal terminology for target-language contexts necessitates the active participation of "native" translators.

4.3 Standardization of Translation of Terminology in Laws and Regulations

The translation of legal terminology constitutes the core task in the standardized translation of laws and regulations. From a practical perspective of legal text translation, the most severe issue affecting translation quality is the arbitrariness and lack of standardization in translating legal terminology, which subsequently undermines the seriousness and authority of legal texts (Xu, 2015: 62). The causes of non-standardized translation of legal terminology are multifaceted. Achieving standardization in the translation of legal terminology requires not only translators to enhance their professional competence but also proactive leadership from the organizational departments responsible for translating laws and regulations. Furthermore, it demands collaborative efforts from experts in jurisprudence, linguistics, and translation studies to conduct in-depth research and discussion on the subject.

4.3.1 Translators Must Continuously Enhance Their Professional Expertise

Legal translation, as a representative form of specialized translation, spans knowledge across three major disciplines: linguistics, translation studies, and jurisprudence. To excel in legal translation, one must be proficient in both law and bilingual communication. Legal translation primarily targets elite audiences, demanding high-quality outcomes and presenting significant technical challenges. In this sense, legal translators are themselves part of the social elite. As the first gatekeepers of the translation process and mediators between two languages, translators' competence directly impacts the accuracy of legal terminology translation. Translating legal terminology is only one part of comparative legal studies, yet precise translation requires translators not only to possess legal knowledge but also to holistically understand different national legal systems. Each term must be meticulously examined, with careful consideration of its connotations and denotations. Only such an approach yields precise and practice-tested terminology translation. To accurately translate legal terminology, translators must strengthen their legal knowledge, enhance their specialization, and build a foundation in comparative Chinese-English linguistics. By conducting multidisciplinary and multi-level comparisons between legal English and legal Chinese, translators can study their distinctive features and similarities in areas such as linguistic ontology, socio-cultural contexts, customs, and legal systems, thereby identifying patterns and methods for interlingual conversion.

4.3.2 Constructing a Terminology Translation Database

The standardization and normalization of legal terminology directly influence the processes of legislation, compliance, law enforcement, and adjudication. In the information age, establishing a terminology database is a crucial means of achieving the specialization, standardization, unification, and normalization of legal terminology. According to relevant national standards in China, it is necessary to standardize legal terminology through the creation of a legal terminology database (Xiang, 2006; Jia, 2007). "Modern society has entered the digital era. Without the aid of digital technology, the efficiency of translation standards consultation relying entirely on human effort would be very low. Hasselgard's research found that using computer database technology to build parallel corpora can significantly improve the efficiency of translation studies" (Li & Dong, 2015: 231).

It is contended that constructing a terminology translation database is also an effective management of linguistic assets. Linguistic assets refer to "language resources formed by past transactions and events, owned or controlled by an enterprise, which will bring economic benefits to the enterprise. Based on the main characteristics of language services, linguistic assets can be divided into two categories: terminology and translation memory" (Wang & Wang, 2012: 118). Of course, unlike translation projects undertaken by translation companies, the translation of Chinese laws and regulations is typically organized by the enacting bodies (such as the Legislative Affairs Office of the State Council or local legislative affairs offices). The purpose of translation is not economic profit but legal and cultural exchange. The linguistic assets generated from translating laws and regulations are owned and controlled by government legal departments. "The primary function of translation memory is to eliminate repetitive tasks for translators, thereby improving efficiency. By storing text segments as translation units using existing source and target texts, one or more translation memory databases can be established" (Wang & Wang, 2012: 120). Therefore, strengthening the management of these linguistic assets can elevate the efficiency of their utilization to new heights, placing the translation of laws and regulations on a more standardized and normalized track. The establishment of a terminology translation database should be led by national legislative bodies or national-level legal departments (such as the Legislative Affairs Office of the State Council), organizing translation departments across regions to compile standardized translations and continuously update and expand the database over time.

4.3.3 Re-standardizing the Terminology Translation Database

Establishing a terminology translation database is only the first step in standardizing the translation of legal terminology. Ongoing management and research of the database are still required. On one hand, "the terminology management process includes analyzing and collecting existing data, extracting terms, translating terms, using terms, and maintaining terms" (Wang & Wang, 2012: 122–123). All things are constantly evolving, and creating a terminology translation database does not mean the work is done once and for all. Existing databases require continuous maintenance, updates, and adaptation to the times. Regular updates are necessary to phase out obsolete terms and incorporate new ones, ensuring the database remains relevant and dynamic. On the other hand, further standardization of the terminology translation database is needed to continuously enhance its "value". The extraction of terminology translation is based on original corpora, and these terms still require in-depth discussion by experts. Further efforts are needed to ensure the accuracy of terminology translation. "Low-level, repetitive compilation of dictionaries and databases is futile; they cannot solve major problems. They may partially facilitate translation convenience but hardly achieve the standardization and unification of legal terminology translation. Clearly, standardized English translations of legal terms require further standardization. Organizing experts to update and supplement existing standardized outcomes is the fundamental solution to the problem" (Qu, 2012: 75).

4.4 Conclusion

In summary, the standardization of legal terminology translation is, in essence, a strategic endeavor to optimize the efficacy of legal discourse dissemination through systematic knowledge engineering. The continuous enhancement of translators' professional competence, the intelligent construction of terminology databases, and the dynamic re-standardization of translation resources collectively form the infrastructure that ensures the accurate cross-border transmission of legal texts.

First of all, as frontline practitioners in cross-system legal dialogue, translators' professional capabilities directly determine the precision of terminology conversion. The interdisciplinary knowledge structure required for legal translation, encompassing jurisprudence, linguistics, and the institutional culture of target countries, makes it a highly specialized intellectual activity. This professionalism is reflected not only in the mastery of conceptual systems but also in the sensitive grasp of legislative intent behind legal provisions. Translators must engage in ongoing comparative legal studies to establish rational frameworks for terminology mapping based on an understanding of institutional differences, thereby avoiding interpretive deviations caused by cultural presuppositions.

Secondly, the construction of terminology databases essentially transforms decentralized translation practices into inheritable and iterative public linguistic assets. Digital management not only addresses translation efficiency but, more importantly, establishes a cross-departmental and cross-hierarchical terminology reference system through the accumulation of standardized translation repositories. When legislative bodies, judicial institutions, and translation departments share the same terminology platform, the consistency of legal interpretation is technically safeguarded. This mechanism is particularly suited to China's multi-level legislative system, effectively coordinating terminology usage between central and local authorities, as well as between comprehensive and specialized laws.

Lastly, the continuous updating and re-standardization of databases are crucial to maintaining the vitality of the terminology system. Legal terminology is inherently dynamic: new legislation gives rise to new concepts, judicial practice enriches terms with new connotations, and the integration of international law introduces foreign terminology. Regular reviews and revisions of terminology databases by interdisciplinary teams comprising legal and linguistic experts serve both as quality checks of existing translations and as scholarly responses to the evolution of legal concepts. This dynamic maintenance mechanism ensures that the terminology system maintains the stability of core concepts while promptly reflecting the development of the legal system.

These three layers of mechanisms are nested to form a closed loop: professional translators produce high-quality initial translations, terminology databases enable knowledge accumulation and sharing, and expert maintenance ensures system evolution. When this collaborative mechanism functions effectively, legal terminology translation transcends mere linguistic conversion to become a precise bridge connecting different legal civilizations. It not only enhances the quality of individual translations but also strengthens the internal coherence of the legal system through systematic terminology management, enabling Chinese legal concepts to be expressed clearly, consistently, and contemporaneously in international dialogues. While such efforts may appear technical, they profoundly impact the clarity and acceptability of cross-border legal communication, laying a linguistic foundation for the exchange and mutual learning of legal civilizations.

References

Baker, M. 2004. *Routledge encyclopedia of translation studies*. Shanghai: Shanghai Foreign Language Education Press.

Bao, K. 2011. Non-equivalence of English-Chinese legal terminology and its translation strategies. *Chinese Science & Technology Translators Journal* 4.

Dickerson, R. 1986. *The fundamentals of legal drafting*. 2nd ed. Boston: Little, Brown.

Dong, X. 2015a. On the "equivalent" translation of English-Chinese legal terminology. *Journal of Xi'an International Studies University* 3.

Dong, X. 2015b. *Legal English translation case tutorial*. Beijing: Beijing Jiaotong University Press; Tsinghua University Press.

Dong, X. 2016. *Research on the standardization of legislative language in China*. Beijing: Beijing Jiaotong University Press.

Du, J., F. Zhang, and L. Yuan. 2004. Problems and solutions in the English translation of Chinese laws and regulations. *Chinese Translators Journal* 3.

Du, J. 2004. *Forensic linguistics*. Shanghai: Shanghai Foreign Language Education Press.

Fan, H. 2014. A review of major translation errors in the English version of the General Principles of the Civil Law of the People's Republic of China. *Chinese Translators Journal* 4.

Fan, H. 2017. A discussion on the English translation of several legal terms in the Copyright Law of the People's Republic of China. *Chinese Translators Journal* 1.

Garner, B. A. 2009. *Black's law dictionary*. 9th ed. St. Paul: West Publishing Co.

Institute of Linguistics, Chinese Academy of Social Sciences, ed. 2016. *Contemporary Chinese dictionary*. 7th ed. Beijing: The Commercial Press.

Jia, L. 2007. The path to legal terminology standardization: Building a legal term bank. *Journal of Shanxi Institute of Economic Management* 2.

Jiang, J. 1994. Legal terminology and its motivation. *Journal of Guizhou Police Officer Vocational College* 4.

Li, J., and X. Dong. 2015. Standardization and countermeasures in the translation of local regulations and rules: A study based on translation practice in Jiangsu Province. *Southeast Academic Research* 4.

Li, Z. 1998. *An initial exploration into forensic linguistics*. Beijing: Law Press.

Liu, F. 2013. On four methods for achieving unified Chinese-English translation of legal terminology. *Chinese Translators Journal* 6.

Liu, R. 2010. On the accuracy of legal terminology translation. *Foreign Language Research* 4.

Liu, W. 2003. Classification of English legal terms and analysis of translation examples. *Terminology Standardization & Information Technology* 3.

Liu, Y. 1999. On the characteristics of legal terminology. *Journal of Political Science and Law* 2.

Pan, Q. 1997. *Cross-century Chinese legal language*. Shanghai: East China University of Science and Technology Press.

Pan, Q. 2004. *Evaluation and analysis of Chinese legal language*. Shanghai: Lexicographical Publishing House.

Qu, W. 2012. Problems and causes in the translation of Chinese legal terminology for foreign audiences: With remarks on the standardization of Chinese legal term translation in recent years. *Chinese Translators Journal* 6.

Qu, W. 2017. On word selection in the English translation of legal terminology. *Journal of University of Shanghai for Science and Technology (Social Science Edition)* 3.

Qu, W., and W. Shi. 2012. *A course in legal English reading and translation*. Shanghai: Shanghai People's Publishing House.

Šarčević, S. 1997. *New approach to legal translation*. The Hague: Kluwer Law International.

Song, B. 2012. *Legal language*. Beijing: China University of Political Science and Law Press.

Sun, G., ed. 1997. *Grand dictionary of chinese law (jurisprudence volume)*. Beijing: China Procuratorial Press.

Teng, C., and F. Kong. 2008. *English-Chinese legal translation: Theory and practice*. Hangzhou: Zhejiang University Press.
Wang, H., and H. Wang. 2012. *Practical translation project management*. Beijing: China Translation & Publishing Corporation Ltd.
Wang, L. 2004. *A brief discussion on the standardization of legal document terminology*, 2. Terminology Standardization & Information Technology.
Wu, C. 2016. Exploring the translation of legal terms: Based on considerations of term equivalence and concept transfer. *Shanghai Journal of Translators* 6.
Xiang, Q. 2006. Considerations on building an English-Chinese public security legal terminology database. *Supplement to the Journal of Sun Yat-sen University* 9.
Xie, B. 2003. *The compact dictionary of Anglo-American law*. Beijing: Law Press.
Xu, D. 2015. Text selection, style mastery and terminology translation: Thoughts on compiling legal translation textbooks. *Chinese Translators Journal* 3.
Yang, S. 2003. On legal terminology. *Journal of Politics and Law* 6.
Ying, S., and X. Liu. 1999. *Lectures on the administrative reconsideration law of the People's Republic of China*. Beijing: China Fangzheng Press.
Zeng, Q., ed. 2000. *Concise dictionary of law*. Shanghai: Shanghai Lexicographical Publishing House.
Zhang, F. 2016. *Legal English translation course*. Beijing: Peking University Press.
Zhang, F. 2017. *A contrastive study of Chinese and Western legal language and culture*. Beijing: Peking University Press.
Zhang, T. 2001. The evolution of U.S. housing policy and its lessons. *Chinese & Foreign Real Estate Herald* 7.
Zhao, G. 2018. Legal terminology translation from the perspective of "equivalence". *Language Education* 3.
Zhao, P. 2017. A study on the translation patterns of legal terminology: Taking the English translation of terms in the Exit-Entry Administration Law as an example. *Legal and Economy* 9.
Zhong, R., and J. Wu. 1994. Legal texts must adhere to the law of identical translated names. *Chinese Translators Journal* 5.
Zhou, Y., M. Gu, Y. Gao, and Y. Zheng, eds. 1991. *Grand dictionary of law*. Beijing: China University of Political Science and Law Press.

Chapter 5 Translation of Words and Expressions in Laws and Regulations

Abstract This chapter delves into the nuanced translation of words and expressions in Chinese laws and regulations, focusing on five core dimensions: the translation of fuzzy legal expressions, which requires balancing flexibility with legal certainty; the translation of legal terms with distinctive Chinese characteristics, necessitating context-sensitive adaptation to convey unique socio-legal concepts; the translation of common terms used in legal texts, where ordinary language assumes specialized meanings; the differentiation and translation of synonyms in legislative language, a critical task for maintaining precision and avoiding ambiguity; and the translation of synonymous or near-synonymous terms, which reflects the stylistic and rhetorical features of Chinese legal drafting. Together, these aspects highlight the complex interplay between linguistic accuracy, legal functionality, and cultural specificity in the translation of Chinese legislative texts.

Keywords Fuzzy legal expressions · Legal terms with Chinese characteristics · Synonyms · Translation

In linguistic communication, words play a vital role, as all linguistic units larger than words are composed of them. Words form phrases, sentences, discourse, and texts, while the process of combining words into sentences gives rise to grammatical rules or syntax. The renowned British linguist Wilkins (1972: 11) noted, "Without grammar, very little can be conveyed; without vocabulary, nothing can be conveyed at all". Vermeer (1992: 147) similarly emphasized, "Knowing words is the key to understanding and being understood. Learning a new language largely involves learning new words. Grammatical knowledge alone does not yield high language proficiency". As the fundamental unit of legal language, integrating sound, form, and meaning, legal words has long been a core subject and primary area of linguistic research. It constitutes an essential component throughout the entire process of learning and applying legal language. In the English translation of laws and regulations, the translator's grasp of the breadth and depth of legal words directly influences their legal language proficiency and translation competence.

X. Dong, Y. Zhang, *On Translation of Laws and Regulations in China*,
https://doi.org/10.1007/978-981-95-9406-1_5

The translation quality of words directly impacts the authority of legal texts and the effectiveness of cross-border communication. Precise lexical conversion is not merely a linguistic issue but a critical factor in ensuring that legal concepts remain undistorted in cross-system dialogues. The translator's command over the breadth and depth of legal vocabulary determines the consistency of legal interpretation in international exchanges and the dissemination efficacy of institutional discourse. This necessitates that translation practices be grounded in a deep understanding of the underlying logic of legal systems, with systematic lexical development safeguarding the rigor of legal texts, thereby laying a linguistic foundation for the mutual learning of legal cultures across borders.

5.1 Translation of Fuzzy Legal Words and Expressions

As a specialized branch of prescriptive language, legal language possesses a distinct stylistic character, with accuracy being its most crucial feature. However, the rapid pace of societal change makes it impossible for finite laws and regulations to cover every conceivable scenario, thus rendering the use of fuzzy expressions in legal texts unavoidable. Williams, in his seminal work Law and Language, observed: "The language constituting legal provisions is, to a greater or lesser extent, inherently ambiguous. While the core meanings of words are clear, their boundaries become increasingly blurred toward the edges. The peripheral meanings at the margins of language are nebulous and highly prone to dispute, making it difficult to determine whether they fall within or outside the scope of the term's extension… This is not due to legislative oversight but is an unavoidable characteristic of any language" (Liu 2003: 31). His analysis precisely articulates the objective existence of fuzziness in legal language. Legal fuzziness refers to the semantic indeterminacy of certain legal provisions or expressions, reflecting uncertainties in the classification, boundaries, or states defined by law. It is typically employed when the nature, scope, extent, or quantity of legal facts cannot be precisely delineated (Chen 2006: 114). In both legal provisions and judicial practice, the use of fuzzy expressions in legal language is pervasive.

5.1.1 Causes for Fuzziness of Legal Language

Fuzziness is an inherent attribute of legal language, permeating all stages of legislation, judiciary, and law enforcement. The manifestations of fuzziness in legal language are diverse, and its causes are complex, arising from both objective and subjective factors. These primarily include the following aspects:

(1) The Infinity of Objective Phenomena and the Limitations of Human Cognition

The objective world is vast and infinitely complex. Human cognitive abilities are limited, often allowing only a partial understanding of many objective phenomena, which makes it difficult to describe them fully and precisely through language. No matter how deeply humans understand objective phenomena, the inherent inadequacy of language in fully encapsulating them remains unresolved.

Laws regulate various social relations in society. However, due to the limitations of human cognition, legislators cannot exhaustively list all social relations and their associated legal phenomena when drafting laws. This inevitably results in legal gaps and imperfections. To enhance the inclusiveness and ensure the stability of laws, legislators must employ fuzzy expressions to bridge the gap between limited human cognition and the infinite complexity of legal phenomena.

(2) The Essential Nature of Natural Language

The fuzziness of legal language primarily stems from the inherent uncertainty of natural language itself. The renowned British legal philosopher Herbert Hart argued that words possess both a "core meaning" and a "penumbra". Within the "core meaning", the meaning of a word is clear and definite, whereas in the "penumbra", its meaning is unconstrained and entirely open-ended. The fuzziness of language arises precisely from this "penumbral structure" of words (Hart 1996: 129).

Language serves as the vehicle for legal thought. Regarding the relationship between law and language, the British philosopher David Hume asserted: "Law and legal systems are purely linguistic forms. The world of law begins with language, and laws are established and promulgated through words…" (Shu 1995: 348). This illustrates that issues in legal language are fundamentally rooted in the nature of language itself. The fuzziness of legal language is objectively determined by the inherent uncertainty of natural language.

(3) The General Nature of Legal Principles

Laws are characterized by universality and generality, meaning they are not targeted at specific individuals or organizations and can be applied repeatedly rather than just once. To ensure the broad applicability of laws, legislators often employ fuzzy expressions to expand their scope of coverage. Legal phenomena in real life are diverse and varied, making it impossible for humans to quantify all such phenomena or describe them in precise language. In addressing these phenomena, the formulation of legal provisions with universal guiding significance requires abstraction, generalization, induction, judgment, and reasoning, all of which necessitate the use of highly generalized and fuzzy language (Yang 2006: 70).

5.1.2 Functions of Fuzzy Legal Words and Expressions

The ultimate purpose of law lies in "resolving disputes and clarifying boundaries", which demands a high degree of precision in legal language to avoid ambiguity in expression. However, this does not mean that legal language excludes the use of fuzzy expressions. On the contrary, fuzzy expressions occupy a significant proportion of legal language and serve unique legal functions:

(1) Ensuring the Rigor of Law

Legal phenomena are complex and ever-changing. It is impractical to exhaustively enumerate all possible subjects of action, motives, methods, and outcomes in legal provisions. To ensure the comprehensiveness and completeness of legal norms, legislators must employ fuzzy expressions to encompass as many uncertainties as possible. For example, Article 22 of the *National Security Law* stipulates: "*Any citizen or organization has the right to report or lodge a complaint with the superior national security authority or relevant departments regarding any actions by national security authorities or their personnel that exceed their authority, constitute abuse of power, or involve other illegal acts. The superior national security authority or relevant departments shall promptly investigate the facts and take responsibility for handling the matter*". Since legislators cannot list all possible circumstances, the term "other" is used after enumerating several major illegal acts. This approach highlights key points while covering general cases, ensuring that legal expression is comprehensive and leaves no gaps, thereby maximizing the effectiveness of combating crimes.

(2) Enhancing Judicial Flexibility

As Francis Bacon noted, "the best laws leave the least room for judicial discretion". This indicates that laws must possess a certain degree of flexibility and elasticity to allow room for their application. Fuzzy expressions, with their unclear boundaries and strong adaptability and inclusiveness, meet the flexibility required by legal language. For instance, when a judge convicts a perpetrator under Article 35 of the *Criminal Law*, which states: "*If judicial personnel abuse their authority to commit acts specified in the preceding three paragraphs jointly with others, they shall be given a heavier punishment…*". The fuzziness of the term "从重处罚 (heavier punishment)" allows the judge to impose a penalty within the statutory range based on the specifics of the case. Thus, fuzzy expressions in legal provisions grant judicial personnel and institutions a certain degree of discretion, enabling them to exercise subjective initiative, adhere to the principles of "freedom, fairness, order, and efficiency", and accurately determine penalties according to specific circumstances, thereby upholding the fairness and justice of the law.

(3) Reflecting the Humanistic Spirit of Law

The essence of jurisprudence is the study of humanity. In the application of law, attention must be paid to the respect and care for individuals inherent in the law itself (Yuan 2009: 186). While law covers all aspects of social life, when it comes to sensitive topics such as state secrets and personal privacy, the law has both the responsibility to clarify them and the obligation not to fully disclose them. To reflect the humanistic care of the law, the use of fuzzy expressions becomes particularly necessary. For example, when describing the circumstances of cases involving serious violations of citizens' personal rights, such as rape, insult, defamation, or sexual harassment, fuzzy expressions can be appropriately employed. This approach protects the personal privacy of the parties involved, upholds public morality, informs the public of the case, and maintains the dignity of the law.

5.1.3 *Strategies for Translation of Fuzzy Legal Words and Expressions*

Mellinkoff (1953: 12) observed: "Legal language can be described as a language full of expressions of generality, fuzziness, and flexibility". This perspective underscores the irreplaceable role of fuzzy expressions in legal texts and highlights the importance of their translation. Specifically, fuzzy expressions in laws and regulations can be handled through the following methods:

(1) Literal Translation: Fuzziness for Fuzziness

Literal translation of fuzzy expressions refers to the direct conversion of fuzzy terms between two languages. Sometimes, legislators deliberately use fuzzy language for specific purposes when drafting laws. In such cases, literal translation best reflects the legislative intent and preserves the original fuzzy information.

Example 1:

第六条 国家安全机关在国家安全工作中依法行使侦查、拘留、预审和执行逮捕以及法律规定的其他职权。

Article 6 The State security organs shall exercise, in the work of State security, the functions and powers of investigation, detention, preliminary examination and execution of arrest according to law and other functions and powers as stipulated by the law.

Example 2:

第一百一十八条 当事人一方因不可抗力不能履行合同的，应当及时通知对方，以减轻可能给对方造成的损失，并应当在合理期限内提供证明。

Article 118 Either party that is unable to fulfill the contract due to the force majeure shall notify the other party in time in order to reduce losses possibly inflicted to the other party, and shall provide evidence thereof within a reasonable period of time.

In the examples above, terms such as "其他 (other)" and "合理 (reasonable)" are fuzzy expressions that do not provide clear boundaries or scope. For instance, the term "reasonable period" is subject to individual interpretation, and such fuzzy language broadens the applicability of the law, maintains flexibility in its enforcement, and allows room for discretion. In such contexts, translators should adopt a "fuzziness for fuzziness" strategy to fully and accurately convey the meaning of the source text.

(2) Free Translation: Transforming Fuzziness into Precision

If literal translation fails to achieve formal or semantic equivalence between the source and target texts, or if it prevents target-language readers from experiencing the same effect and understanding as source-language readers, translators may appropriately handle fuzzy expressions in the source text based on its underlying intent. This involves converting fuzzy information in the target language into relatively precise language to preserve the original connotation.

Example 1:

第一百四十八条 扶养适用与被扶养人有最密切联系的国家的法律。

Article 148 Maintenance of a spouse after divorce shall be bound by the law of the country to which the spouse is most closely connected.

Article 148 of the *General Principles of Civil Law* addresses the applicable law for maintenance relationships in foreign-related civil matters. The term "被抚养人" (the person to be maintained) is fuzzy in the source text, but it should not be blindly translated as a fuzzy term in English. According to Article 147 of the *General Principles of Civil Law*, which states: "*Marriage between a citizen of the People's Republic of China and a foreigner shall be governed by the law of the place where the marriage is contracted, and divorce shall be governed by the law of the place where the court handling the case is located*", the term "被抚养人" here refers specifically to a spouse after divorce. Therefore, the translator renders it as "spouse after divorce" to prevent conveying misleading information to target-language readers and avoid disputes over the scope of legal application in judicial practice.

(3) Addition

When translating fuzzy expressions into the target language, translators may appropriately supplement them to make the translation more complete in meaning and to convey the original content more faithfully and fluently. Consider the following examples:

Example 1:

第四十四条 海上货物运输合同和作为合同凭证的提单或者其他运输单证中的条款，违反本章规定的，无效。

Article 44 Any stipulation in a contract of carriage of goods by sea or a bill of lading or other similar documents evidencing such contract that derogates from the provisions of this Chapter shall be null and void.

Example 2:

第六条 凡在中华人民共和国领域内犯罪的，除法律有特别规定的以外，都适用本法。

Article 6 This Law shall be applicable to anyone who commits a crime within the territory and territorial waters and space of the People's Republic of China, except as otherwise specifically provided by law.

In Example 1, the term "其他运输单证" (other transport documents) is fuzzy. The translator adds "similar" to clarify its meaning. In Example 2, the term "中华人民共和国领域" (territory of the People's Republic of China) refers to all areas within China, including land, territorial waters, and airspace. Thus, the translator should not simply translate it literally as "the territory of the People's Republic of China" but instead supplement it as "the territory and territorial waters and space of the People's Republic of China".

(4) Omission

For fuzzy expressions in the source text that serve no practical purpose or are included to prevent loopholes and preempt issues, translators may omit them in translation to avoid redundancy. Consider the following example:

Example 1:

第二十五条 政府指导价、政府定价的具体适用范围、价格水平，应当根据经济运行情况，按照规定的定价权限和程序适时调整。

Article 25 The specific applicable scope and price level of the government-guided prices and government-set prices shall be adjusted at an appropriate time in the light of the economic performance and in pursuance of the pricing authority and procedures provided for.

In the example above, the term "情况" (situation) is a categorical term commonly used in Chinese. As Joan Pinkham notes: "While categorical terms serve their purpose in Chinese, they add no meaningful or stylistic value when included in English sentences…" (Pinkham 2000: 3–45). Therefore, categorical terms such as "情况" (situation), "行为" (behavior), and "状态" (state), which frequently appear in laws and regulations, are often omitted in translation.

5.2 Translation of Legal Terms with Chinese Characteristics

The legal system with Chinese characteristics is a product of China's social development. Its formation is shaped by cultural traditions, political systems, legislative frameworks, and other factors, closely tied to China's national conditions. This means that many of its expressions bear distinct Chinese characteristics and are unique to China's legal system. Legal terminology with Chinese characteristics constitutes the core component of China's legal language, reflecting the typical features of its legal system. The translation of such terminology serves as a crucial window to showcase China's achievements in the rule of law. High-quality translation of legal terminology plays a positive role in shaping the positive image of the Chinese government, enhancing international understanding of China, safeguarding China's legitimate rights and interests in international exchanges, and strengthening China's international discourse power.

When translating legal terminology with Chinese characteristics, three principles should be followed: accuracy, flexibility, and contemporaneity. Accuracy is the soul of legal text translation. Legal texts are highly formal and rigorous, and as the fundamental components of such texts, the translation of terminology must be free of any deviation, as inaccuracies would directly undermine the normative quality of the entire text. Flexibility is reflected in the translation's ability to fully convey the original meaning while aligning with the thinking habits of foreign readers, without compromising the essence of Chinese characteristics. Contemporaneity means that the translation of terminology must keep pace with the times. The socialist legal system with Chinese characteristics is dynamic and open to development, evolving alongside China's economic and social progress. In this process, new legal terminology will emerge, and translations of existing terms may require adjustments. Therefore, terminology translation must be continuously updated.

5.2.1 Strategies for Translation of Legal Terms with Chinese Characteristics

The quality of translating legal terminology with Chinese characteristics directly impacts China's international image in the rule of law. However, due to differences in legal systems and understanding, these terms with Chinese characteristics can sometimes be difficult to translate in international communication. It is often unavoidable that translations may fall short due to the lack of exact equivalents in foreign languages (Cao 2017: 123). Therefore, translators must adopt flexible approaches, ensuring accuracy while employing domestication, foreignization, or a combination of both, depending on the specific communicative purpose and context.

(1) Foreignization

Due to the unique nature of socialist legal terminology with Chinese characteristics, foreignization has become the primary translation strategy. Foreignization emphasizes the source language, preserving linguistic and cultural differences and conveying the original content in a manner consistent with the source language's expression. This approach is reflected in translation techniques such as transliteration and literal translation, with literal translation being the most commonly used method for translating legal terminology with Chinese characteristics. Such terminology reflects China's unique legal institutions, legal thinking, and the spirit of the rule of law. Employing foreignization can maximally retain the cultural distinctiveness of these terms, avoid semantic deviation, and facilitate the global dissemination of "Chinese characteristics". Consider the following examples:

Legal Terms with Chinese Characteristics	Translation
中国特色社会主义法律制度	the socialist system of laws with Chinese characteristics
全国人民代表大会	the National People's Congress
地方政府	local people's government
人民法院	people's court
人民调解	people's mediation
公安部	Ministry of Public Security

It is evident that these Chinese expressions lack direct equivalents in English. Therefore, literal translation is recommended to preserve their linguistic form and cultural connotations. This process essentially involves coining new terms. These "Chinese-style translations" remain faithful to the original texts, serving as a genuine window for the international community to understand China's legal development. They represent a form of international language that adheres to the basic norms of English while retaining Chinese characteristics. Consequently, both Chinese and foreign media tend to adopt foreignized translations.

While this source-reader-centered foreignization strategy has its merits, not all "foreignized" translations achieve the desired effect. For example, the Chinese legal concept of "死缓" (death penalty with reprieve) is a unique form of death penalty execution in China. Some texts have literally translated it as suspension of execution for death sentence. Although this translation may seem appropriate, it fails to explain what "死缓" actually entails, lacking substantive meaning. "死缓" refers to a system in which criminals who are sentenced to death but do not require immediate execution are given a 2-year reprieve, during which they undergo labor reform to assess their potential for rehabilitation. Therefore, its appropriate translation should be death sentence with a 2-year reprieve and forced labor. This example demonstrates that while the foreignization strategy is effective, it cannot resolve all translation challenges, making "domestication" equally essential.

(2) Domestication

While the nature of socialist legal terminology with Chinese characteristics emphasizes foreignization as the primary translation strategy, aimed at promoting the global dissemination of Chinese legal culture represented by such terminology, the essence of translation from a textual perspective is an act of domestication that caters to foreign readers (Yu 2015: 40). All translation activities must take into account the expressive habits and needs of the target audience. When foreignized terminology is cumbersome or fails to achieve its communicative purpose, translators should adopt domestication as a strategy. For example, "事业单位" refers to social service organizations established by the government using state-owned assets, engaged in activities such as education, science and technology, culture, and health, with a certain degree of public welfare. Thus, it should be translated as public institutions, which is far more accurate than the term business entities found in some texts. In translating legal terminology with Chinese characteristics, foreignization takes precedence, while domestication serves as a beneficial supplement. Relying solely on either foreignization or domestication in a one-size-fits-all approach is ineffective. Translators must analyze specific contexts and cannot generalize.

5.2.2 Standardization of Translation for Legal Terms with Chinese Characteristics

The standardization of legal terminology translation refers to the activities aimed at achieving uniformity and consistency in translating specialized concepts within the legal domain. In the translation of Chinese laws and regulations, many legal terms with Chinese characteristics suffer from non-standard translations, primarily manifested in inappropriate translations of the terms themselves and inconsistencies in translating the same term across different texts or within the same text. The confusion in the translation of legal terminology can easily lead to ambiguity, significantly undermining the seriousness and stability of the law. Therefore, it is necessary to standardize their translations. As He (2011: 18) noted, the precision and consistency in translating Chinese legal terminology into foreign languages are requirements for new forms of legal exchanges between China and other countries.

China places great emphasis on standardizing legal terminology and has achieved some results to date. For example, the Department of Translation, Review, and Foreign Affairs of the Legislative Affairs Office of the State Council published the *Chinese-English Glossary of Terms in the Laws and Regulations of the People's Republic of China* in 1998 and the *Handbook of Common Sentence Patterns for Legal Translation* in 2005. These two handbooks have since become essential guides for translators of laws and regulations. Despite these achievements, it is undeniable that the standardization of laws and regulations remains a challenging and ongoing task. On one hand, the state must continue to strengthen the standardization of terminology translation; on the other hand, translators must consciously choose standardized professional terminology in their work.

5.3 Translation of Common Terms in Laws and Regulations

Common terms in laws and regulations refer to frequently occurring words in legal texts. They are also among the most representative vocabulary in legal documents. To a certain extent, accurately translating these terms lays the foundation for the correct translation of a law or regulation. Over long-term translation practice, these common terms have developed established translations, some with one or multiple renderings. While some of these translations have proven effective, others remain subject to debate, making their standardization essential. This section focuses on the translation of nine commonly used terms in laws and regulations, analyzing their appropriate renderings and proposing standardized approaches.

5.3.1 Translation of "制定"

The term "制定" refers to the creation or establishment of laws, also known as "legislation". In Chinese laws and regulations, "制定" is primarily translated in two ways: formulate and enact. For example:

Example 1:

第一条 为了发展社会主义商品经济，促进技术进步，改进产品质量，提高社会经济效益，维护国家和人民的利益，使标准化工作适应社会主义现代化建设和发展对外经济关系的需要，制定本法。

Article 1 This Law is formulated with a view to developing the socialist commodity economy, promoting technical progress, improving product quality, increasing social and economic benefits, safeguarding the interests of the State and the people and suiting standardization to the needs in socialist modernization and in the development of economic relations with foreign countries.

Example 2:

第一条 为了加强对档案的管理和收集、整理工作，有效地保护和利用档案，为社会主义现代化建设服务，制定本法。

Article 1 This Law is enacted with a view to strengthening the management, collection and arrangement of archives and effectively protecting and using archives in the service of socialist modernization.

Currently, in domestic legal documents, the phrase "制定法律" is often rendered as formulate law, and cross-referencing among documents suggests that formulate has become a customary usage (Fu 2003: 67). However, translating "制定" as formulate is not entirely appropriate. According to the Oxford Advanced Learner's Dictionary, formulate has two main meanings: to create or prepare something carefully, giving particular attention to the details; to express your ideas in carefully chosen words. The Longman Dictionary of Contemporary English further provides common collocations for the first meaning of formulate, such as formulate a policy/plan/strategy, etc. Thus, formulate corresponds to the Chinese meaning of "构想、规划或清楚地阐明" (to conceive, plan, or articulate clearly) and is typically followed by terms like "policy", "plan", or "strategy". It is not equivalent to "制定" in the context of legislation.

A more formal and accurate expression for "制定(法律法规)" in legal contexts is enact. The Longman Dictionary defines enact as "to pass a law", and Black's Law Dictionary provides a similar definition: "to make into law by authoritative act; to pass". Therefore, "制定法律" should be translated as enact law, and "制定法条" as enact clause. In conclusion, "制定" should be translated as enact rather than formulate in the context of legislative acts.

5.3.2 Translation of "公布"

In Chinese laws and regulations, "公布" is commonly used to indicate the official announcement or proclamation of laws, administrative regulations, etc., and in this context, it is equivalent to "颁布" (promulgation). Consider the following example:

Example 1:

1988年9月5日第七届全国人民代表大会常务委员会第三次会议通过 1988年9月5日中华人民共和国主席令第六号公布 自1989年5月1日起施行。

Adopted at the Third Meeting of the Standing Committee of the Seventh National People's Congress on September 5, 1988 and promulgated by Order No. 6 of the President of the People's Republic of China on September 5, 1988.

Here, "公布" refers to the act of a government body making drafted laws, regulations, or decrees known to the public. Therefore, promulgate should be used, meaning "to announce a law officially and publicly". However, it is important to note that promulgate is a formal and official term, and its subject should typically be laws, decrees, or regulations.

When "公布" is used to indicate the disclosure of information, results, facts, or other matters to the public, translating it as promulgate may sound overly formal or even forced. In such cases, terms like publish or announce are more appropriate and natural.

Example 2:
第二十八条 城市规划经批准后，城市人民政府应当公布。
Article 28 The plan for a city shall be announced by the people's government of the city after it is approved.

Example 3
第二十四条政府指导价、政府定价制定后，由制定价格的部门向消费者、经营者公布。
Article 24 After the government-set and guided prices are determined, they shall be made public by the price departments.

5.3.3 Translation of "遵守"

Laws grant people their rights while also stipulating the obligations they must fulfill. The term "遵守" is frequently used in Chinese laws and regulations to express mandatory provisions. Depending on the subject and context, it can be translated in various ways, as illustrated below:

(1) When the Subject is a Person or Organization

In Chinese laws and regulations, "遵守" often follows a subject that is a person or organization. In such cases, it can be translated as abide by or observe. Abide by is more formal and carries a stronger tone than observe, making it the more common choice in official legal translations.

Example 1:
第七条 现役军人必须遵守军队的条令和条例，忠于职守，随时为保卫祖国而战斗。
Article 7 Active servicemen must abide by the rules and regulations of the army, faithfully discharge their duties and always be ready to fight for the defense of the motherland.

Example 2:
第九条供电企业和用户应当遵守国家有关规定，采取有效措施，做好安全用电、节约用电和计划用电工作。
Article 9 Power supply enterprises and users shall both observe the relevant regulations of the State by adopting efficient measures to achieve the safe, economical and planned use of power.

(2) When the Subject is a Thing

When the subject is an inanimate entity such as a law, plan, or project, "遵守" can be translated as observe, comply with, conform to, in compliance with, or in conformity with.

Example 1:

第二条 制定和实施城市规划，在城市规划区内进行建设，必须遵守本法。

Article 2 This Law shall be observed when the plan for a city is being formulated or implemented, or when construction is being carried out within a planned urban area.

Example 2:

第十三条　新建、改建、扩建的建设项目，必须遵守国家有关建设项目环境保护管理的规定。

Article 13 Every project under construction, renovation or expansion must conform to the regulations of the State governing environmental protection.

5.3.4 Translation of "规定"

In legal contexts, "规定" can function both as a noun and a verb. As a noun, it is typically translated as provision. As a verb, it generally has three possible translations: prescribe, provide for (or provide), and stipulate.

"Prescribe", as defined in *Black's Law Dictionary*, means "t*o dictate, ordain, or direct; to establish authoritatively (as a rule or guideline)*". It emphasizes the authoritative establishment or determination of a law, carrying a connotation of command or mandate. "Provide for (or provide)" carries the implicit meaning of "supplying" and is more neutral and objective than prescribe, often used to indicate that "a certain clause provides for….". "Stipulate" is primarily used in contracts or agreements to mean "agree" but can also be used in laws and regulations to convey "agree" or "stipulate". In summary, all three can convey the meaning of "stipulate" in legal contexts, with subtle differences in nuance.

Example 1:

第四十七条……行政长官的产生办法由附件一《澳门行政长官的产生办法》规定。

Article 47 The specific method for selecting the Chief Executive is prescribed in Annex I Method for the Selection of the Chief Executive of the Macao Special Administrative Region.

Example 2:

第十三条……婚前保健工作规范和婚前医学检查项目由国务院卫生行政部门规定。

Article 13 …The work norms of pre-marital health care and the items of pre-marital medical examination shall be provided for by the administrative department of public health under the State Council.

Example 3:

第十一条 招用人员简章应当包括用人单位基本情况、招用人数、工作内容、招录条件、劳动报酬、福利待遇、社会保险等内容，以及法律、法规规定的其他内容。

Article 11 The employment brochure shall include basic information about the employer, number of workers to be employed, types of work, qualifications for employment, labor remunerations, welfare treatments, social insurance, etc., as well as other contents stipulated in laws and regulations.

5.3.5 Translation of "批准"

In legal contexts, "批准" refers to the process whereby an authorized body, in accordance with statutory authority and conditions, reviews applications or submitted matters from parties and decides whether to grant permission. Common collocations in Chinese laws and regulations include "报……批准" (to be submitted to… for approval) and "经/由……批准" (subject to the approval of…). "报……批准" is often translated as be submitted to… for approval. "经/由……批准" is more formally rendered as be subject to the approval of…, though it may also be translated as be approved by….

Example 1:

第二十一条 省、自治区、直辖市的土地利用总体规划，报国务院批准。

Article 21 The overall planning for land utilization of the provinces, autonomous regions and municipalities directly under the Central Government shall be submitted to the State Council for approval.

Example 2:

第十一条 监狱的设置、撤销、迁移，由国务院司法行政部门批准。

Article 11 The establishment, abolition or move of a prison shall be subject to the approval of the department of judicial administration under the State Council.

5.3.6 Translation of "实施"

"实施" is another high-frequency verb in Chinese laws and regulations, referring to the execution or enforcement (of laws, policies, etc.). It is commonly translated as implement, conduct, carry out, or put into practice, all of which convey the meaning of making something that has been initiated happen. These terms can often be used interchangeably depending on the context.

Example 1:

第十五条 有关部门依法将纳税人、扣缴义务人遵守本法的情况纳入信用信息系统，并实施联合激励或者惩戒。

Article 15 The relevant departments shall, in accordance with the law, include information on the compliance of taxpayers and withholding agents with this Law in their credit information systems, and implement joint incentives or sanctions.

Example 2:

第七条 国务院生态环境主管部门对全国土壤污染防治工作实施统一监督管理；国务院农业农村、自然资源、住房城乡建设、林业草原等主管部门在各自职责范围内对土壤污染防治工作实施监督管理。

Article 7 The ecological and environmental department of the State Council shall conduct uniform supervision and administration of the prevention and control of soil pollution across the country; and the agriculture and rural affairs, natural resources, housing and urban-rural development, forestry and grassland, and other departments of the State Council shall conduct supervision and administration of the prevention and control of soil pollution within their respective competence.

5.3.7 *Translation of* "强制"

In Chinese laws and regulations, "强制" is translated in three ways: compulsory, mandatory, and coercive. Although all three convey the meaning of "compulsory", they are not without differences. The *Compact English-Chinese Dictionary of Anglo-American Law* explains the distinction between "compulsory" and "mandatory" as the former refers to requirements imposed by law or legal procedures, while the latter emphasizes "commanding or obligatory behavior". Based on this analysis, consider the following example:

Example1:

违反本条例规定生产、储存、运输、经营、携带、使用、销毁易燃易爆危险物品的，由公安机关消防机构责令停止违法行为，可以对易燃易爆危险物品采取查封、扣押等强制措施。

In case of the violations against the provisions of these Regulations in manufacturing, storing, transporting, operating, carrying, using and/or destroying dangerous flammable or explosive goods, the fire department of the public security organ shall order the violator to stop such illegal acts, and may take such coercive measures as sealing up and/or seizing the dangerous flammable or explosive goods, etc.

The above sentence lists specific means related to "强制措施" (coercive measures), aligning with the meaning of coercive as "relating to or using force". Therefore, using coercive to convey "强制" in this context is appropriate.

5.3.8 *Translation of* "转让"

"转让" is a high-frequency term in laws and regulations, referring to the transfer of one's property, lawful rights, interests, or entitlements. Depending on the nature of the item being transferred, "转让" is generally translated in three ways: transfer, assign, and negotiate. According to the *Compact English-Chinese Dictionary of Anglo-American Law*, these terms are defined as follows: "*transfer, the conveyance of (ownership) rights from one person to another, or the transfer of property rights, titles, etc; assign, the conveyance of personal property or movable assets, especially the transfer of personal or movable property; negotiate, the transfer of a bill of exchange or other negotiable instrument from one person to another, making the transferee the holder of the instrument*".

From these definitions, it can be concluded that transfer is a broad term referring to all forms of conveyance. Assign and negotiate are more specific: assign emphasizes the transfer of property, while negotiate pertains to the transfer of negotiable instruments. Translators must choose the appropriate term based on the nature of the item being transferred. The following three examples illustrate the correct usage of these terms in Chinese laws and regulations:

Example 1:

第二十四条　国有不可移动文物不得转让、抵押。建立博物馆、保管所或者辟为参观游览场所的国有文物保护单位，不得作为企业资产经营。

Article 24 State-owned unmovable cultural relics may not be transferred or mortgaged. A state-owned protected historical and cultural site, on which a museum, preservation institute is established or which is used as a tourist site, may not be operated as the assets of an enterprise.

Example 2:

第四十八条　中标人应当按照合同约定履行义务，完成中标项目。中标人不得向他人转让中标项目，也不得将中标项目肢解后分别向他人转让。

Article 48 The bid winner shall perform duties and complete the bidding project, as specified in the contract. The bid winner shall neither assign the project to any other person nor dismember the project and then assign the project in part to other persons.

Example 3:

第二百八十一条　按照规定可以背书转让的票据持有人，因票据被盗、遗失或者灭失，可以向票据支付地的基层人民法院申请公示催告。依照法律规定可以申请公示催告的其他事项，适用本章规定……

Article 281 The holder of an instrument negotiable by endorsement according to the relevant provisions may, if the instrument is stolen, lost or extinguished, apply to the basic people's court at the place of payment of the instrument for an announcement to urge declaration of claims…

5.3.9 *Translation of* "以上", "以下", *and*"……以上……以下"

In Chinese laws and regulations, the translations for "以上", "以下", and "……以上……以下" vary widely, but not all are appropriate.

Example 1:

惯窃、惯骗或者盗窃、诈骗、抢夺公私财物数额巨大的，处五年以上十年以下有期徒刑；

Habitual thieves, cheats, or those who steal, cheat, or rob a huge amount of public or private property shall be sentenced to imprisonment between five to ten years;

Example 2:

经营者违反本法第十三条规定进行有奖销售的，监督检查部门应当责令停止违法行为，可以根据情节处以一万元以上十万元以下的罚款。

Where an operator makes sales with prizes attached in contravention of the provisions of Article 13 of this Law, the relevant control and inspection authority shall order it or him to desist from the illegal act and may, according to circumstances, impose on it or him a fine of more than RMB 10,000 yuan and less than RMB 100,000 yuan.

In Chinese laws and regulations, unless otherwise specified, "以上" and "以下" typically include the baseline number. However, expressions such as between… to or more than… less than imply "between… and…" or "greater than… and less than…", which narrows the scope compared to the inclusive meaning of "……以上……以下". Therefore, using these translations for "……以上……以下" in the above examples is inaccurate. Additionally, common erroneous translations for "以上" include over or beyond, while "以下" is often mistranslated as under or below.

The accurate and relatively standardized translations for "以上" and "以下" are not less than and not more than, respectively. For "……以上……以下", the appropriate translations are between not less than… and not more than… or not less than… but not more than…. These expressions mean "including and not exceeding… while not falling below…" and accurately correspond to the inclusive meaning of "……以上……以下" in Chinese legal provisions.

5.4 Differentiation and Translation of Synonyms in Laws and Regulations

Accuracy is the soul of legal translation, as the authority and solemnity of the law are reflected through the precision of language. To ensure the accuracy of legal translation, the careful selection of words by translators is particularly important. Laws and regulations contain a large number of synonyms, often grouped in pairs or sets, with many similarities in meaning and usage. Without careful differentiation, confusion in translation between these words is inevitable. This section enumerates six groups of easily confused terms in laws and regulations. Based on a meticulous analysis of the meaning of each group of terms, their correct translations are explored, aiming to provide insights and references for the in-depth study of legal translation.

5.4.1 Differentiation and Translation of "罚金" and "罚款"

"罚金" refers to a criminal penalty imposed by a people's court, requiring an individual or entity convicted of a crime to pay a specified amount of money to the state. It is a form of criminal punishment. "罚款" encompasses two meanings: judicial fines, which is a coercive measure imposed by a people's court in civil or administrative litigation, requiring a person or entity obstructing legal proceedings to pay a specified amount of money and administrative fines, which is a penalty imposed by an administrative authority on individuals or entities violating administrative regulations, requiring payment of a specified amount of money. Both terms involve the demand by state authorities for specific persons to pay a certain amount of money to the state within a stipulated period.

In the translation of laws, regulations, and normative documents, "罚金" and "罚款" are primarily expressed as fine and penalty. Analysis of English translations of Chinese laws and regulations reveals that, when "罚金" or "罚款" appears individually, fine generally refers to "罚金" (criminal penalty), while penalty may refer to either "罚金" or "罚款". When both terms appear in the same sentence, fine typically refers to "罚金", and penalty refers to "罚款".

Example 1:

第二百一十五条　公司违反本法规定，应当承担民事赔偿责任和缴纳罚款、罚金的，其财产不足以支付时，先承担民事赔偿责任。

Article 215 Where a company violates any provision of this Law, it shall bear the corresponding civil liabilities of compensation, and shall pay the corresponding fines and pecuniary penalties; if the property thereof is not enough to pay for the compensation, it shall bear the civil liabilities first.

Example 2:

第二十八条第一项　处罚款、罚金、追缴、没收财产或者违反国家规定征收财物、摊派费用的，返还财产。

Paragraph 1 of Article 28 in case of imposition of a fine or penalty, recovery or confiscation of property, or expropriation of property and article, or appointment of expenses in violation of the provisions of the state, the property shall be returned.

5.4.2 Differentiation and Translation of "过错" *and* "过失"

"过错" refers to an imputable and reprehensible act committed by a person under a subjective state of negligence, recklessness, intention, or even malice. "过失" refers to a psychological state where a person should have foreseen that their actions might cause socially harmful consequences but failed to do so due to negligence, or having foreseen them, lightly believed they could be avoided. Legally speaking, both "过失" and "过错" pertain to subjective errors on the part of the actor. The scope of "过错" is broader, encompassing both "过失" (negligence) and "故意" (intention). "过失" is merely one form of "过错". In most cases, "过错" leads to civil liability, while "过失" can result in criminal liability. In translations of Chinese laws and regulations, the term related to "过错" is fault, while "过失" is translated as negligence.

Example 1:

第二十六条劳动合同依照本法第二十六条规定被确认无效，给对方造成损害的，有过错的一方应当承担赔偿责任。

Article 26 Where a labor contract is confirmed invalid under Article 26 of this Law and any damage is caused to the other party, the party at fault shall be liable for compensation.

Example 2:

第四十三条　财产代管人因故意或者重大过失造成失踪人财产损失的，应当承担赔偿责任。

Article 43 Where the property custodian causes damage to the absentee's property intentionally or with gross negligence, the custodian shall assume compensatory liability.

5.4.3 *Differentiation and Translation of* "执业人员" *and* "从业人员"

"执业人员" refers to individuals who meet the conditions stipulated by law, have obtained the corresponding professional certificates in accordance with the law, and are engaged in providing services to the public, such as lawyers holding a lawyer's certificate or doctors holding a medical license. "从业人员" refers to individuals engaged in a specific industry or providing services. The key distinction lies in whether the individual holds a relevant professional certificate. If a person working in a certain field has not obtained the required professional certificate, they are considered "从业人员" (employees or staff) in that field; otherwise, they are "执业人员" (practitioners). Based on this understanding, translators of Chinese laws and regulations often render "执业人员" as practitioner, while "从业人员" is defined as "员工、职员" and translated as employee or staff.

Example 1:

第十六条 公证员是符合本法规定的条件，在公证机构从事公证业务的执业人员。

Article 16 A notary shall be a notarial practitioner who meets the conditions as prescribed by this Law and is working in a notarial office.

Example 2:

第四十条 从业人员有依法接受职业培训和继续教育的权利和义务。

Article 40 Employees shall have the right and obligation to receive vocational training and continuing education according to law.

5.4.4 *Differentiation and Translation of* "抵押" *and* "质押"

Both "抵押" and "质押" are important forms of security interests in rem under the law. Due to the similarity in their names, they are often conflated.

Article 33 of the *Security Law of the People's Republic of China* stipulates: "本法所称抵押，是指债务人或者第三人不转移对本法第三十四条所列财产的占有，将该财产作为债权的担保。债务人不履行债务时，债权人有权依照本法规定以该财产折价或者以拍卖、变卖该财产的价款优先受偿 (*Mortgage as used in this Law means that a debtor or a third party, without transferring the possession of the property listed in Article 34 of this Law, uses such property as security for the performance of an obligation. If the debtor fails to perform the obligation, the creditor shall have the right to convert the property into money or to auction or sell the property in accordance with the provisions of this Law, and to have priority in being paid with the proceeds therefrom*)". From the definition alone, it is generally inappropriate for Chinese translators to render "抵押" as mortgage. The reason is that mortgage is a form of security that requires the transfer of property rights to the creditor, equivalent to what is commonly referred to as "mortgage financing" today. However, as the boundaries of property rights transfer in Anglo-American law regarding mortgage have become increasingly blurred, it is not entirely incorrect for Chinese translators to use mortgage to denote "抵押". In common law systems, the term that more closely corresponds to the meaning of "抵押" is charge, which means that the mortgagor does not need to transfer ownership of the property to the mortgagee but only grants the mortgagee certain specific rights. Hong Kong law translates this as "押记" (charge) (Song 2011: 90). In summary, "抵押" can be translated as mortgage or charge, but based on the analysis of translations of Chinese laws and regulations, "抵押" is almost universally rendered as mortgage.

In contrast to "抵押", which does not involve the transfer of possession of the collateral, "质押" refers to the transfer of possession of certain property by the debtor or a third party to the creditor, with the latter holding the property as security for the former's payment of money or performance of an obligation. The corresponding term for "质押" in common law systems is pledge, which means "security by a pledge of property".

5.4.5 Differentiation and Translation of "注销" and "吊销"

In legal contexts, the terms "注销行政许可" (cancellation of administrative permits) and "吊销营业执照" (revocation of business licenses) are frequently mentioned. What distinguishes the two? "吊销" is a punitive legal action taken by administrative authorities to forcibly terminate an entity's operating rights, qualifications, or licenses, such as "business licenses", "permits", or "certificates". It typically appears in the liability provisions of laws and regulations and is imposed when the subject has violated relevant legal or regulatory provisions".注销" refers to a procedural action applied for according to legal procedures and executed by competent state authorities. It represents a normal termination process and does not involve value judgments; it is purely a procedural act.In Chinese laws and regulations, "吊销" is typically translated as revoke, while "注销" is translated as cancel.

Example 1:

第九条 有下列情形之一的，由省、自治区、直辖市人民政府司法行政部门撤销准予执业的决定，并注销被准予执业人员的律师执业证书……

Article 9 Under either of the following circumstances, the justice administrative authority of a province, autonomous region or municipality directly under the Central Government shall revoke a decision on approving the practice of law, and cancel the lawyer's practicing certificate of the person whose practice of law is approved…

Example 2:

第八十五条 保险公司违反法律、行政法规，被金融监督管理部门吊销经营保险业务许可证的，依法撤销。由金融监督管理部门依法及时组织清算组，进行清算。

Article 85 An insurance company shall be dissolved in the event that its insurance license is revoked by the financial supervision and regulation department due to the violation of laws, or administrative regulations. The financial supervision and regulation department shall promptly appoint a liquidation task force to carry out the liquidation procedures.

5.4.6 Differentiation and Translation of "修订" and "修正"

In legal contexts, "修订" refers to the comprehensive modification of laws and regulations by statutory authorities, including significant changes to the names and structures of legal texts, which can be termed as a "comprehensive revision". On the other hand, "修正" refers to the modification of specific clauses or minor content within laws and regulations, which can be termed as a "partial amendment". These two terms correspond to revise and amend in English, respectively.

Example 1:

根据1992年9月4日第七届全国人民代表大会常务委员会第二十七次会议《关于修改〈中华人民共和国专利法〉的决定》第一次修正。

Amended in accordance with the Decision of the Standing Committee of the Seventh National People's Congress on Amending the Patent Law of the People's Republic of China at its 27th Meeting on September 4, 1992.

Example 2:

第二十五条 本细则由经贸部负责解释，由经贸部自行修订。

Article 25 The authority to interpret and revise the Detailed Rules resides in MFERT.

5.5 Translation of Synonymous or Near-Synonymous Terms in Laws and Regulations

In Anglo-American law, the use of synonymous or near-synonymous terms is relatively common. Early discussions on this phenomenon and its translation were presented by Yang (1998) and Dong Xiaobo (2004) in their research papers. Later scholars, including Li and Zhang (2006), Qu and Shi (2012), Wang (2013), Zhang (2016), and Zhang (2017), also addressed the translation of such terms in their monographs. However, these discussions and studies have primarily focused on English legal texts. In fact, Chinese legislation also contains synonymous or near-synonymous terms. Although these terms constitute only a small portion of Chinese laws and regulations, they reflect the uniqueness of the Chinese language and the fundamental characteristics of legal texts. Currently, few scholars have systematically examined synonymous or near-synonymous terms in Chinese legislation or explored their translation. This section discusses such terms in Chinese laws and regulations and summarizes general translation principles.

5.5.1 Synonymous or Near-Synonymous Terms in Anglo-American Law

The precision and highly formulaic nature of legal terminology stem from the inherent need of law to pursue certainty and authority. In the legal documents of the Anglo-American legal system, including statutes, case law documents, contracts, wills, trust agreements, and other normative texts, a unique linguistic phenomenon is prevalent: the juxtaposition of two or three semantically similar or identical words within a single sentence. This structure typically manifests as "doublets" or "triplets", whose essence lies in constructing a semantic composite through adoption of multiple synonymous terms, thereby ensuring logical comprehensiveness and interpretive uniqueness in legal expression. Such expressions are not mere rhetorical redundancy but a specialized form developed by legal language to prevent interpretive ambiguity and strengthen normative force. As scholars have noted, "The use of synonyms in legal texts not only reflects the solemnity of legal language and the precision of legal style but also serves as an essential mechanism for achieving complete and accurate communication of legal meaning through semantic complementarity and mutual delimitation" (Zhang 2016: 13).

In the Anglo-American legal tradition, many such synonymous structures have solidified into conventional expressions with specific legal connotations, widely accepted in judicial practice and academic research. Additionally, a significant number of synonymous couplets are employed as rhetorical strategies to pursue precision and avoid semantic ambiguity. The table below lists common examples of synonymous couplets found in Anglo-American legal texts (Zhang 2016: 64–66; Zhang 2017: 74).

Synonymous Terms	Synonymous Terms
acknowledge and confess	act and deed
adjust, compromise, and settle	adopted by me or born to me
advice, opinion, and direction	agree and covenant
aid and abet	all and every
all and singular	alter or change
annul and set aside	any and all
assign, transfer	assume and agree
attorney and counselor at law	attorney or lawyer
bind and obligate	build, erect or construct
business, undertaking	buy or purchase
by and through	by and with
cancel and set aside	cancel and terminate
cease and desist	cease and come to an end
cease and terminate	chargeable or accountable
changes and modifications	children and issue
conjecture and surmise	constable or sheriff
convey and transfer	costs charges and expenses
damaged or destroyed	deem and consider
execute and perform	documents and writings
due and collectible	due and owing
due and payable	each and all
each and every	engage,hire and employ
entering or breaking	entirely and completely
evidencing and relating to	excess and unnecessary
fair and equitable	fair and reasonable

Synonymous Terms	Synonymous Terms
false and fraudulent	final and conclusive
finish and complete	fit and proper
fit and suitable	for and during
for and in consideration of	for and on behalf of
force and effect	fraud and deceit
free and clear	free and unfettered
free and without consideration	from and after
full and complete	full force and effect
furnish and supply	give and grant
give and bequeath	goods and effects
good and sufficient	have, hold and possess
heed and care	heirs and devisees
hold and keep	if and when
in and for	in and to
in my stead and place	in truth and in fact
indebtedness and liabilities	interpretation or construction
keep and maintain	kind and character
larceny or theft or stealing	last will and testament
legal and binding	let or hindrance
levies and assessments	lien, charge or encumbrance
loans or advances	loss or damages
lot, tract or parcel	made and entered into
made and provided	made, ordained and appointed
make, declare, and publish	maintenance and upkeep
meet and just	mend, maintain, and repair
mentioned or referred to	mind and memory
minor or child or infant	modified and changed
nature or description	nominate, constitute
null, void and of no force	obligation and liability
obey, observe and comply with	observe, perform
of and concerning	ordain and establish
order and direct	order, adjudge, and decree
over, above	own or possess
pardon or forgive	part and parcel
pay, satisfy, and discharge	peace and quiet
perform and discharge	performance or observance
place, install or affix	possession and control
power and authority	property or chattels or goods
provisions and stipulations	release and discharge
relieve and discharge	remise, release and quitclaim
rented or loaned	rest and remainder
revoked and annulled	right, title and interest
rights and remedies	rules and regulations
save and except	seized and possessed
save and except	shun and avoid

Synonymous Terms	Synonymous Terms
sell, transfer, and dispose of	situate, lying, and being in
signed, published	staff and workers
sole and exclusive	suffer or permit
stipulate and agree	supersede and displace
suit, claim or demand	terms and conditions
term or covenant	then and in that event
terminate, cancel o revoke	true and correct
to have and to hold	type and correct
truth and veracity	unless and until
understood and agreed	void and of no effect
vacate, surrender	void and of no value
void and of on force	act and deed

The use of synonymous terms is to convey a shared meaning through lexical accumulation. "The piling up of several synonyms is essentially a matter of form. To enable readers to maximize their understanding of the source text and overcome cultural barriers is an inescapable responsibility of the translator. If this unique phenomenon in Anglo-American legal language is not appropriately handled by the translator, readers will inevitably find themselves lost in confusion, unable to discern the intention behind the verbose original text. Therefore, when dealing with synonymous couplets, translators must take responsibility: identify the common meaning they pursue and express it directly with a single Chinese word. Profession is profession, tariff is tariff, clarity and directness are paramount" (Yang 1998: 27). Additionally, scholars such as Li and Zhang (2006: 93) and Qu (2012: 159) also contend that, in the translation process, synonymous repetitive phrases should generally be condensed into a single term.

Synonymous Terms	Translation
aid and abet	同谋
attorney or lawyer	律师
acknowledge and confess	承认
annul and set aside	取消，注销，废除
buy or purchase	购买
free and clear	没有义务
cease and desist	终止
heirs and devisees	继承人
part and parcel	重要部分
minor or child or infant	未成年人
null and void	无效的
last will and testament	遗嘱
goods and chattels	财产
provisions and stipulations	规定
terms and conditions	条件
larceny or theft or stealing	盗窃

5.5.2 *Synonymous Terms in Chinese Laws and Regulations*

In written Chinese expression, there exists a notable abundance of repetitive phrases. Pinkham (2000: 63) refers to these as "redundant twins" or repetitive parallel phrases, such as "帮助和支持" (help and assistance), "意见和建议" (views and opinions), "鼓励和支持" (encourage and promote), "讨论和探讨" (discuss and debate), "认真仔细" (prudent and cautious), "情感和感情" (sentiments and feelings), and so forth. Evidently, such repetitive expressions are acceptable, even necessary, in Chinese to avoid ambiguity, emphasize meaning, provide balance and symmetry, or simply for phonetic harmony and structural parallelism. Pinkham (2000: 66–68). categorizes these repetitive parallel phrases into three types: basic synonyms, the meaning of one word is virtually the same as that of the other; terms with inclusive meanings, the meaning of one word is contained in or implied by the other; and non-substantive terms, the meaning of one word is so fuzzy and general that it cannot be differentiated from the other. In fact, legal language in legal texts often overlaps with ordinary language, and the repetitive parallel phrases commonly found in Chinese expression also appear in Chinese legislative texts. Similar repetitions frequently occur in China's laws and regulations.

(1) Basic Synonyms

Example 1:

第十九条 县级以上地方人民政府应当健全特困人员供养制度，对无劳动能力、无生活来源且无法定赡养、抚养、扶养义务人，或者其法定赡养、抚养、扶养义务人无赡养、抚养、扶养能力的老年人、残疾人以及未满16周岁的未成年人，给予特困人员供养。

The *Contemporary Chinese Dictionary* (seventh edition) defines "扶养" as "*to raise; to bring up a child*" (2016: 399), and "抚养" as "t*o care for and nurture; to raise children*" (2016: 404). Both terms essentially mean "to raise a child", with no significant distinction between them.

Example 2:

第一条 为贯彻落实尊重劳动、尊重知识、尊重人才、尊重创造的方针，推动科学技术进步，调动科学技术工作者的积极性和创造性，加快创新型省份建设，根据《国家科学技术奖励条例》，结合本省实际，制定本办法。

The *Contemporary Chinese Dictionary (seventh edition)* defines "贯彻" as "*to thoroughly implement or embody (policies, principles, spirit, methods, etc.)*" (2016: 483), and "落实" as "*to put into practice; to make plans, policies, measures, etc. concrete and achievable*" (2016: 864). Again, there is no great difference in meaning therebetween.

(2) Terms with Inclusive Meanings

Example 1:

第二条 本省行政区域内特种设备的生产(包括设计、制造、安装、改造、修理)、经营、使用、检验、检测和特种设备安全的监督管理，适用本条例。

The *Contemporary Chinese Dictionary (seventh edition)* defines "检测" as "*to inspect and measure*" and "检验" as "*to inspect and verify; to examine and confirm*" (2016: 635). "检测" inherently includes the meaning of "检验".

(3) Non-Substantive Terms

Example 1:
第一条 为了完善劳动合同制度，明确劳动合同双方当事人的权利和义务，保护劳动者的合法权益，构建和发展和谐稳定的劳动关系，制定本法。

In the phrase "构建和发展", the term "发展" (develop) adds minimal semantic value. The sentence remains fully coherent even if "发展" is omitted.

(4) Rhyming and Parallel Terms

In both Chinese and Western legal history, greater attention has been paid to the "truth" and "goodness" of the law, achieving fairness and justice to resolve disputes, while the "beauty" of legal language has largely been overlooked". Much of the earliest law produced by humanity was preserved or transmitted in the form of poetry… Law expressed in poetic form is known as poetic law" (Ge 1998: 4). Over the long historical process, legal language has gradually evolved into a professionalized language, yet its poetic characteristics have been partially retained. The poetic features of legal language are primarily reflected in two aspects: on the one hand, in legal English, numerous pairs of synonyms or synonymous repetitions are guided by "and/or", where two or three near-synonyms appear in a single sentence; on the other hand, legal English also exhibits a wealth of synonymous or near-synonymous parallel usages with alliterative features, contributing to its poetic quality (Wang 2013: 179–180). For example: *damaged or destroyed*, *aid and abet*, *each and every*, *false and fraudulent*, and so on. Similar lexical phenomena exist in Chinese laws and regulations. To achieve formal uniformity or poetic effect, there is often a reliance on the accumulation of parallel vocabulary or the use of four-character structures. Such repetition not only enhances the accuracy of legal language and emphasizes the intended meaning but also makes the text rhythmic, structurally balanced, and memorable for readers.

(a) Rhythming Words

Rhythmic repetition in Chinese involves continuously combining new words around a core vocabulary to form an open group. For example, based on "诉" (lawsuit), terms such as "本诉" (original lawsuit), "反诉" (counterclaim), "上诉" (appeal), "申诉" (petition), and "抗诉" (protest) are formed. Similarly, from "刑" (penalty), terms like "减刑" (commutation), "缓刑" (probation), "判刑" (sentencing), "徒刑" (imprisonment), and "死刑" (death penalty) are derived.

Example 1:
新闻媒体应当开展养老服务宣传，在全社会营造敬老、养老、助老、爱老氛围。

(b) Parallel Words

Example 1:

第七十九条 公安机关交通管理部门及其交通警察实施道路交通安全管理，应当依据法定的职权和程序，简化办事手续，做到公正、严格、文明、高效。

第二十五条 交通信号灯、交通标志、交通标线的设置应当符合道路交通安全、畅通的要求和国家标准，并保持清晰、醒目、准确、完好。

The two articles above have all used parallel vocabulary to address the specific requirements for certain deeds. These parallel vocabulary, though different in meaning, have all achieved uniformity in form, making the expression of law more precise and clear.

5.5.3 Translation of Synonymous Terms in Laws and Regulations

The civil law system and the common law system are fundamentally different, with their legal terminology and vocabulary belonging to distinct systems. The lexical expressions in China's laws and regulations carry Chinese characteristics and may not always find exact equivalents in the common law system. While synonymous parallel phrases in common law texts may be translated as a single term, the complexity of such phrases in China's laws and regulations means there is no uniform approach to their translation. Different methods must be chosen based on specific contexts. We propose three main approaches: equivalent translation, omission, and translation that preserves poetic features (e.g., rhythm and rhyme).

(1) Translation of Basic Synonymous Terms

(a) Equivalent Translation

Example 1:

第一百七十四条 担保期间，担保财产毁损、灭失或者被征收等，担保物权人可以就获得的保险金、赔偿金或者补偿金等优先受偿。被担保债权的履行期未届满的，也可以提存该保险金、赔偿金或者补偿金等。

Article 174 In case of damage or destruction, loss or requisition of the mortgaged property during the period of guarantee, the holder of the security interest shall have priority in having his claim paid with the insurance monies, compensations or indemnities. The holder of security interest may also have the insurance monies, compensation or indemnities deposited with a third party before the time limit for payment of the guaranteed claim expires.

It is noteworthy that in the translations below, the conjunction "or" is consistently used between synonyms. This practice originates from the communicative purpose of legal texts, which is to ensure that all possibilities related to actors, entities, time, and actions are included within the provision, thereby granting the legal rule a broader scope of application (Wang 2013: 37).

(b) Omission in Translation

Omission is employed because the semantic difference between two coordinated terms is minimal and often self-evident. Even if one term is omitted in the English translation, the overall meaning of the sentence remains unaffected.

Example 1:

第十九条 县级以上地方人民政府应当健全特困人员供养制度，对无劳动能力、无生活来源且无法定赡养、抚养、扶养义务人，或者其法定赡养、抚养、扶养义务人无赡养、抚养、扶养能力的老年人、残疾人以及未满16周岁的未成年人，给予特困人员供养。

Article 19 The local people's government at or above the county level shall complete a system supporting the especially poor people, grant support of the especially poor to those who are incapable of work, have no income source and have no persons with statutory obligations to support, or the elderly, the disabled and minors under 16 years of age whose legal support persons do not possess the capacity to support them.

(2) Translation of Terms with Inclusive Meanings

For lexical combinations with inclusive semantic relationships, such as "建立和健全" (establish and improve), where "健全" implies further refinement on the basis of "建立", or "保护和改善" (protect and improve), where "改善" inherently presupposes "保护", such phrases are generally translated using equivalent methods to convey the complete legal meaning.

Example 1:

第二条 本省行政区域内特种设备的生产(包括设计、制造、安装、改造、修理)、经营、使用、检验、检测和特种设备安全的监督管理，适用本条例。

Article 2 These Regulations shall apply to the production(including design, manufacture, installation, renovation, and repair), trading, use, inspection and examination of special equipment within the administrative region of this Province, as well as the safety supervision and administration of special equipment.

(3) Translation of Non-Substantive Terms

Chinese contains many terms that lack substantive meaning, and their parallel usage may serve to enhance the rhythmic quality of expression. In many cases, omitting some of these terms does not hinder the overall meaning of the sentence. During translation, strategies such as equivalence translation can be adopted to preserve the linguistic characteristics of Chinese, or methods like pursuing "alliteration" or "end rhyme" can be employed to create a poetic effect. For example, translating "持续健康" as "sustainable and sound" or "安全和畅通" as "safe and smooth" achieves an alliterative poetic quality.

Example 1:

第三条 国家巩固和发展公有制经济，鼓励、支持和引导非公有制经济的发展。

Article 3 The State consolidates and develops the public sectors of the economy, and encourages, supports and guides to the development of the non-public sectors of the economy.

(4) Translation of Rhyming and Parallel Words

(a) Translation of Rhyming Words

For rhyming parallel phrases in Chinese, equivalent translation is generally adopted. The "core term" may be repeated consistently and meticulously, or it may be extracted and presented only once, with appropriate omission in translation.

As for equivalent translation, here is an example.

Example 1:

第二条 本办法所称的职业学校教育是指学历职业教育，包括初、中、高等职业学校教育；职业培训是指非学历职业教育，包括从业前培训、转业培训、学徒培训、在岗培训、转岗培训以及其他职业培训。

Article 2 The vocational school education as mentioned in these Measures refers to diploma vocational education, including elementary, secondary and higher vocational school education; job training refers to non-diploma vocational education, including pre-service training, re-employment training, apprentice training, on-the-job training, job-transfer training and other forms of vocational training.

As for omission, here is an example.

Example 2:

第二十二条 鼓励养老服务组织为老年人提供助餐、助浴、助行、助洁、助购、助医、助急等服务。

Article 22 Organizations of supporting services for the aged shall be encouraged to provide the aged with such services as assistance in catering, bathing, transportation, cleaning, shopping, seeing a doctor and emergency aid.

In this example, the repetitive structure "助X" (assistance in X) is simplified by extracting the common term "assistance" and listing the specific actions (catering, bathing, etc.) without repeating the core term for each item. This approach preserves the meaning while adapting to the conciseness expected in English legal texts.

(b) Translation of Parallel Words

The formal uniformity in laws and regulations is often reflected in their parallel structures. In translation, one may strive for equivalent rendering or attempt to convey the "poetic" characteristics of legal language through parallelism.

As for translation of two-character parallel words, one may adopt equivalent translation. Adjectives and verbs can be translated directly as adjectives or verbs, or they can be rendered through nominalization, translating adjectives into nouns and verbs into nouns. "Nominalization is frequently used in legal documents because it achieves an objective effect. Although legal writing advocates the use of 'basic verbs,' nominalization remains a stylistic feature of legal writing" (Li and Zhang 2006: 37). Here is an example.

Example 1:

第七十九条 违反本办法规定，截留、挤占、挪用、私分社会救助资金、物资的，由有关部门责令追回；有违法所得的，没收违法所得；对直接负责的主管人员和其他直接责任人员依法给予处分。

Article 79 Where there is any case in violation of these Measures, in which social assistance funds and materials are detained, misappropriated, diverted or divided privately, relevant departments shall recover them; where there is illegal income, it shall be confiscated; the person directly in charge or persons directly responsible shall be given a sanction.

What's more, one may also use words preserving poetic alliteration or rhyme to achieve nominalization of parallel words, here is an example.

Example 2:

第三十二条 物权受到侵害的，权利人可以通过和解、调解、仲裁、诉讼等途径解决。

Article 32 Where the property right is encroached on, the oblige may have the matter settled by means of conciliation, mediation, arbitration or litigation.

Such deliberate lexical patterning reflects the aesthetic dimension of legal drafting, where formal elegance reinforces textual clarity and mnemonic resonance without compromising juridical precision. The translator's choice to cluster semantically related terms with phonetic harmony aligns with the stylistic conventions of legal English, which often employs lexical pairing or listing for emphasis, clarity, and rhetorical force.

(5) Translation of Three-Character Parallel Words

In Chinese, the phenomenon of three-character parallel phrases often ends with "X性" to denote a certain attribute, creating a repetitive and rhythmic pattern through rhyming. While nominalization can be used in translation, achieving complete rhyme in English is challenging.

Example 1:

第一条 为了加强统计管理和监督，规范统计行为，维护统计调查对象的合法权益，保障统计资料的真实性、准确性、完整性和及时性，发挥统计服务经济社会发展的作用，根据《中华人民共和国统计法》等法律、行政法规，结合本省实际，制定本条例。

Article 1 These Regulations are enacted in accordance with the Statistics Law of the People's Republic of China and other laws and administrative regulations, in light of the specific situation of this Province and for the purposes of strengthening the administration of and supervision on statistics, regulating statistical acts, protecting the legal rights and interests of the objects of statistical investigations, guaranteeing the authenticity, accuracy, completeness, and promptness of statistical materials and putting into play the role of statistics in the economy and social development.

The Chinese phrase "真实性、准确性、完整性和及时性" exemplifies a parallel structure ending with the suffix "-性", emphasizing attributes through rhythmic repetition. In the English translation, these are rendered as "authenticity, accuracy, completeness, and promptness". While the suffix-based rhyming pattern in Chinese is lost, the English version retains lexical parallelism and conceptual clarity. The translation employs nominalizations ("authenticity", "accuracy", etc.) to preserve the formal tone of legal language, though it does not replicate the phonetic harmony of the original. This reflects a functional compromise, prioritizing legal precision and readability over strict poetic equivalence.

(6) Translation of Four-Character Parallel Words

As a formulaic language, legislative drafting inevitably employs certain standardized expressions in vocabulary or syntax. The parallel use of four-character structures is common in Chinese laws and regulations, particularly in provisions related to principles, guidelines, and similar contexts, reflecting vocabulary expressions with Chinese characteristics. These four-character structures often utilize modifier-head, subject-predicate, and verb-object constructions. The consecutive parallel structures may or may not be consistent in form, and the translation method generally involves equivalent translation, assessing and selecting nominalized forms, verbs, participles, or adjective equivalents based on the part-of-speech characteristics of the original terms.

Example 1:

第五十九条 文化等有关部门及其工作人员违反本条例规定，玩忽职守、滥用职权、徇私舞弊的，对直接负责的主管人员和其他直接责任人员依法给予处分；构成犯罪的，依法追究刑事责任。

Article 59 Where government organs like the cultural department and their personnel, in violation of these Regulations, neglect their duties, abuse their powers, or engage in malpractice for personal gains, leading persons directly in charge and other persons directly responsible for it shall be given administrative sanctions according to law; where a crime is constituted, the criminal liabilities shall be investigated according to law.

The Chinese source text employs three parallel four-character idioms: "玩忽职守" (neglect of duties), "滥用职权" (abuse of powers), and "徇私舞弊" (malpractice for personal gains). These idioms follow a verb-object structure and carry strong evaluative connotations. In the English translation, they are rendered as verb phrases: "neglect their duties", "abuse their powers", and "engage in malpractice for personal gains". The translation preserves the parallel structure through the use of three verb phrases while adapting the syntax to fit English legal conventions. The choice of verbs ("neglect", "abuse", "engage in") maintains the active voice and legal gravity of the original, ensuring functional equivalence in describing prohibited conduct. This approach demonstrates how four-character idioms in Chinese legislative texts can be effectively translated by analyzing their syntactic and semantic features and selecting appropriate grammatical forms in the target language.

The use of synonymous terms in laws and regulations allows for varied interpretations and explanations. From the perspective of legal language accuracy, the repetition of synonyms helps encompass the unexpressed nuances of legal language, ensuring completeness and inclusiveness of meaning. However, from the standpoint of legal language standardization, using multiple words with identical meanings to convey the same idea violates the principle of precision required in legislative language. The use of synonymous terms in Chinese laws and regulations and their translation deserve further exploration to draw the attention of both legislators and translators. We believe that with the continuous improvement and advancement of legislative techniques, the use of synonymous terms in China's laws and regulations will undoubtedly become more standardized in the future.

Given that similar phenomena exist in common law systems, the translation of synonymous terms in laws and regulations into English must be approached on a case-by-case basis. There is no absolute conclusion regarding the translation method. Translators must remain faithful to the linguistic form of the laws and regulations, accurately conveying the meaning of the Chinese legislative texts, while also considering the reading habits of the target audience. Additionally, attention should be paid to the aesthetic qualities of legal language, allowing translators to exercise their subjectivity to the greatest extent possible.

5.6 Conclusions

This chapter systematically examines the translation of words and expressions in laws and regulations, revealing from the perspective of national governance how linguistic transformation profoundly impacts the authority, enforceability, and international dissemination of legal texts. Regarding the translation of fuzzy legal expressions, the study emphasizes the need to achieve a dynamic balance between flexibility and normative precision through functional equivalence while upholding legal certainty, thereby avoiding the undermining of governance efficacy due to excessive rigidity or arbitrary interpretation. Concerning the translation of legal terms with Chinese characteristics, the chapter highlights that such terminology serves as a linguistic vehicle for the socialist rule of law system with Chinese characteristics. Its translation must balance cultural fidelity with target-language acceptability to accurately convey China's governance philosophy and institutional strengths. With respect to the specialized conversion of ordinary vocabulary in legal contexts, the research uncovers the unique institutional connotations carried by everyday language in legal texts, noting that translation quality directly affects the operationality and transnational applicability of legal provisions. In terms of distinguishing and translating synonyms and near-synonyms, the chapter provides an in-depth analysis of how carefully crafted lexical variations in legal texts reflect legislative precision and governance logic. It underscores the necessity of systematic comparison and contextual restoration during translation to prevent ambiguity in rights and obligations arising from semantic confusion. Overall, this chapter demonstrates that the translation of legal vocabulary is not merely a linguistic technical issue but a critical extension of national governance capacity in the linguistic dimension. It directly influences the construction of legal transparency, the enhancement of international discourse power, and the establishment of cross-system institutional trust mechanisms. Advancing the standardization and scientization of related translation work holds profound strategic significance for strengthening the international recognition and institutional competitiveness of China's rule of law system.

References

Cao, Y. 2017. Translation of Chinese-characteristic legal terms in external reporting: Taking relevant reports in *China Daily* as examples. *The Press* 5.

Chen, H. 2006. The rationality and applicable scope of fuzzy legal language. *Journal of Anqing Normal University (Social Science Edition)* 2.

Dong, X. 2004. Research on vagueness of English legislative language and its removal. *Foreign Languages and Their Teaching* 2.

Fu, W. 2003. Translation of near-synonyms and synonyms in legal documents. *Chinese Translators Journal* 4.

Ge, H. 1998. *Jurisprudence*. Beijing: China University of Political Science and Law Press.

Hart, H. L. A. 1996. *The concept of law*. Translated by Zhang Wenxian. Beijing: Encyclopedia of China Publishing House.
He, H. 2011. English translation of several keywords in Chinese administrative law. *Administrative Law Review* 3.
Joan Pinkham. 2000. *The translator's guide to Chinglish. Proofread by Jiang Guihua*. Beijing: Foreign Language Teaching and Research Press.
Li, K., and X. Zhang. 2006. *Legal texts and legal translation*. Beijing: China Translation & Publishing Corporation.
Liu, W. 2003. Classification of English legal terms and analysis of translation examples. *Terminology Standardization & Information Technology* 3.
Mellinkoff, David. 1953. *Language of the law*. Texas University Press.
Qu, W., and W. Shi. 2012. *A course in legal English reading and translation*. Shanghai: Shanghai People's Publishing House.
Shu, G. 1995. Development directions of German legal philosophy after World War II. *Journal of Comparative Law* 4.
Song, L. 2011. *Essentials of legal terminology translation*. Beijing: China University of Political Science and Law Press.
Vermeer, A. 1992. Exploring the second language learner lexicon. In *The construct of language proficiency*, ed. L. Verhoeven and J. H. A. L. de Jong. London: Benjamins Publishing Company.
Wang, J. 2013. *Research on legal translation*. Chengdu: Sichuan University Press.
Wilkins, D. A. 1972. *Linguistics in language teaching*. London: Arnold.
Yang, Y. 1998. A brief discussion on synonymous and near-synonymous words in Anglo-American legal language. *Shanghai Journal of Translators for Science and Technology* 4.
Yang, D. 2006. The influence of fuzziness in legal language on the legal system. *Journal of Yunnan University Law Edition* 7.
Yu, X. 2015. Domestication and foreignization in the Russian translation of Chinese-characteristic political terms. *Journal of Tianjin Foreign Studies University* 4.
Yuan, H. 2009. Functions and translation of fuzzy words in legal English. *Journal of Hunan University of Science and Engineering* 5.
Zhang, F. 2016. *Legal English translation course*. Beijing: Peking University Press.
Zhang, F. 2017. *A contrastive study of Chinese and Western legal language and culture*. Beijing: Peking University Press.

Chapter 6
Translation of Syntactic Structures in Laws and Regulations

Abstract This chapter investigates the translation of syntactic structures characteristic of Chinese legislative texts into English, with a focus on the systematic rendering of fixed patterns across different functional sections. It analyzes the translation of recurring structures in general provisions, definitional clauses, obligation clauses, right-granting clauses, liability clauses, and supplementary provisions, highlighting how syntactic choices affect legal precision, enforceability, and cross-jurisdictional comprehensibility. Special attention is given to the ubiquitous "的" structure and its functional equivalents in English, examining strategies to preserve logical relationships while adapting to target-language legal conventions. By emphasizing syntactic consistency and context-aware adaptation, this chapter provides a framework for producing legally sound, linguistically coherent translations that support China's engagement with international legal discourse.

Keywords Translation of syntactic structures · Legislative drafting conventions · Cross-jurisdictional adaptation

Legal language, as a specialized register formed through the historical evolution of legal systems and legal culture, is essentially a highly institutionalized professional discourse system. Its development profoundly reflects the inherent demand of the national governance system for linguistic standardization. The formulaic characteristics of legal language are not merely superficial structural features but rather the institutionalized representation of legal authority, stability, and predictability at the linguistic level. At the macro level, legal texts adopt a tripartite structure of "General Provisions—Specific Provisions—Supplementary Provisions", along with a hierarchical organization of "articles", "paragraphs", "subparagraphs", "items", and "points", constructing a logically rigorous and clearly layered normative system. This structural design itself responds linguistically to the demarcation of powers and responsibilities, procedural justice, and systematic management in national governance. At the micro level, legal language employs highly fixed terminological collocations, syntactic structures, and expressive paradigms to form a symbol

X. Dong, Y. Zhang, *On Translation of Laws and Regulations in China*,
https://doi.org/10.1007/978-981-95-9406-1_6

system with binding force, ensuring uniformity in legal interpretation while reducing cognitive costs in law enforcement and judicial processes.

The formulaic nature of legal language serves as a crucial linguistic foundation for achieving the goal of building a "China under the rule of law". It curbs arbitrariness in legal interpretation through standardized textual structures, enhances the efficiency of cross-border legal communication through uniform expressive models, and strengthens the international discourse power of the national legal system through institutionalized linguistic forms. Therefore, a deep understanding and accurate application of formulaic legal language are not only technical requirements for legal translation but also fundamental competencies for participating in global legal governance and disseminating the civilization of Chinese rule of law. Thus, this chapter takes the study of the formulized structure of legal texts as its starting point, focusing on the translation of common syntactic patterns in the general provisions and supplementary provisions of laws and regulations, as well as in definition clauses, obligation clauses, rights clauses, liability clauses, and the "的" structure within specific provisions.

6.1 Translation of Fixed Syntactic Structures in the General Provisions

General provisions, also known as the general principles or overarching framework of a law, serve to clarify the purpose and spirit of the legislation while providing a cohesive structure for the entire text. The general provisions of a law fulfill three primary functions: first, they serve as a legislative guide. The general provisions establish the tone, framework, norms, and guiding principles of the entire law, ensuring it forms an organic and internally consistent whole while avoiding contradictions and enhancing content completeness; second, they act as an enforcement guide. The effective implementation of a law, essential to achieving its legislative purpose, relies heavily on the general provisions. On one hand, they guide law enforcement officers in applying specific provisions; on the other hand, when specific provisions do not directly address real-world situations, the general provisions offer a basis for appropriate action; and third, they provide an interpretive function for legal principles. Laws and regulations consist of abstract provisions that generalize specific issues into broader concepts and principles. In many cases, interpreting specific provisions without reference to the general provisions can obscure their true meaning. Thus, the general provisions play a critical role in clarifying legal principles (Jiang, 2003: 3).

Chinese laws and regulations generally include a section on general provisions, which typically cover the legislative purpose, objectives, legal basis, scope of application, fundamental principles, interpretation of legal terms, and the competent authorities. These elements reflect the legislative spirit of the law and serve as its "guiding framework". Legal language is highly proceduralized and follows established conventions of expression. Almost every law or regulation includes fixed sentence patterns in its general provisions, such as: "为了……制定本法", "根据/依据……", "结合……", and "……适用本法". Below is a summary of common translation approaches for these sentence patterns.

6.1.1 Translation of "为了……制定本法"

In the general provisions section, legislators frequently use purpose clauses to explain the rationale behind the legislation. The basic sentence pattern for purpose clauses in Chinese is "为了……" (in order to...), which can be translated as "for the purpose of…", "in order to…", "with a view to…", "with the purpose of…", "to…", etc. Among these, "for the purpose of", "in order to", and "with a view to" convey a stronger sense of purpose and are therefore more commonly used. In particular, "for the purpose of" is considered more formal and standardized, as recommended in the *Handbook of Common Sentence Patterns for Legal Translation and Review* compiled by the Legislative Affairs Office of the State Council. The verb "制定" (to formulate) is commonly translated as "formulate", "enact", "promulgate", or "develop", with "formulate" and "enact" being the most widely accepted translations.

Example 1

第一条　为保守国家秘密，维护国家的安全和利益，保障改革开放和社会主义建设事业的顺利进行，制定本法。

Article 1 This Law is formulated for the purpose of guarding State secrets, safeguarding State security and national interests and ensuring the smooth progress of reform of the opening to the outside world and socialist construction.

Example 2

第一条　为了规范保险活动，保护保险活动当事人的合法权益，加强对保险业的监督管理，促进保险事业的健康发展，制定本法。

Article 1 This Law is formulated for the purpose of regulating insurance activities, protecting the legitimate rights and interests of the parties involved, strengthening supervision and regulation of the insurance industry and promoting its healthy development.

6.1.2 Translation of "根据/依据……"

The legal basis for legislation refers to the laws, regulations, and other normative documents that legislative bodies rely on when formulating specific legal instruments. It addresses the issue of legislative legitimacy (Wang & Zhang, 2012: 105). The fixed syntactic pattern for such clauses is "根据/依据…" (in accordance with/pursuant to/under). While "according to" is a common translation, it is relatively colloquial and carries a lower register, making it less suitable for formal legal documents. For instance, "依法办事" (acting in accordance with the law) may be translated as "according to law". To reflect the formality of legal language, "根据/依据" is often rendered as "in accordance with", "under", or "pursuant to". Among these, "in accordance with" is the most standardized expression used in the general provisions of laws to denote "based on" or "in compliance with". Consider the following examples:

Example 1

第一条 为了防范和惩治恐怖活动，加强反恐怖主义工作，维护国家安全、公共安全和人民生命财产安全，<u>根据</u>宪法，制定本法。

Article 1 This Law is formulated <u>in accordance with</u> the Constitution for the purpose of preventing and punishing terrorist activities, improving counterterrorism work, and safeguarding national security, public security and the security of people's lives and property.

Example 2

第一条 为了保障适龄儿童、少年接受义务教育的权利，保证义务教育的实施，提高全民族素质，<u>根据</u>宪法和教育法，制定本法。

Article 1 This Law was formulated <u>in accordance with t</u>he Constitution and the Education Law for the purpose of guaranteeing the right to compulsory education of school-age children and adolescents, ensuring the implementation of the compulsory education policy and promoting the quality of the whole nation.

The choice among "in accordance with", "under", and "pursuant to" involves nuanced distinctions in legal drafting. "*In accordance with*" typically denotes general compliance with broader legal principles or frameworks. "*Under*" often indicates authorization or operation within a specific statutory scheme (e.g., under the provisions of Article X). "*Pursuant to*" emphasizes direct procedural or substantive derivation from a legal source. In Chinese legislative translations, "in accordance with" has emerged as the preferred formulation for constitutional and foundational references, reflecting its formal tone and systematic alignment with China's hierarchical legal structure. This terminological consistency supports both domestic legal coherence and the intelligibility of Chinese law in comparative international contexts.

6.1.3 *Translation of "结合……"*

Another common structure in the general provisions of laws is "结合…" ("taking into account" or "in light of"). This expression frequently appears in the first article of local regulations and rules, as such instruments are formulated by provinces based on national laws and administrative regulations while considering their local specific conditions. The standard translation of "结合…" is "in light of", though it is occasionally rendered as "in the consideration of", albeit less commonly.

Example 1

第一条 为了惩罚犯罪，保护人民，根据宪法，**结合**我国同犯罪作斗争的具体经验及实际情况，制定本法。

Article 1 This law is formulated in accordance with the Constitution and in light of the concrete experience of China launching a struggle against crime and the realities in the country for the purpose of punishing crime and protecting the people.

Example 2

第一条 中华人民共和国民事诉讼法以宪法为根据，结合我国民事审判工作的经验和实际情况制定。

Article 1 The Civil Procedure Law of the People's Republic of China is formulated in accordance with the Constitution and in light of civil trial experience and actual circumstances of civil trials in China.

The use of "结合…" in legislative texts reflects the principle of adapting national legislation to local realities, a key feature of China's legislative system that balances uniformity with flexibility. This expression signifies the integration of practical experience and contextual factors into the legislative process, emphasizing the empirical and pragmatic dimensions of lawmaking. In translation, "in light of" effectively conveys this adaptive and contextualized approach, while "in the consideration of", though less common, may be used to highlight deliberative or evaluative aspects. The consistent use of such phrasing in local regulations underscores the importance of contextual relevance in China's legal framework, supporting both regional autonomy and national coherence.

6.1.4 Translation of "……适用本法"

The applicability of a law determines the relationship between individuals or entities and the legal norms it establishes. Therefore, legislators typically specify the scope of application in the general provisions of a law. In China's legislative practice, clauses defining the scope of application commonly follow the patterns "...适用本法" or "本法适用于...". These are typically translated as "...apply to...", "...be applicable to...", or "...be governed by...". Among these, "...apply to..." is widely accepted and is recommended in the *Handbook of Common Sentence Patterns for Legal Translation and Review* compiled by the Legislative Affairs Office of the State Council.

Example 1
第一条　在中华人民共和国境内建设、运营、维护和使用网络，以及网络安全的监督管理，适用本法。

Article 1 This Law shall apply to the construction, operation, maintenance and use of the network as well as the supervision and administration of cybersecurity within the territory of the People's Republic of China.

The phrasing "...适用本法" serves as a critical jurisdictional and operational clause, delineating the spatial, personal, and substantive boundaries of a law's authority. In translation, the modal auxiliary "shall" in "This Law shall apply to..." reinforces the normative and mandatory nature of the provision, aligning with the imperative tone of legislative language. The choice of "apply to" over alternatives such as "be applicable to" or "be governed by" reflects a preference for active, direct expression in statutory drafting, enhancing clarity and enforceability. This formulation not only ensures consistency across Chinese legislative translations but also facilitates cross-jurisdictional comprehension, supporting the integration of China's legal framework into global discourse on governance and regulation.

6.2 Translation of Fixed Syntactic Structures in the Definition Clauses

Legal language, as a clear, universal, and definitive norm, must express its meanings with considerable precision to minimize ambiguity. Definition clauses within a law provide accurate and authoritative interpretations of specialized terms used in that law (Zhu & Zhang, 2009: 246). In legal texts, definition clauses, also referred to as interpretive clauses for legal terms or concepts, are provisions where legislators explicitly define concepts, terms, or expressions that appear in laws or regulations, incorporating them as integral components of the legal text's structure. Definition clauses are indispensable parts of legal texts, serving as prerequisites for the application of other legal norms and providing systematic connections and support for the normative functions of the law.

In Chinese laws and regulations, definition clauses can be found in the general provisions, specific provisions, and supplementary provisions, with the highest frequency occurring in the general provisions. Some experts argue that placing definition clauses in the general provisions is the most appropriate approach, as early clarification of legal terms, regulated subjects, and scope of application helps readers accurately understand the meaning of the law more efficiently. However, definition clauses may also appear in the specific and supplementary provisions, though for ease of reading, they are often placed in the early sections of these parts. The common sentence patterns used to express definitions in Chinese legal texts are relatively fixed, primarily falling into four categories: "…是…", "…是指…", "…包括…", and "…即…".

6.2.1 *Translation of "…是…"*

The structure "...是..." is one of the most common sentence patterns in Chinese legal texts used to define the meaning of legal concepts. Its use reflects the solemn and normative characteristics of legal language. Common English translations include the simple present tense of the verb "be", "shall be", or "refer to".

Translated as the Simple Present Tense of the Verb "Be"

When the law explains an objective fact, "是" can be directly translated into the simple present tense of the verb "be", with its form varying according to the subject's number.

Example 1

第十六条　劳动合同<u>是</u>劳动者与用人单位确立劳动关系、明确双方权利和义务的协议。建立劳动关系应当订立劳动合同。

Article 16 A labor contract <u>is</u> the agreement reached between a laborer and an employing unit for the establishment of the labor relationship and the definition of the rights, interests and obligations of each party. A labor contract shall be entered into where a labor relationship is to be established.

The translation of "...是..." into the simple present tense of "be" reflects the distinction in legal English between descriptive provisions (stating what is) and prescriptive provisions (stating what shall be). This aligns with common law drafting conventions where definitions and factual descriptions use the present tense, while obligations and requirements employ "shall". The example illustrates this clearly: the definitional clause ("A labor contract is...") establishes the nature of the concept, while the operational clause ("A labor contract shall be entered into...") imposes a mandatory action. This syntactic distinction enhances legal precision by separating conceptual foundation from normative command, a practice that supports both domestic legal clarity and cross-jurisdictional comprehension in comparative law contexts.

Translation as "Shall Be"

In legal texts, the modal verb "shall" is typically used to express specific provisions and requirements, reflecting legally enforceable obligations. When "...是..." is translated as "shall be", it carries the connotation of "shall" or "must".

Example 1

第三条 中华人民共和国港务监督机构，是对沿海水域的交通安全实施统一监督管理的主管机关。

Article 3 The harbor superintendence agencies of the People's Republic of China shall be the competent authorities responsible for the unified supervision and administration of traffic safety in the coastal waters.

The translation of "...是..." as "shall be" introduces a normative dimension that transcends mere definitional description. In this context, "shall be" operates as a performative utterance that not only identifies the designated authority but also legally constitutes its jurisdictional status. This usage reflects the civil law tradition's integration of institutional designation with mandatory authorization, distinguishing it from common law drafting conventions where "is" might suffice for descriptive institutional definitions. The choice of "shall be" here embodies the Chinese legislative technique of combining constitutive and prescriptive functions within a single formulation, thereby reinforcing the binding nature of administrative designations. This approach aligns with the principle of legal certainty while ensuring the provision carries both explanatory force and enforceable authority in maritime governance frameworks.

Translated as "Refer to"

The "...是..." structure can also be commonly translated as "refer to", indicating an explanatory function. In this context, "是" is equivalent to "是指" (meaning "refers to").

Example 1
第二条本法所称合同是平等主体的自然人、法人、其他组织之间设立、变更、终止民事权利义务关系的协议。

Article 2 A contract in this Law refers to an agreement among natural persons, legal persons or other organizations as equal parties for the establishment, modification of a relationship involving the civil rights and obligations of such entities.

The use of "refer to" in translating the "...是..." structure serves a specific terminological definition function within legal texts. This formulation is particularly appropriate when the text explicitly introduces a statutory definition, as seen in phrases like "本法所称..." ("as referred to in this Law..."). The choice of "refer to" over "is" or "shall be" signals to the reader that what follows is an authoritative, self-contained definition that establishes the precise meaning of a term within the specific legal instrument. This aligns with common law drafting techniques where "means" or "refers to" are standard markers for definitional clauses. Such precision in translation not only maintains the normative integrity of the source text but also facilitates accurate interpretation and application in comparative legal analysis, particularly in contexts requiring unambiguous cross-system conceptual alignment.

6.2.2 *Translation of "…是指…"*

The structure "…是指…" is widely used in legal texts to express concepts or definitions. Like "…是…", it denotes the connotative definition of a legal concept. Both share similarities in translation, as they can be rendered as "refer to". However, it is important to note that "是指" in legal texts can also be translated as "mean".

Translated as "Mean"

The most common translation of "是指" is "mean", and this applies equally in legal texts, where it serves an explanatory function.

Example 1
第四十六条　本法所称枪支，是指以火药或者压缩气体等为动力，利用管状器具发射金属弹丸或者其他物质，足以致人伤亡或者丧失知觉的各种枪支。

Article 46 "Firearms" in this law means those which are driven by powder or compressed air, discharge metal shots or other substances through a tube-shaped appliance and may cause deaths or injuries or losing of consciousness.

The translation of "是指" as "mean" in legal definitions reflects the functional equivalence approach in legal translation, where precision and clarity take precedence over literal correspondence. While "refer to" suggests a broader or more conceptual linkage, "mean" conveys a direct, authoritative definition, which is particularly suited to statutory interpretation. This choice aligns with common law drafting traditions where definitions are often introduced by "means" to establish unambiguous legal meanings. The example illustrates how the translation captures both the technical specifications and the legal consequences of the defined term, thereby ensuring the operational effectiveness of the provision in enforcement and judicial application.

Translated as "Refer to"

Another translation of "是指" in legal texts is "refer to". Compared to "mean", "refer to" is more formal and standardized, making it more frequently used in legal translations.

Example 1

第二条 本法所称对外贸易，<u>是指</u>货物进出口、技术进出口和国际服务贸易。

Article 2 The term "foreign trade" as mentioned in this law <u>refers to</u> the import and export of goods and technologies and international service trade.

Example 2

第二条　　本法所称公司<u>是指</u>依照本法在中国境内设立的有限责任公司和股份有限公司。

Article 2 The term "company" as mentioned in this Law <u>refers to</u> a limited liability company or a joint stock company limited set up within the territory of the People's Republic of China in accordance with the provisions of this law.

The use of "refer to" in translating "是指" reflects a deliberate choice to align with the formal and precise nature of legal terminology. Unlike "mean", which may carry broader semantic associations, "refer to" emphasizes direct, definitive reference to a specific legal concept or category. This aligns with common law drafting conventions where statutory definitions use "means" for exhaustive definitions and "includes" for illustrative ones, while "refers to" often serves as a bridge between general language and legal technicality. In comparative legal linguistics, this translation choice facilitates cross-jurisdictional clarity by maintaining consistent terminological boundaries, thereby supporting the accurate transmission of Chinese legal concepts into international legal discourse. The pattern "as mentioned in this Law" further reinforces the self-referential nature of statutory definitions, a feature common in civil law systems that enhances systemic coherence.

6.2.3 Translation of "…包括…"

Legal concepts encompass both their intension (connotation) and extension (denotation). When enumerating or delineating the extension of legal concepts, the commonly used structure is "…包括…". In legal translation, two frequent renderings for "…包括…" are "…include…" and "…cover…", with the former being more widely adopted.

Translated as "Include"

As in other textual contexts, "包括" in legal documents is most commonly translated as "include" in the vast majority of cases.

Example 1
第三百六十五条　技术咨询合同<u>包括</u>就特定技术项目提供可行性论证、技术预测、专题技术调查、分析评价报告等合同。

Article 365 Technical consulting contracts <u>include</u> contracts for provision of feasibility studies, technical forecast, specialized technical investigation, and analysis and evaluation report, etc. in respect of a particular technical project.

The translation of "…包括…" as "include" reflects the principle of extensional definition in legal drafting, where the scope of a legal term is clarified through non-exhaustive enumeration. This aligns with international legal drafting conventions where "include" typically signals an illustrative rather than exhaustive list, preserving flexibility for judicial interpretation. The use of "include" instead of "cover" or "comprise" follows common law preferences for inclusive rather than restrictive definitional language. This terminological choice supports both legal precision and adaptability, allowing courts to extend application to analogous cases while maintaining conceptual boundaries, a crucial consideration in China's evolving legal system where new technical and commercial scenarios continually emerge.

Translated as "Cover"

The phrase "...包括..." can be translated not only as "...include..." but also as "... cover...", though the latter is used less frequently.

Example 1
第二十一条　前款规定的审慎经营规则，包括风险管理、内部控制、资本充足率、资产质量、损失准备金、风险集中、关联交易、资产流动性等内容。

Article 21 Prudential rules and regulations referred to in the preceding paragraph shall cover, among others, risk management, internal controls, capital adequacy rates, asset quality, loan loss reserves, risk concentrations, connected transactions and liquidity management.

The choice of "cover" instead of "include" in this context reflects a nuanced difference in legal drafting semantics. While "include" typically suggests a non-exhaustive enumeration, "cover" implies broader conceptual scope and regulatory comprehensiveness. In banking supervision terminology, "cover" conveys that the prudential rules encompass the specified domains as essential components, rather than merely listing examples. The phrase "among others" further reinforces the non-exhaustive nature of the list while maintaining the authoritative tone characteristic of financial regulatory texts. This translation choice aligns with international financial regulatory discourse where "cover" is often used to describe the scope of supervisory frameworks. Such terminological precision supports cross-jurisdictional understanding in global financial regulation and enhances the normative force of the provision in both domestic and international contexts.

6.2.4 Translation of "…即…"

The term "即" literally means "that is to say". It is often used to define or explain the meaning of a previously established concept, serving as a judgment about a legal term whose meaning has already been established. In English translation, it has two primary renderings: "mean(s)" or an appositive introduced by "that is".

Translated as "Mean(s)"

The first way to translate "即" is as "mean(s)". In this usage, "即" is equivalent to "就是", and the two are often interchangeable.

Example 1
第五条下一级只有本级预算的，下一级总预算即指下一级的本级预算。

Article 5 Where the next lower level has only the budget of the government at the corresponding level, the totalized general budget at the next lower level means the budget of the government at the corresponding level.

The translation of “即” as “mean(s)” reflects its role in providing precise, authoritative clarification within a legal definition. This usage aligns with the drafting principle that legal definitions should be explicit and unambiguous. The verb “mean” is preferred in such contexts because it directly establishes semantic equivalence, thereby strengthening the normative clarity of the provision. This approach is consistent with international legal drafting practices, where terms such as “means” are used to introduce exhaustive definitions, while “includes” is used for non-exhaustive illustrations. In comparative law contexts, this syntactic choice facilitates accurate cross-jurisdictional interpretation by minimizing interpretive discretion and emphasizing definitional rigor.

Translated as an Appositive Structure Introduced by “That Is”

The second translation method for “……即……” is the appositive structure “that is, …”, which provides supplementary explanation for the preceding content.

Example 1
第八十五条　中华人民共和国国务院，即中央人民政府，是最高国家权力机关的执行机关，是最高国家行政机关。

Article 85 The State Council, that is, the Central People’s Government, of the People’s Republic of China is the executive body of the highest organ of state power; it is the highest organ of state administration.

The use of the appositive structure “that is” to translate “即” reflects a sophisticated approach to legal drafting where explanatory information is integrated seamlessly into the sentence structure while maintaining grammatical precision. This construction serves two key functions in legal translation: (1) it preserves the authoritative tone of constitutional language while clarifying institutional relationships, and (2) it follows international conventions for legislative drafting where explanatory phrases are typically enclosed within commas or parentheses. The example demonstrates how this technique achieves both semantic accuracy and syntactic elegance, presenting the Central People’s Government not merely as an alternative name but as the formal institutional designation of the State Council. Such translation choices support constitutional clarity and facilitate comparative constitutional analysis by maintaining structural parallels with how other legal systems denote official titles and institutional relationships in foundational documents.

6.3 Translation of Fixed Syntactic Structures in the Obligation Clauses

Legal obligations, as a concept symmetrical to legal rights, refer to the mandatory responsibilities that subjects of legal relationships must fulfill according to law. They are stipulations or implicit provisions within legal norms, realized through legal relationships, serving as a binding mechanism whereby subjects, through relatively restrained acts or omissions, ensure that right-holders obtain benefits. When obligated subjects fail to perform or improperly perform their obligations, they are subject to sanctions by state coercive power and bear corresponding liability.

Legal obligations include affirmative obligations and negative obligations. Affirmative obligations refer to duties that must be performed through affirmative acts. In contrast, negative obligations, relative to affirmative obligations, require individuals to refrain from certain acts as prescribed by law. In legal texts, sentences indicating affirmative obligations include phrases such as "必须…", "应当…", and "有义务……/有……义务" while sentences indicating negative obligations include phrases such as "禁止…", "不得…", and "不能…".

6.3.1 Translation of "应当…"

In legal contexts, "应当……" expresses an obligatory norm, indicating a mandatory requirement imposed by law upon subjects in specific situations. This formulation encompasses both specific requirements for legal subjects and potential legal consequences, as well as reflecting the legislator's value orientation. In translation, "应当" is typically rendered as "shall" in English legal texts.

Example 1

第八条　税务机关依照前款规定做出纳税调整，需要补征税款的，**应当**补征税款，并依法加收利息。

Article 8 Where tax authorities make tax payment adjustments under the preceding paragraph, which requires collection of taxes in arrears, such taxes in arrears shall be collected, together with interest thereon in accordance with the law.

The translation of "应当" involves cross-system correspondence in expressing legal obligations. In the common law tradition, "shall" carries clear mandatory force and is commonly used to denote legal duties or compulsory norms. However, contemporary international legal English practice shows a trend toward minimizing the use of "shall", with alternatives such as "must" or active voice constructions gaining preference for clarity. The translation of Chinese "应当" must consider three dimensions: the degree of mandatory force in legal theory, the normative nature of the provision in context, and the linguistic conventions of the target legal system. Currently, "shall" remains the primary equivalent in English translations of Chinese laws and regulations, aligning with traditional legal English usage and maintaining consistency with international legal texts. Nevertheless, for international treaties or cross-border legal instruments, attention must be paid to potential interpretive ambiguities associated with "shall". Alternatives like "must" or "is required to" may be employed when necessary to enhance precision. This approach balances fidelity to the source text with the evolving norms of global legal drafting, supporting both the authority of domestic legislation and its accessibility in transnational contexts.

6.3.2 Translation of "必须…"

"应当……" generally indicates a legal obligation that subjects are expected to comply with under normal circumstances, reflecting the principle of conduct for the obligated party. In contrast, "必须" denotes a mandatory requirement that subjects must fulfill as stipulated by laws and regulations, emphasizing legal and factual necessity and reinforcing the imperative expectation, thereby underscoring the solemnity and authority of the law (Chen, 2003: 13). In translation, "必须" corresponds to "must" in legal English.

Example 1

第十一条 生产药品所需的原料、辅料，<u>必须</u>符合药用要求。

Article 11 The raw and supplementary materials used for the production of pharmaceuticals <u>must</u> conform to the requirements for medicinal use.

The distinction between "应当" (shall) and "必须" (must) in Chinese legislative language reflects a gradation in normative force within the civil law tradition. While "应当" implies a general obligation that permits exceptions under justifiable circumstances, "必须" expresses an absolute mandate allowing no discretion. In legal English, this distinction is typically mapped onto the "shall"/"must" dichotomy, though with important caveats. "Must" conveys stronger deontic modality and is increasingly preferred in modern plain-language legal drafting for its clarity and reduced ambiguity. The example demonstrates how "必须" is translated as "must" to emphasize the non-negotiable nature of quality standards in pharmaceutical production, a domain where public safety considerations elevate the normative force to an imperative level. This translation choice aligns with international regulatory language (e.g., WHO guidelines, ICH standards) and reinforces the harmonization of Chinese pharmaceutical regulations with global norms. The consistent use of "must" for "必须" across Chinese legislative translations enhances predictability for international stakeholders and supports China's integration into transnational regulatory regimes.

6.3.3 Translation of "有义务....../有......义务"

In Chinese laws and regulations, common expressions for indicating obligatory norms include "有义务.../有...义务" ("have the duty to.../have the obligation to.../it is the duty of..."). Corresponding English translations include "it is the duty of...", "have the duty to...", and "have the obligation to...".

Example 1
第五十二条　中华人民共和国公民有维护国家统一和全国各民族团结的义务。

Example 2
第四十九条 父母有抚养教育未成年子女的义务，成年子女有赡养扶助父母的义务。

Article 49 Parents have the duty to rear and educate their children who are minors, and children who have come of age have the duty to support and assist their parents.

Example 3
第十一条　任何单位和个人都有义务保护水环境，并有权对污染损害水环境的行为进行检举。

Article 11 All entities and individuals have the obligation to protect water environment, and have the right to report to authorities acts polluting or damaging water environment.

The translation of obligatory norms in Chinese legislation reflects a nuanced approach to conveying legal duties in English. The choice between "duty" and "obligation" often depends on contextual and jurisprudential distinctions: "duty" typically denotes a broader moral or legal responsibility, while "obligation" may imply a more specific, legally enforceable requirement. In comparative law, such differentiation aligns with common law traditions where "duty" often correlates with foundational legal or civic responsibilities, whereas "obligation" may arise from contractual or statutory mandates. The use of "it is the duty of…" in constitutional contexts emphasizes the fundamental nature of the responsibility, while "have the obligation to…" in environmental law underscores actionable and enforceable duties. This terminological precision not only enhances the clarity and enforceability of translated texts but also facilitates their integration into international legal discourse, supporting China's engagement with global normative frameworks.

6.3.4 Translation of "不得…"/"不能…"

Prohibitive clauses in legal texts are commonly expressed as "不得…" or "不能…". Among these, "不得…" is the most frequently used prompt, reflecting clear restrictions on the conduct of legal subjects while balancing solemnity and conciseness (Zhang, 2010: 95). In translation practice, "不得…" or "不能…" can be rendered as "shall not…" or "may not…". It should be noted that although both can express prohibitive norms, there is a subtle semantic difference: "shall not" emphasizes the prevention of anticipated behavior, while "may not" focuses on "revoking relevant permissions".

Example 1

第十一条　居民个人向扣缴义务人提供专项附加扣除信息的，扣缴义务人按月预扣预缴税款时应当按照规定予以扣除，<u>不得</u>拒绝。

Article 11 Where a resident individual provides the withholding agent with information on special additional deductibles, the withholding agent shall, when withholding and prepaying taxes on a monthly basis, make deductions as required, and <u>shall not</u> refuse to do so.

Example 2

第十六条　经审核批准用地的外商投资企业，应当遵守土地管理法律、法规、规章的有关规定，<u>不得</u>买卖或者以其他形式非法转让土地使用权。

Article 16 Foreign-funded enterprises that have been approved to use land upon examination shall comply with the relevant provisions of land administration laws, regulations and rules, and <u>may not</u> trade or illegally assign in other forms land use rights.

The choice of English translation for "不得…" ("shall not" or "may not") reflects the semantic stratification of prohibitive norms in common law systems: "shall not" typically corresponds to mandatory prohibitions with absolute binding force, while "may not" is often used to revoke permissions or negate specific authorizations (discretionary restrictions). In Example 1, "shall not refuse" emphasizes the unconditional obligation of the withholding agent, representing a typical mandatory prohibition of conduct. In Example 2, "may not trade…" implies restrictions on specific actions related to the acquired land use rights, focusing on the boundaries of rights exercise. This distinction is particularly critical in cross-system translation, as it must remain faithful to the prohibitive strength of the source text while aligning with the expressive conventions of the target legal system. In current Chinese legal translation practice, "shall not" has gradually become the standard translation for absolute prohibitions, while "may not" is often used for conditional or authority-bound restrictions, reflecting the precise transmission of legislative intent and the functional equivalence of legal norms.

6.3.5 *Translation of "禁止…"*

The expression "禁止…" signifies legal restrictions on the actions that subjects of legal relations must not perform. In English, it is commonly translated as "prohibit…", "…be prohibited", "forbid…", or "…be forbidden".

Example 1
第三条 国家<u>禁止</u>任何形式的家庭暴力。

Article 3 The state <u>prohibits</u> any form of family violence.

Example 2
第五条证券的发行、交易活动，必须遵守法律、行政法规；<u>禁止</u>欺诈、内幕交易和操纵证券市场的行为。

Article 5 The issuance and trading of securities shall abide by laws and administrative regulations. Any fraud, insider trading or manipulation of the securities market <u>shall be prohibited</u>.

The translation of "禁止…" involves nuanced choices between active and passive constructions ("prohibit" vs. "be prohibited") as well as lexical selection ("prohibit" vs. "forbid"). In legal English, "prohibit" typically implies formal statutory prohibition with institutional authority, while "forbid" may carry a more general or moral connotation. The active form ("prohibits") emphasizes the agency of the regulating body (e.g., the state), whereas the passive form ("shall be prohibited") focuses on the normative status of the prohibited act itself. Example 1 uses the active voice to assert the state's authoritative stance, while Example 2 employs the passive voice to establish an objective legal norm. In contemporary Chinese legislative translation, "prohibit" has become the preferred term for formal legal prohibitions, reflecting its stronger juridical tone and alignment with international legal discourse.

6.4 Translation of Fixed Syntactic Structures in the Right Clauses

In laws and regulations, provisions that stipulate the rights enjoyed by legal subjects in accordance with the law are referred to as rights provisions. These provisions form an essential component of legal texts and are distributed across the general provisions, specific provisions, and supplementary provisions of laws. In the structural framework of legal texts, rights provisions should be prioritized. The primary functions of rights provisions in legal texts are twofold: first, to declare the rights of legal subjects, and second, to stipulate the safeguards for these rights.

Regarding the fixed sentence patterns for rights provisions, Article 127 of the *Guangdong Provincial People's Congress Standing Committee's Norms on Legislative Techniques and Procedures (Trial)* specifies that rights provisions generally follow the authorized subject and commonly employ phrases such as "有……权利", "有权……", "可以……", "不受侵犯", and "不受……干涉". This section will explore the translation of these five types of emblematic structures.

6.4.1 Translation of "有……权利/有权……"

The phrases "有…权利" and "有权…" are typical expressions used in legal provisions to grant rights. Their English equivalents mainly include "enjoy the right to…", "be entitled to…", "have the right to…", "have the authority to…", "have the power to…", and "be empowered to…".

Example 1
第二十条 农民专业合作社成员<u>享有下列**权利**</u>……

Article 20 The members of a farmer's professional cooperative may <u>enjoy the following rights…</u>

Example 2
第四条 劳动者依法<u>享有</u>职业卫生保护<u>的**权利**</u>。

Article 4 Employees shall <u>be entitled to</u> occupational health protection according to law.

Example 3
第十一条 人民检察院有权对行政诉讼实行法律监督。

Article 11 The people's procuratorates shall have the authority to exercise legal supervision over administrative litigation.

Example 4
第五十八条 县级以上人民政府或者其授权的部门在处理水事纠纷时，有权采取临时处置措施，有关各方或者当事人必须服从。

Article 58 When handling any dispute concerning water, the people's government at or above the county level, or the competent department authorized by such a government, shall have the power to take temporary measures with which the parties must comply.

The translation of "有权…" involves nuanced differentiation based on the nature of the right or authority granted. The use of "may enjoy the right…" (as in Example 1) often denotes discretionary entitlements, while "shall be entitled to…" (Example 2) emphasizes legally guaranteed rights. The phrases "have the authority to…" (Example 3) and "have the power to…" (Example 4) reflect institutional or administrative powers conferred by law. The choice among these expressions in translation must align not only with the source text's intent but also with the functional equivalents in common law drafting traditions. In comparative legal linguistics, such distinctions are essential for accurately conveying whether a provision grants a subjective right, an institutional competence, or an administrative discretion, a precision that supports both domestic legal certainty and the transnational comprehensibility of Chinese legislation.

6.4.2 *Translation of* "可以"

The expression "可以…" denotes the rights of a legal subject, specifically the right to act or refrain from acting, without compulsion. It indicates that the legal subject has the autonomy to decide whether to engage in certain legal conduct, and whatever choice is made within the permitted scope will be recognized and protected by law. The fixed translation of "可以…" in legal texts is "may…".

Example 1
第十二条 对外贸易经营者可以接受他人的委托，在经营范围内代为办理对外贸易业务。

Article 12 A foreign business operator may accept the entrustment of other people and handle foreign trade businesses on their behalf within its scope of business.

The translation of "可以…" as "may…" aligns with the common law convention of using modal verbs to distinguish between discretionary rights ("may") and mandatory obligations ("shall"). This linguistic choice reflects the conceptual distinction in legal systems between permissive norms and imperative norms. In comparative legal linguistics, "may" serves as a marker of authorized discretion, enabling legal subjects to exercise agency within defined boundaries. The consistent use of "may" in translating Chinese permissive clauses supports cross-jurisdictional comprehensibility, particularly in international trade and commercial contexts where clarity regarding rights and autonomy is essential. This practice also underscores the functional equivalence approach in legal translation, where the focus is on preserving the normative effect of the source text rather than adhering strictly to literal correspondence.

6.4.3 Translation of "不受侵犯"

The expression "不受侵犯" indicates that the lawful rights and interests of legal subjects shall not be infringed upon by other individuals or organizations. Its English linguistic structures include: (1) shall/may not be infringed upon; (2) may not be encroached upon; (3) be inviolable; (4) shall not be violated; (5) be protected from infringement, among others.

Example 1
第三十七条 律师在执业活动中的人身权利<u>不受侵犯</u>。
Article 37 The personal rights of a lawyer in practicing law <u>shall not be infringed upon</u>.

Example 2
第十三条 公民的合法的私有财产<u>不受侵犯</u>。
Article 13 The lawful private property of citizens <u>may not be encroached upon</u>.

Example 3
第四条 精神障碍患者的人格尊严、人身和财产安全<u>不受侵犯</u>。
Article 4 The personality, dignity, and personal and property safety of the patients with mental disorders <u>are inviolable</u>.

Example 4
第二十六条 导游在执业过程中，其人格尊严受到尊重，人身安全<u>不受侵犯</u>，合法权益受到保障。
Article 26 During the process of practicing, a tour guide's personal dignity shall be respected, personal safety shall not be violated, and lawful rights and interests <u>shall be protected</u>.

The translation of "不受侵犯" demonstrates the nuanced gradation of legal protection in English legal drafting. "Shall not be infringed upon" (Example 1) reflects an active prohibition against interference, typically used for rights subject to specific legal action. "May not be encroached upon" (Example 2) carries a more passive connotation, often applied to property rights where encroachment implies gradual or indirect violation. "Inviolable" (Example 3) represents the strongest formulation, denoting absolute and inherent protection, frequently used for fundamental rights. "Shall not be violated" (Example 4) emphasizes explicit breach of established boundaries. These distinctions align with the civil law tradition's categorization of rights into absolute and relative protections, while adapting to common law's preference for gradations of enforceability. The variation in translation also reflects China's legislative hierarchy, constitutional protections ("inviolable") versus ordinary statutory protections ("shall not be infringed"), demonstrating how linguistic choices in translation systematically convey the normative weight of legal provisions across different tiers of legislation.

6.4.4 Translation of "不受……干涉"

Another common pattern in rights-provision clauses is "不受……干涉", where the subject typically refers to legally permissible actions undertaken by legal entities. English equivalents include "free from interference" and "without interference from".

Example 1
第四条 商业银行依法开展业务，<u>不受</u>任何单位和个人的<u>干涉</u>。

Article 4 Commercial banks shall carry out business in accordance with laws <u>free from any interference</u> by entities or individuals.

Example 2
第六条　人民法院依照法律规定对民事案件独立进行审判，<u>不受</u>行政机关、社会团体和个人的<u>干涉</u>。

Article 6 The people's courts shall try civil cases independently in accordance with law, <u>without interference from</u> any government agency, social group or individual.

The translation of "不受……干涉" as "free from interference" or "without interference from" underscores the legal protection of institutional autonomy and judicial independence. This formulation establishes a negative-rights framework that shields authorized actions from external disruption, reflecting constitutional principles of separation of powers and institutional integrity. The choice between prepositional ("without interference from") and adjectival ("free from interference") structures allows for syntactic flexibility while maintaining normative clarity. In comparative legal contexts, such phrasing aligns with international human rights instruments that guarantee freedom from undue interference, thereby facilitating cross-jurisdictional dialogue on institutional safeguards and rule-of-law standards. The consistent use of this pattern in Chinese legislation reinforces the systemic commitment to protected spheres of legal action, whether in commercial autonomy or judicial independence.

6.5 Translation of Fixed Syntactic Structures in the Liability Clauses

Liability clauses in legal texts refer to provisions that express the legal relationship of remedial rights arising from unlawful acts infringing upon rights or legal interests, embodying the normative effect of sanctions. Simply put, liability clauses can be defined as provisions in legal texts that indicate the content of liability (Li, 2015: 37).

The vast majority of current Chinese laws and regulations include liability clauses, which specify the civil, administrative, and criminal liabilities that actors must bear. Common civil liabilities include compensation for losses, payment of liquidated damages, payment of damages for emotional distress, cessation of infringement, removal of obstacles, elimination of dangers, return of property, restoration to the original condition, and rehabilitation of reputation. Types of administrative penalties include warnings, fines, administrative detention, confiscation of illegal gains, confiscation of illegal property, orders to suspend production or business operations, temporary suspension or revocation of permits, and temporary suspension or revocation of licenses. Criminal penalties encompass principal punishments such as public surveillance, criminal detention, fixed-term imprisonment, life imprisonment, and the death penalty, as well as supplementary punishments such as deprivation of political rights, imposition of fines, and confiscation of property. Fixed sentence patterns or phrases in liability clauses of Chinese laws and regulations include "构成犯罪的", "处…", and "给予/予以…".

6.5.1 Translation of "构成犯罪的"

The common and more formal approach to translating "构成犯罪的" in Chinese laws and regulations is "constitute a crime". Given the implicit conditional nature of the clause, it is appropriately rendered as a conditional sentence in English, which may be expressed in either passive or active voice.

Example 1

第六十八条　违反本法规定，侵害劳动者合法权益，造成财产损失或者其他损害的，依法承担民事责任；构成犯罪的，依法追究刑事责任。

Article 68 Any person who, in violation of the provisions of this Law, infringes a worker's legitimate rights and interests and causes the loss or losses of property or any other damage shall bear civil liability in accordance with the law; where the violation constitutes a crime, criminal liability shall be investigated in accordance with the law.

Example 2

第二十四条　执法机关及其工作人员违法行政或者不作为，致使公民、法人或者其他组织的合法权益、公共利益遭受损害的，对直接负责的主管人员和其他直接责任人员依法给予行政处分；构成犯罪的，依法追究刑事责任。

Article 24 If law enforcement departments and their staff do not perform their duties according to law or neglect their duties, thus damaging the legitimate rights and interests of citizens, legal persons or other organizations, the person directly in charge and other person directly responsible shall be subject to administrative sanctions in accordance with laws; if a crime is constituted, criminal responsibility shall be investigated according to law.

The consistent translation of "构成犯罪的" as "constitutes a crime" or "a crime is constituted" reflects a standardized approach in Chinese legislative translation, aligning with common law conventions for describing criminal liability triggers. The conditional structure, often introduced by "where" or "if", accurately conveys the threshold nature of the provision, which links substantive violations to procedural consequences. This phrasing also demonstrates the hierarchical logic of Chinese legal sanctions, where civil or administrative liability precedes potential criminal escalation. The subsequent clause "依法追究刑事责任" is uniformly rendered as "criminal liability shall be investigated/prosecuted according to law", emphasizing the mandatory and procedural dimension of criminal enforcement. This parallel structure reinforces the principle of legality and ensures cross-jurisdictional clarity in texts addressing transnational compliance or judicial cooperation.

6.5.2 Translation of "处…(罚款/徒刑)"

The phrase "处" (punish/impose) in Chinese legal texts is commonly used to express prohibitive norms. In legal provisions containing "处", the subject of the sentence is often a "的" (de) structure, aiming to highlight the offender and the criminal act, while the predicate "处" indicates the sanction imposed on the offender and the criminal conduct. In Chinese laws and regulations, there are two common structures for "处" sentences: "处...(罚款/罚金)"and "处...徒刑". Below are the common methods for translating these structures into English.

Translation of "处...(罚款/罚金)"

In China's laws and regulations regarding administrative legal liability of counterparts, property penalties constitute the largest proportion, primarily including three categories: imposing fines, confiscating illegal gains, and confiscating illegal property. Among these, imposing fines is the predominant measure. In translation, "处......罚款/罚金" is rendered differently depending on the subject.

When the Subject Is the Law Enforcement Agency

When the subject is the law enforcement agency, the predicate "处......罚款/罚金" is typically translated as "impose a fine/penalty on/upon sb" or "impose a fine/penalty of...". While both "fine" and "penalty" legally refer to monetary penalties, the latter has a broader scope, encompassing a wider range of sanctions, including monetary penalties, labor reform, imprisonment, and others.

Example 1
第五十六条　机动车驾驶人有下列行为之一的，由公安机关交通管理部门<u>处</u>以二百元<u>罚款</u>......

Article 56 The traffic control department of the public security organ shall <u>impose a fine of</u> RMB200 yuan on the vehicle driver who commits any one of the following acts:

Example 2
第十五条　外国企业违反本法第八条、第九条、第十条、第十二条规定的，税务机关可以酌情<u>处以罚金</u>。

Article 15 The tax authorities may, acting at their discretion, <u>impose a penalty on</u> any foreign enterprise which has violated the provisions of Article 8, 9, 10 and 12 of this Law.

The translation of "罚款/罚金" into "fine" or "penalty" reflects functional distinctions within the legal taxonomy of sanctions. While "fine" strictly denotes a monetary penalty, "penalty" encompasses a broader spectrum of punitive measures, aligning with the gradational nature of administrative sanctions in Chinese law. The syntactic choice of "impose on/upon" emphasizes the authoritative action of the enforcement entity, reinforcing the hierarchical relationship between regulatory bodies and subjects. This translation strategy not only preserves the normative force of the original but also accommodates comparative legal interpretations, as "penalty" in common law systems similarly includes both pecuniary and non-pecuniary sanctions. Such precision in terminology supports the cross-jurisdictional intelligibility of Chinese administrative law, particularly in contexts involving international compliance and enforcement cooperation.

When the Subject Is an Organization or Individual

When the subject of a legal liability clause is an organization or individual represented by a "的" structure, the phrase "处……罚款/罚金" should be translated in the passive voice. There are generally three translation approaches: "be imposed a fine/penalty of…", "be fined…", and "is liable to…".

Example 1

第二十三条 违反本办法第六条、第二十条、第二十一条规定的，由县级以上质量技术监督行政部门责令限期改正，可处1000元以上10000元以下罚款。

Article 23 Violators of the provisions of Article 6, Article 20 or Article 21 of these Measures shall be ordered to rectify the violation within the prescribed time limit by the administrative department for quality and technical supervision at and above the county level, and may be imposed a fine of not less than RMB1, 000 yuan but not more than RMB10, 000 yuan.

Example 2

第六十五条　违反本条例第五十一条第一款、第二款规定的，责令改正，可以处一万元以上五万元以下罚款。

Article 65 Those who have violated the provisions of Sections 1 and 2 of Article 51, shall be instructed to rectify, and may be fined not less than 10,000 to no more than 50,000 yuan.

Example 3

第三十条　公共停车场(库)经营者、道路停车场管理者违反本办法第十五条第(一)、(二)、(三)、(四)、(六)项和第二十三条规定，可处以警告或者200元以上2000元以下的罚款……

Article 30 The operator of a public parking lot (garage) or the administrator of a curb-side parking area who violates the provisions under Article 15, Items (1), (2), (3), (4), (6) and Article 23 of these Procedures is liable for a warning or a fine of between not less than 200 yuan and not more than 2000 yuan…

The passive constructions "be imposed a fine", "be fined", and "is liable to" reflect the legal principle that penalties are administered by authoritative bodies rather than initiated by the violator. This syntactic choice reinforces the state's monopoly on punitive authority while maintaining the formal tone of statutory language. The variation among the three structures demonstrates functional flexibility: "be imposed a fine" emphasizes the procedural aspect of penalty imposition, "be fined" focuses on the resulting obligation, and "is liable to" introduces a conditional legal exposure. These translations align with common law drafting conventions where passive voice predominates in penalty clauses to underscore the objectivity of legal consequences. The consistent use of modal verbs like "may" or "shall" further clarifies the discretionary or mandatory nature of the penalty, enhancing cross-jurisdictional comprehensibility while preserving the normative hierarchy of Chinese administrative law.

When the Subject Is a Fine or Penalty

When emphasizing fines or penalties in legal provisions concerning property sanctions, the fine or penalty may be placed in the subject position for translation. In such cases, the phrase "处……罚款/罚金" can be rendered as "a fine/penalty of… may be imposed".

Example 1

第四十一条 违反本法规定，食品生产经营过程不符合卫生要求的，责令改正，给予警告，可以<u>处</u>以五千元以下的<u>罚款</u>；拒不改正或者有其他严重情节的，吊销卫生许可证。

Article 41 If, in violation of this Law, any food producer or marketer does not comply with the hygiene requirements, he shall be ordered to set it right and given a disciplinary warning, and <u>a penalty o</u>f not more than 5,000 yuan may <u>be imposed</u>; if he refuses to set it right or other serious circumstances are involved, his hygiene license shall be revoked.

The syntactic repositioning of fines or penalties as the subject in English translations reflects the common law drafting convention of emphasizing the sanction itself as an independent legal consequence. This construction aligns with the passive voice often used in penalty clauses to maintain formal and impersonal tone, while the modal verb "may" preserves discretionary enforcement authority. The translation accurately captures the conditional nature of the penalty while conforming to the standardized sentence pattern of Anglo-American statutory language. This approach enhances cross-jurisdictional comprehensibility by presenting the penalty as a distinct legal outcome rather than embedding it within a complex verbal phrase, thereby supporting clearer interpretation in international legal contexts.

Translation of "处…徒刑"

The expression "处……徒刑" is a typical sentence pattern in Chinese laws and regulations for indicating the criminal liability that responsible parties shall bear. In translation, it conventionally corresponds to "be sentenced to… imprisonment".

Example 1

第一百零九条　破坏电力、煤气或者其他易燃易爆设备，危害公共安全，尚未造成严重后果的，<u>处</u>三年以上十年以下<u>有期徒刑</u>。

Article 109 Whoever sabotages electric power or gas facilities or other inflammable or explosive equipment and thereby endangers public security, if serious consequences have not yet resulted, shall <u>be sentenced to fixed-term imprisonment</u> of not less than three years and not more than ten years.

The translation of "处……徒刑" into "be sentenced to…imprisonment" aligns with the syntactic conventions of common law criminal statutes, where passive constructions ("be sentenced to") are commonly used to denote judicial imposition of penalties. The phrase "fixed-term imprisonment" corresponds to the civil law concept of determinate sentences, distinguishing it from indefinite or life imprisonment. This translation approach maintains the normative precision of the original while ensuring cross-jurisdictional comprehensibility. The structure also reflects the hierarchical logic of criminal law drafting, where the description of the offense precedes the specification of the penalty, following a "conduct-consequence-punishment" sequence common to both Chinese and Anglo-American legal traditions. Notably, the use of "not less than…and not more than…" preserves the exact statutory sentencing range, demonstrating how formulaic legal language can achieve both linguistic equivalence and functional fidelity across legal systems.

6.5.3 Translation of "给予/予以…(警告/处分)"

The verbs "给予/予以" in China's legal liability clauses carry a negative semantic prosody, commonly used by legislators to express penalties for violations of legal provisions through the structure "给予 + specific measure". Frequent collocations include "给予/予以警告" (give a warning) and "给予/予以处分" (impose a sanction). Translations of "给予/予以" include "give", "impose", and "be subject to", followed by the object "warning" or "sanction".

Translation of "给予/予以…警告"

Example 1
第二十四条 ……逾期未改正的，给予警告，并可以视情节轻重处二百元以上二千元以下罚款。

Article 24 …where he fails to make the rectifications within the prescribed time limit, a warning shall be given, and a fine not less than RMB200 yuan but not more than RMB2, 000 yuan shall concurrently be imposed on him according to the seriousness of the case.

Example 2
第三十二条 非银行金融机构违反本规定者，外汇管理部门有权视其情节给予警告、罚款、停业整顿直至吊销《经营外汇业务许可证》的处罚。

Article 32 In violation of the present provisions by non-bank financial institutions, foreign exchange control departments shall have the right to impose warning, penalties, suspension of business for consolidation and even to revoke foreign exchange business license.

The translation of "给予/予以" as "give" or "impose" reflects the enforcement mechanism of administrative penalties in Chinese law. The passive construction "a warning shall be given" emphasizes the procedural formality and mandatory nature of the penalty, aligning with the objective tone of legal provisions. Meanwhile, "impose" conveys the authoritative application of sanctions by regulatory bodies. The syntactic variation, using passive voice for procedural descriptions ("a warning shall be given") and active voice for regulatory actions ("impose warning"), highlights the distinction between procedural compliance and discretionary enforcement. This nuanced translation approach ensures that the legal intent of deterrence and correction is accurately communicated while maintaining consistency with common law drafting conventions for penalty clauses.

Translation of "给予/予以…处分"

Example 1
第二十八条 国家工作人员在计量监督管理过程中滥用职权、徇私舞弊、玩忽职守的，由有权机关按照管理权限依法给予处分；构成犯罪的，依法追究刑事责任。

Article 28 Where any government functionary neglects his duties, engages in malpractice for personal gains, or abuses his powers in the supervision and administration of metrology, the competent authority shall impose sanction within its administrative authority; if the behavior constitutes a crime, it shall be investigated for criminal liability according to law.

Example 2
第五十条 国家工作人员违法失职，损害残疾人的合法权益的，由其所在单位或者上级机关责令改正或者<u>给予行政处分</u>。

Article 50 Where government functionaries neglect their duties, in violation of the law, and infringe upon the lawful rights and interests of disabled persons, the units to which they belong or their higher authorities shall instruct such persons to rectify their wrong doings or <u>subject them to administrative sanctions</u>.

The translation of "给予处分" as "impose sanction" or "subject to administrative sanctions" reflects the hierarchical and procedural nature of disciplinary actions in China's administrative legal system. The use of "impose" conveys the authoritative application of penalties by competent authorities, while "subject to" emphasizes the subordinate position of the penalized party within the administrative hierarchy. This linguistic choice aligns with the principle of ultra vires in administrative law, where disciplinary power must be exercised within defined jurisdictional boundaries ("within its administrative authority"). The parallel structure in Example 2, "instruct to rectify or subject to sanctions", illustrates the escalating severity of administrative responses, from corrective measures to punitive actions. These translations maintain the normative gravity of disciplinary provisions while ensuring cross-jurisdictional comprehensibility, particularly in contexts where administrative sanction systems may differ significantly between civil law and common law traditions. The consistent rendering of "处分" as "sanction" (rather than "punishment" or "penalty") appropriately captures its disciplinary rather than criminal nature, preserving the conceptual distinction between administrative and criminal liability in Chinese law.

6.6 Translation of Fixed Syntactic Structures in the Supplementary Provisions

The supplementary provisions of a law refer to the collective body of articles that serve as auxiliary content supporting the general and specific provisions of the legislation (Huang & Yang, 2002: 110). A normative legal document typically comprises three parts: general provisions, specific provisions, and supplementary provisions. The general provisions address substantive legal matters such as legislative purpose, legal basis, fundamental principles, scope of application, and competent authorities. The specific provisions elaborate on normative content, including the rights, obligations, and procedures pertaining to the regulated subjects. The supplementary provisions, on the other hand, address operational aspects related to the implementation of laws and regulations, such as effective dates, repeal of existing laws, and delegated provisions, while also supplementing any ambiguities unresolved in the general and specific provisions. Like the main text, the supplementary provisions of a law possess equal and distinct legal force (Xu & Sun, 1993: 53), primarily serving auxiliary and supplementary functions.

The supplementary provisions of China's current laws and regulations cover a wide range of content, which can be summarized to include the following aspects: effective dates of laws and regulations, repeal or retention of previously related laws and regulations, duration and time limits of laws and regulations, applicable subjects and scope of laws and regulations, resolution of legal conflicts, definition of legal terminology, implementing agencies or authorities, delegated provisions, fee regulations, transitional provisions, retroactivity, and legal liability. Among these, clauses related to the implementation of laws, repeal of prior laws, and resolution of legal conflicts appear most frequently across various laws and regulations. Common related phrases include "自……起施行", "……同时废止", "另行规定/制定", and "以……为准".

6.6.1 Translation of "自……起施行"

The phrase "自……起施行" indicates that a law or regulation becomes effective from a specified date after its promulgation. The expression "自……起" has a fixed equivalent in legal English: "as of", which functions similarly to "as from" or "starting from". The term "施行" can be translated in several ways, including "come into effect", "enter into force", "take effect", and "be effective". Among these, the first two are considered more formal.

Example 1
第四十五条 本条例<u>自</u>1996年10月1日<u>起施行</u>。
Article 45 These Regulations shall <u>enter into force</u> as of October 1, 1996.

Example 2
第七十四条 本法<u>自</u>1993年9月1日<u>起施行</u>。
Article 74 This Law shall <u>come into effect</u> as of September 1, 1993.

The translation of "自……起施行" as "shall enter into force as of" or "shall come into effect as of" follows established conventions in international legal drafting where temporal precision is paramount. The use of "as of" rather than simpler alternatives like "on" or "from" reflects a technical preference for unambiguous temporal demarcation in statutory instruments. The modal verb "shall" underscores the normative force of the provision, transforming a descriptive date into a binding temporal boundary. Notably, "enter into force" is often preferred in treaties and international instruments, while "come into effect" appears more frequently in domestic legislation, a distinction observed but not rigidly maintained in Chinese legislative translations. This phrasing aligns with the Vienna Convention on the Law of Treaties terminology while adapting to national legislative practices, demonstrating how Chinese legal translation navigates between domestic specificity and international interoperability.

6.6.2 *Translation of "……*同时废止"

When a new legal instrument is enacted to replace an existing one with similar content, the new instrument must specify the termination of the prior law's effect in its supplementary provisions. The fixed phrase used is "...同时废止". The term "同时" can be translated as the adverb "simultaneously" or the phrase "as of the same date", while "废止" may be rendered as "annul", "abolish", "repeal", "abrogate", "nullify", and so forth.

Example 1
第三十五条 1951年6月月公布的《保守国家机密暂行条例》同时废止。
Article 35 The Provisional Regulations on Guarding State Secrets promulgated in June 1951 shall be annulled as of the same date.

Example 2
第七十条 《中华人民共和国城市规划法》同时废止。
Article 70 The City Planning Law of the People's Republic of China shall be abolished simultaneously.

The translation of "同时废止" as "shall be annulled as of the same date" or "shall be abolished simultaneously" embodies the principle of legal continuity and systematic coherence in legislative updates. The choice of terms such as "annulled" or "abolished" reflects the permanent and formal termination of legal effect, distinguishing it from temporary suspensions or partial invalidations. In common law drafting, "repeal" is often the preferred term for statutory revocation, while "annul" may imply retroactive nullification. The phrasing "as of the same date" explicitly clarifies the temporal alignment of legal succession, preventing normative gaps or overlapping jurisdictions. This formulation not only ensures legislative clarity but also aligns with international norms for legal transition, supporting the harmonization of China's legal system with global best practices in legislative drafting and implementation.

6.6.3 *Translation of* "另行规定/制定"

For important matters not covered by the existing provisions of the law, supplementary provisions must specify that these matters are subject to separate regulations, commonly expressed as "…另有规定/制定" and translated as "shall be formulated separately".

Example 1
第八十二条 宗教学校教育由国务院另行规定。

Article 82 Regulations on education in religious schools shall be formulated by the State Council separately.

The clause "…另行规定/制定" is a legislative deferral mechanism that reflects China's layered regulatory system. By stipulating that certain matters "shall be formulated separately", the law reserves space for specialized or evolving regulations without delaying the enactment of the primary statute. This approach balances legislative efficiency with regulatory precision, allowing detailed rules to be developed by administrative bodies (e.g., the State Council) or specialized agencies based on practical needs and evolving contexts. The translation "shall be formulated separately" preserves the mandatory and future-oriented nature of the provision, emphasizing the obligation to create supplementary rules while maintaining the primacy of the statutory framework. This drafting technique is common in civil law systems and supports the systematic development of legal norms by enabling adaptability and specificity in implementation.

6.6.4 Translation of "以……为准"

Supplementary provisions of laws also address conflicts between the law in question and other laws or regulations. The fixed expression "以……为准" indicates that when conflicts arise between higher-level normative legal documents and lower-level ones, the higher-level document shall apply. The standard translation for this expression is "shall prevail".

Example 1
第四十六条 现行的有关海洋环境保护的规定，凡与本法抵触的，均以本法为准。

Article 46 Where existing provisions concerning marine environmental protection contradict this Law, this Law shall prevail.

The phrasing "以……为准" is a fundamental conflict-of-laws provision that establishes legal hierarchy and normative priority within China's legislative system. Its translation as "shall prevail" precisely conveys the mandatory precedence of higher legal authority, aligning with common law terminology where "prevail" denotes hierarchical supremacy in statutory interpretation. This formulation operates as a meta-rule that governs inter-normative relationships, ensuring systemic coherence while preventing legal fragmentation. In cross-jurisdictional contexts, such clear hierarchy-establishing clauses enhance the predictability of legal application, particularly important for foreign entities navigating China's multi-layered regulatory environment. The consistent use of this construction across Chinese legislation reinforces the constitutional principle of normative hierarchy, which is essential for maintaining the integrity of the socialist legal system with Chinese characteristics.

6.7 Translation of "的" Structure

The "的" structure is a distinctive feature of Chinese legislative texts, bearing strong linguistic characteristics of the Chinese language. It appears with high frequency in Chinese legal documents, primarily serving to make legal writing more concise, rigorous, and solemn. In Chinese laws and regulations, the "的" structure typically takes the following forms: subject-predicate structure + "的", verb-object structure + "的", and prepositional phrase + "的". The "的" structure essentially represents a syntactic form in which the logical subject or actor is omitted, functioning as a nominal element in the sentence. When translating into English, it can be rendered as a conditional clause, a nominal clause, a parallel simple sentence, or a gerund phrase, depending on the context.

The "的" structure in Chinese legislative texts is a linguistic device that condenses complex legal conditions into nominalized phrases, enhancing both brevity and generality. This structure aligns with the Chinese preference for topic prominence and contextual inference, where omitted subjects are recoverable from the discourse. In translation, the choice of rendering, whether as conditional clauses, noun phrases, or gerund constructions, depends on the syntactic norms of legal English and the need for precision. Conditional clauses (introduced by "where") are often favored for their clarity in stipulating legal conditions, while nominalizations maintain the formal tone of legal texts. The translation must also consider the functional equivalence between Chinese nominalizations and English syntactic structures, ensuring that the legal intent is preserved without introducing ambiguity. This linguistic feature underscores the importance of cross-linguistic adaptability in legal translation, particularly in bridging civil law and common law drafting traditions.

6.7.1 Translation as Conditional Clauses

The "的" structure in legal texts serves a hypothetical function, encompassing and highlighting presumed factors within the law to indicate various assumed scenarios in specific contexts. In most cases, the "的" structure in Chinese legal texts can be converted into hypothetical sentences led by "如果" ("if"). Correspondingly, in

English, it is often translated into conditional clauses introduced by conjunctions such as "if", "where", or "when".

Translated as Conditional Clauses Introduced by "if"

The most common usage of the "的" structure in Chinese legal texts is to express the judgment and prediction of potential situations. It can be directly mapped onto sentence patterns such as "如果…就…" ("if… then…") or "只要…就…" ("as long as… then…"). In English, the most common way to express hypothetical situations is through conditional adverbial clauses introduced by "if". Thus, the "的" structure can be translated into conditional clauses led by "if".

Example 1

第三十六条　由于犯罪行为而使被害人遭受经济损失<u>的</u>，对犯罪分子除依法给予刑事处罚外，并应根据情况判处赔偿经济损失。

Article 36 <u>If</u> a victim has suffered financial loss or losses as a result of a crime, the criminal shall, in addition to receiving a criminal punishment according to law, be sentenced to make compensation for the financial loss or losses in the light of the circumstances.

The translation of the "的" structure into "if"-clauses reflects the functional equivalence between Chinese legislative syntax and common law drafting conventions. This transformation preserves the hypothetical and conditional nature of legal provisions while adapting to target-language norms for expressing legal contingencies. The use of "if" establishes a clear cause-effect relationship between the condition (criminal act causing loss) and the legal consequence (compensation order), enhancing the predictability and enforceability of the norm. Such translation choices demonstrate how syntactic restructuring serves not only linguistic accuracy but also jurisprudential clarity, ensuring that conditional legal logic remains intact across linguistic and systemic boundaries.

Translated as Conditional Clauses Introduced by "Where"

In legal texts, the conjunction "where" at the beginning of a sentence often carries conditional implications. Alongside "if", these two structures constitute the highest proportion of conditional sentences across various legal contexts. Compared to "if", "where" tends to introduce more complex conditional clauses and conveys a tone of greater objectivity and formality.

Example 1
第七十条　债权人分立、合并或者变更住所没有通知债务人，致使履行债务发生困难的，债务人可以中止履行或者将标的物提存。

Article 70 Where the obligee fails to notify the obligor of its separation, merger, or change of the domicile, thereby making it difficult for the obligor to perform its obligations, the obligor may suspend its performance or escrow the subject matter.

The use of "where" as a conditional marker in legal translation reflects the formal and systematic nature of legislative language. While "if" typically introduces hypothetical or specific conditions, "where" is often employed to denote legal circumstances or states of affairs that trigger statutory consequences, thereby enhancing the text's normative authority. This distinction aligns with drafting conventions in common law jurisdictions, where "where" clauses are used to establish legal contingencies within a broader regulatory framework. The example illustrates how "where" effectively captures the procedural conditionality embedded in Chinese legislative syntax, translating a complex causal relationship ("致使…") into a logically structured English conditional clause. Such translation choices not only preserve the legal precision of the source text but also ensure that the target version conforms to internationally recognized standards of legal drafting, facilitating cross-jurisdictional comprehensibility and enforcement.

Translated as Conditional Clauses Introduced by "When"

When expressing the conditions for the application of laws and regulations, conditional clauses introduced by "when" can be interchanged with those introduced by "if" or "where" to indicate hypothetical situations. However, unlike the latter two, "when"-led conditional clauses often carry a stronger temporal implication.

Example 1
第四十条　格式条款具有本法第五十二条和第五十三条规定情形的，或者提供格式条款一方免除其责任、加重对方责任、排除对方主要权利的，该条款无效。

Article 40 When standard terms are under the circumstances stipulated in Articles 52 and 53 of this Law, or the party which supplies the standard terms exempts itself from its liabilities, increases the liabilities of the other party, and deprives the material rights of the other party, the terms shall be invalid.

The choice of "when" over "if" or "where" in translating conditional clauses reflects nuanced semantic differences in legal drafting. While "if" typically introduces hypothetical conditions and "where" designates general conditions or scenarios, "when" implies an expectation of occurrence, blending hypotheticality with temporal anticipation. This distinction is particularly significant in legislative texts where conditions are not merely abstract possibilities but anticipated events within legal operations. The use of "when" in Article 40 of the Contract Law suggests that the described circumstances are foreseeable outcomes in contractual practice, thus emphasizing the normative readiness of the legal system. This translation strategy aligns with functional equivalence principles, ensuring that the anticipatory nature of Chinese legal conditions is preserved in the target language while maintaining syntactical precision required for enforceable legal instruments.

6.7.2 Translated as Nominal Clauses

The "的" structure in Chinese legal language is frequently used as a subject to denote a representative concept or refer to a specific category of persons or groups. Due to its nominal nature, it requires translation into a nominal component in English. Accordingly, it can be rendered as a subject clause introduced by "whoever" or as an attributive clause structured as "any + noun + who/that/which".

Translated as Subject Clauses Introduced by "Whoever"

When the omitted logical subject refers to a person in a general sense, the "的" phrase structure can be translated into a subject clause introduced by "whoever".

Example 1

第五十一条　侵害残疾人的合法权益，造成财产损失或者其他损失、损害的，应当依法赔偿或者承担其他民事责任。

Article 51 Whoever infringes upon the lawful rights and interests of a disabled person and causes property or other losses or damage shall compensate for the losses or damage according to law or bear other civil liabilities.

The translation of "的" phrase structures into "whoever" clauses represents a sophisticated adaptation of Chinese legislative syntax to common law drafting conventions. This transformation achieves three critical function. First, universalization of legal subjects. "Whoever" establishes an open class of potential violators, aligning with the inclusive nature of Chinese legal provisions that address general categories of actors. Second, syntactic normalization. It converts the typically postpositive Chinese conditional structure into a prepositive English subject-predicate framework, enhancing readability for target-language legal professionals.

Third, jurisprudential precision. The choice of "whoever" over alternatives like "any person who" or "those who" creates immediate legal agency, emphasizing active responsibility rather than passive description.

This translation approach demonstrates how functional equivalence operates at the syntactic level: while Chinese legislative technique often relies on contextual implication of subjects, English legal drafting requires explicit grammatical subjects to establish clear agency. The "whoever" construction thus serves as a bridge between these differing legal linguistic traditions, preserving the normative scope of the original while meeting target-language expectations for unambiguous subject specification. Notably, this pattern appears most frequently in provisions establishing universal prohibitions or obligations, reflecting its utility in translating broadly applicable legal norms.

Translated as Attributive Clauses Introduced by "Any + Noun + Who/That/Which"

When "的"字结构 expresses nominal concepts, it can also be translated as attributive clauses introduced by "any + noun + who/that/which". Unlike "whoever", this construction requires the translator to supply a specific subject based on context, thereby clarifying the referent and narrowing the scope of legal application.

Example 1
第一百二十五条　在公共场所、道旁或者通道上挖坑、修缮安装地下设施等，没有设置明显标志和采取安全措施造成他人损害<u>的</u>，施工人应当承担民事责任。

Article 125 <u>Any constructor who</u> engages in excavation, repairs or installation of underground facilities in a public place, on a roadside or in a passageway without setting up clear signs and adopting safety measures and thereby causes damage to others shall bear civil liability.

The use of "any + noun + who/that/which" as a translation strategy for "的"字结构 serves to precisely define the legal subject and limit the scope of liability. This construction enhances legal clarity by explicitly identifying the responsible party (e.g., "any constructor") rather than relying on the more generic "whoever". In common law drafting, "any + noun + relative clause" is a conventional method to specify subjects of obligations while maintaining generality within defined parameters. This approach aligns with the principle of legal certainty, ensuring that normative texts are both inclusive of all relevant actors and restrictive in their application. In comparative legal translation, such phrasing bridges the conceptual gap between Chinese nominalizations and English syntactic specificity, facilitating cross-jurisdictional comprehension of liability frameworks. The use of "shall" further reinforces the mandatory nature of the obligation, consistent with the prescriptive tone of civil liability provisions.

6.7.3 *Translated as Gerund Phrases*

In Chinese legal provisions, the structures "有下列行为之一的" or "有以下情况之一的" are often used to introduce multiple parallel "的"structures. These phrases can be translated as conditional clauses introduced by conjunctions such as if, where, in case of, or in the event of. Multiple parallel structures can be rendered as a series of gerund phrases with consistent syntactic form.

Example 1

企业法人有下列情形之一的，除法人承担责任外，对法定代表人可以给予行政处分、罚款，构成犯罪的，依法追究刑事责任:

(一)超出登记机关核准登记的经营范围从事非法经营的；

(二)向登记机关、税务机关隐瞒真实情况、弄虚作假的；

(三)抽逃资金、隐匿财产逃避债务的；

(四)解散、被撤销、被宣告破产后，擅自处理财产的；

(五)变更、终止时不及时申请办理登记和公告，使利害关系人遭受重大损失的；

(六)从事法律禁止的其他活动，损害国家利益或者社会公共利益的。

Under any of the following circumstances, an enterprise as legal person shall bear liability, its legal representative may additionally be given administrative sanctions and fined and, if the offence constitutes a crime, criminal liability shall be investigated in accordance with the law:

(1) conducting illegal operations beyond the range approved and registered by the registration authority;

(2) concealing facts from the registration and tax authorities and practicing fraud;

(3) secretly withdrawing funds or hiding property to evade repayment of debts;

(4) disposing of property without authorization after the enterprise is dissolved, disbanded or declared bankrupt;

(5) failing to apply for registration and make a public announcement promptly when the enterprise undergoes a change or terminates, thus causing interested persons to suffer heavy loss or losses; or

(6) engaging in other activities prohibited by law, damaging the interests of the state or the public interest.

The gerund form used in translating the enumerated items serves multiple functions in legal drafting. Firstly, it creates grammatical parallelism that enhances the structural clarity and readability of the provision. Secondly, the gerund construction effectively converts descriptive Chinese "的" phrases into active verbal forms that clearly denote prohibited or regulated conduct. This transformation is particularly important in common law legal drafting where precise action-description is crucial for determining violations. Thirdly, the consistent use of gerunds maintains syntactic unity across multiple subparagraphs, which is essential for systematic legal interpretation. This translation approach demonstrates how Chinese legislative style, which often employs nominalized structures, can be effectively adapted to the verb-oriented syntax of English legal language while preserving the normative intent and logical structure of the original provision.

6.8 Conclusion

Syntactic structure serves as the formal carrier through which legal language achieves normative force, determinacy, and enforceability. The quality of its translation directly impacts the accurate transmission of national governance intent in the international arena. Through a systematic analysis of seven categories of fixed syntactic patterns in legal texts, including general provisions, definition clauses, obligation clauses, right clauses, liability clauses, supplementary provisions, and the "的" structure, this chapter reveals the underlying tensions in converting Chinese and English legal sentences. Chinese legislative language emphasizes parataxis and holism, adept at constructing flexible normative spaces through multi-layered modifiers and fluid sentence sequences. In contrast, the English legislative tradition prioritizes hypotaxis and explicit logical connections, requiring clear subjects, unambiguous relationships, and distinct modalities. This structural divergence dictates that syntactic translation cannot remain at the level of superficial correspondence but must accomplish a transition from "grammatical conversion" to "transplantation of governance functions."

The research in this chapter demonstrates that successful syntactic translation requires the establishment of a triple correspondence mechanism. First, at the syntactic level, "functional sentence equivalence" must be achieved, for instance, converting Chinese subjectless sentences into English passive structures or transforming lengthy "的" structure modifiers into English relative clauses. Second, at the logical level, "explicitation of normative intent" must be reconstructed by adding conjunctions, adjusting word order, and clarifying agent-patient relationships, thereby converting implicit legal logic into traceable chains of reasoning for target-language readers. Third, at the pragmatic level, "stylistic authority adaptation" must be accomplished through the selection of modal verbs and control of syntactic complexity, ensuring that translations conform to the stylistic features of common law legislative texts while preserving the solemnity unique to Chinese legal documents.

From the perspective of national governance, the standardization of syntactic translation is not merely a technical issue but a foundational project for enhancing the efficacy of China's international legal communication. Precise syntactic conversion ensures that the international community can interpret Chinese legal provisions predictably, reducing cross-border legal disputes arising from structural ambiguity. A systematic syntactic correspondence framework facilitates comparability between Chinese and foreign legal texts, providing a reliable linguistic basis for transnational rule-of-law cooperation, such as international commercial arbitration and judicial assistance. Furthermore, highly professional syntactic translation serves as a crucial discursive tool for China's participation in international rule-making and the reform of the global governance system.

Future research should expand in three dimensions: first, constructing a "parallel corpus of Chinese-English legal sentences" to reveal patterns of syntactic conversion through big data analysis; second, conducting "comparative studies on the readability of transnational legal texts" to optimize syntactic design from the perspective of audience cognition; third, exploring "AI-assisted syntactic conversion systems" to improve translation efficiency while maintaining the central role of human review. Only by integrating syntactic translation into the strategic framework of national language capacity building can it truly become a bridge connecting China's rule-of-law wisdom with global governance needs, showcasing the clear voice and institutional confidence of Chinese law within the landscape of globalized governance.

References

Chen, J. 2003. On several special sentence patterns expressing legal norms. *Journal of Bijie Teachers College (Comprehensive Edition)*, 4.

Huang, W., and Y. Yang. 2002. *Legislative Science*. Jilin University Press.

Jiang, M. 2003. *Interpretation of Articles and Case Analysis of the Administrative Licensing Law*. Beijing: People's Court Press.

Li, L. 2015. *A Study on the Normative Design of Legal Liability Provisions*. Doctoral dissertation, Shandong University.

Wang, Q. and P. Zhang. 2012. An analysis of the setting of "legislative basis" clauses in legal texts. *Journal of South-Central University for Nationalities (Humanities and Social Sciences)*, 4.

Xu, X., and C. Sun. 1993. Several issues regarding the drafting techniques of legal supplementary provisions. *China Legal Science* 3.

Zhang, F. 2010. *Legal Text Translation*. Shandong University Press.

Zhu, L., and S. Zhang. 2009. *Legislative Science*. 3rd ed. Beijing: China Renmin University Press.

Chapter 7
Translation of Laws and Regulations: Standardization and Prospects

Abstract This chapter explores the standardization of translating Chinese laws and regulations through the lens of translation norm theory, examining deviations from established norms and the factors influencing translational consistency. It analyzes systemic challenges such as terminological inconsistency, structural ambiguity, and cross-jurisdictional conceptual gaps. The discussion proposes multi-level strategies for achieving standardization, including the development of authoritative terminology databases, the implementation of project-based quality-control mechanisms, and the integration of digital tools such as parallel corpora and AI-assisted translation systems. Finally, the chapter outlines future directions for legal translation as a strategic component of China's engagement in global governance, emphasizing the role of standardized translations in enhancing the international credibility and communicative efficacy of Chinese legal discourse.

Keywords Norm theory · Translation norms · Deviation · Legal translation standardization · Translation tools

Since 2015, with the deepening implementation of the central government's policy of streamlining administration and delegating power, and the expanded legislative authority granted to cities with districts under the newly amended Legislative Law, local legislative power has undergone structural expansion nationwide. Taking Jiangsu Province as an example, all ten of its cities with districts have successively obtained legislative authority, leading to an exponential increase in the number of local regulations and rules. Consequently, the demand for translating government regulations and rules is facing unprecedented growth pressure. However, the development of translation work for local government regulations and rules in China currently shows significant regional disparities. According to research, only a few provinces and municipalities such as Jiangsu, Zhejiang, and Shanghai have established relatively regular translation mechanisms, while translation efforts in most regions remain fragmented and reactive. More notably, existing translation outputs generally suffer from systemic issues characterized by "overall low quality and frequent occurrences of mistranslations and omissions" (Dong, 2014: 84).

X. Dong, Y. Zhang, *On Translation of Laws and Regulations in China*,
https://doi.org/10.1007/978-981-95-9406-1_7

From an academic research perspective, a prominent contradiction persists in China's legal translation field: the disconnection between theoretical research and practical needs. There is a scarcity of systematic research outcomes, particularly academic monographs and specialized studies that deeply integrate translation theory with practice and offer direct guidance for translating laws and regulations (Li & Hu, 2002). Since the beginning of the new century, with the increasing activity of local government legislation, research on the translation of government regulations and rules, an emerging field, has remained largely on the periphery of academic attention. The problems exposed in translation practice have not yet received adequate theoretical response or methodological guidance (Li & Dong, 2015). As an officially sanctioned translation activity led by the state, the quality of translating government regulations and rules not only affects the accurate dissemination of legal norms but also directly influences the international representation of national governance efficacy and the global construction of the rule-of-law image of China. Establishing a scientific, standardized, and sustainable translation mechanism has become a critical issue to be addressed in advancing the modernization of the national governance system and governance capabilities.

As the concluding chapter of this book, the author, from the perspective of translation norm theory and drawing on over a decade of practical experience in participating in the translation and review of regulations and rules for the Jiangsu Provincial People's Government, systematically analyzes the existing irregularities in China's translation of regulations and rules and their institutional causes. Furthermore, the author proposes a pathway for constructing a standardized system for translating laws and regulations with Chinese characteristics, aiming to provide theoretical reference and practical solutions for promoting the professionalization and standardization of legal translation work in China.

7.1 Norm Theory in the Field of Translation

Schäffner and Adab (2000) posits that norms are the behavioral standards governing interactions among individuals in society, endowing human actions with predictability. It is precisely the existence of such norms that renders human activities, such as language and translation, predictable and systematic, thereby making them suitable subjects for scientific research and analysis. The exploration of translation norms has undergone multiple developmental stages, giving rise to various schools of thought.

Early translation scholars in China, such as Yan Fu, Qian Zhongshu, and Fu Lei, primarily approached norms from a philological perspective, defining them through reflective insights drawn from their personal translation experiences. For instance, Qian Zhongshu's concept of "transformation" (化境) focused mainly on the treatment of words and sentences in texts, lacking the comprehensiveness and systematicity expected of a theoretical framework. In the late 1970s, translation scholars in China and the West shifted their focus to linguistics, applied linguistics, and discourse analysis. For example, Nida's theory of dynamic equivalence emphasized achieving equivalence between source and target languages according to specific criteria. Since the turn of the new century, some legal translation scholars have built upon earlier foundations to propose more detailed guidelines for legal translation. For instance, Qiu (2000) introduced principles such as the use of solemn vocabulary, accuracy, conciseness, terminological consistency, and the application of specialized terminology. Li and Zhang (2006) proposed six applied operational principles for legal translation: accuracy and precision, consistency and uniformity, clarity and conciseness, professionalism, linguistic standardization, and collaborative work.

While the aforementioned norms have significantly contributed to the advancement of translation, they share a common characteristic: the aspiration to establish a comprehensive set of rules to address translation challenges. Such prescriptive translation norms often overlook the "communicative function of translation within the target culture or context" and disconnect translation from its "socio-cultural and ideological associations" (Yan, 2009: 169). Take the principle of conciseness as an example. This rule rigidly dictates that translated legal texts should employ simple and brief language, a perspective clearly influenced by the Plain Legal English Movement that emerged in the United States in the 1970s. However, this movement arose in response to the extreme difficulty of understanding certain financial legal clauses, which sparked dissatisfaction among lawyers and judges and led to language reform efforts. Times have changed. Today, the subjects regulated by legal texts have become more extensive and complex. Moreover, the inherent characteristics of the source language and various other factors may fundamentally necessitate the use of complex language in legal texts to ensure accuracy and prevent loopholes. Mechanically demanding simplicity and brevity in translation language evidently disregards the socio-developmental factors that shape translation norms.

The guiding significance of translation norm theory for legal translation must be examined within the macro-framework of national governance modernization. Legal translation is not merely a technical act of linguistic conversion but an institutional practice in constructing and disseminating a nation's rule-of-law discourse system internationally. While early translation norms under the philological paradigm embodied practical wisdom, they lacked systematic theoretical support. The equivalence theories emerging from the linguistic turn advanced methodological development but often fell into the technical trap of formal equivalence. Although the specific principles proposed by contemporary legal translation scholars offer operational value, their prescriptive orientation frequently overlooks the dynamism and social embeddedness of translation as a cross-cultural governance act.

From the perspective of national governance, norms for legal translation should transcend the static "checklist of rules" model and shift toward a dynamic "functional adaptation" paradigm. The complexity of legal texts is not a linguistic flaw but an inevitable reflection of governance refinement at the textual level. Taking the principle of conciseness as an example, its mechanical application may lead to the oversimplification or even distortion of China's institutional expressions in international dissemination. Authentic translation norms should balance three critical requirements: ensuring professional precision at the linguistic level, preserving institutional integrity at the jurisprudential level, and achieving cross-cultural acceptability at the communicative level.

The current development of standardization in translating China's laws and regulations requires the construction of a "trinity" theoretical framework: a micro-level system for terminological equivalence, a meso-level mechanism for textual functional adaptation, and a macro-level strategy for converting national governance discourse. This demands that translation norms be rooted in the particularities of China's rule-of-law practice while interfacing with the universality of international legal discourse. They must maintain the authority and stability of legal texts while adapting to the dynamic communication needs of the globalized era.

The evolution of legal translation norms is essentially an extension of national governance capacity in the linguistic dimension. Only by establishing a translation norm system aligned with governance modernization can China ensure that its rule-of-law narrative accurately conveys institutional essence and effectively shapes its rule-of-law image on the international stage, ultimately serving the strategic goal of enhancing the nation's institutional discourse power.

7.2 Deviation from Norms in Translation of Laws and Regulations

The a priori nature of prescriptive translation norms leads to inherent limitations that are difficult to overcome. Current research on translation norms is undergoing a shift from prescriptive to descriptive approaches. In this process, some scholars emphasize the integration of linguistics and sociology, exploring translation norms through empirical evidence that reflects temporal and social characteristics. By describing phenomena, they seek to uncover universal patterns, thereby enabling the systematic prediction of occurrences. Key proponents of this perspective on translation norms include the Israeli scholar Toury and the Finnish scholar Chesterman.

Toury (1995: 56–58) first posited that translation is fundamentally a socio-culturally constrained activity, with translations involving two socio-cultural systems and necessitating choices between them. As standards for measuring such choices, translation norms encompass: preliminary norms involving factors related to the selection of texts for translation; initial norms involving macro-level choices made by translators regarding their orientation toward the source text or the target text; and operational norms involving micro-level choices made during the translation process.

Chesterman (1999: 9–19), deeply influenced by Toury's theory, focused more closely on initial norms and operational norms, which are closely tied to translation behavior. He further categorized translation norms into two major types: first, expectancy norms, which refer to the expectations held by target-language readers regarding the grammatical, stylistic, and acceptability standards of translated works. This category encompasses what Toury termed initial norms and operational norms. And second, professional norms, which are process norms established by professional translators deemed competent by readers of the translation. They primarily include relation norms governing the relationship between the source and target texts, communication norms pertaining to the communicative effectiveness of the translation, and accountability norms addressing the ethical and professional responsibilities of translators.

The descriptive approach to translation norms, as advocated by Toury and Chesterman, provides a robust theoretical framework for analyzing irregularities in the translation of China's laws and regulations. This perspective shifts the focus from rigid prescriptive rules to the dynamic interplay between socio-cultural contexts and translational choices. In the context of Chinese legal translation, expectancy norms reflect the target readership's demands for accuracy, consistency, and formal equivalence, while professional norms underscore the translator's role in mediating between legal systems and ensuring communicative fidelity. The application of these norm categories enables a systematic diagnosis of translation irregularities, such as terminological inconsistency, stylistic mismatches, and cultural misinterpretations, by situating them within broader socio-institutional and professional practice frameworks. This analytical lens not only elucidates the root causes of translation anomalies but also informs the development of norm-based strategies for enhancing the quality and reliability of legal translations in cross-jurisdictional contexts.

7.2.1 Deviation from Initial Norms

The initial norms of translation mainly refer to the macro choices of translators in terms of translation policy and translation directness (Toury, 1995). This macro choice combines many factors such as historical background, social needs, era conditions and the readership it faces, and is closely related to the dominant social and cultural development needs. The current translation of laws and regulations in China began in the new century, which is an official translation led by local governments at all levels. Different from translation activities at any time in China's history, China's current national strength is growing stronger and closer to the international community. Translation activities are turning from foreign translation to Chinese translation. In the process of foreign translation, we need to not only transfer simple information, but also carry forward the socialist core values with Chinese characteristics through translation. Government regulations and rules are the legal text of socialism with Chinese characteristics and the concentrated embodiment of the socialist core values. Their translation bears the heavy responsibility of carrying forward the socialist core values with Chinese characteristics. To do a good job in the translation of government regulations and rules, it is necessary to effectively disseminate legal information to the outside world and strive for the international discourse right, which requires translators not only to translate according to the method of literal translation, but also to make overall consideration. China's government regulations and rules have a short history of foreign translation, and have not formed a complete translation tradition.

Moreover, China's government regulations and rules must reflect different ideologies from those in western countries such as Britain and the United States, and the acceptance of the target readers may decline. Therefore, the degree of translation directness should be appropriately adjusted in translation. In addition, the translation of China's current government regulations and rules also plays a role in restricting the behavior of foreign personnel in China. As the basic function of the legal text, the realization of the function of restricting others' behavior requires that the translation of the legal text clarify what can be done and what cannot be done. There are many legislative languages with Chinese characteristics in China's government laws and regulations. Due to social differences, there are no corresponding concepts in the context of the target language. If these languages are simply translated, they will not enable foreign personnel to clearly grasp the content of the acts to be bound by the legal text. Therefore, it is also necessary to appropriately adjust the directness of the translation of these legislative languages with Chinese characteristics. However, in the process of translation practice, it is not easy for translators to grasp the degree of literal translation. They often affect the acceptance of the translation due to improper macro choices.

For example, the *Regulation of Jiangsu Province on National Defense Education* mentions "supporting the military and giving preferential treatment to family members". This expression cannot find a corresponding concept and ready-made translation in English. Considering that this is a fine revolutionary tradition in China, the translator should strictly and accurately convey the concept of supporting the army and taking care of the families of soldiers and martyrs, so he gave the translation "support the army and extend preferred treatment to the families of services and martyrs". On the surface, this translation is more comprehensive and accurate, but the concept of "martyrs" is easy to arouse the antipathy of the target language readers. Because this word means not only soldiers killed in battle, but also martyrs. After the 9/11 terrorist attacks in the United States, the word "martyrs" is often used to describe the terrorist attackers in the western media. The translation does not properly adjust the direct degree of translation, which affects the readers' acceptance and is not conducive to the establishment of their own discourse power. It is easier for readers to accept it than to simplify it to "support the army and extend preferred treatment to the families of services". Therefore, when translating, the translator should combine the national conditions of China and the habits of the readers in the translation context, and translate the concepts that the readers can understand and accept, rather than find an equivalent translation.

Additionally, generally speaking, the translators involved in the translation of laws and regulations are all native speakers of Chinese, and there are no native speakers of English. This defect may lead to the passive neglect of the acceptance of the target language readers. The acceptance of target language readers is affected by multiple factors such as history, culture and social habits, which is quite complex. And with the social changes, the degree of acceptance also changes accordingly. Although the translator is proficient in English, he is not a native speaker after all, and cannot guarantee an accurate and comprehensive grasp of the acceptance of the target language readers, which leads to the translator's inability to reasonably adjust the translation policy and the degree of translation directness. The active and passive neglect of the target language readers' acceptance makes our translation violate the requirements of the initial norms, which greatly weakens the role of our external translation and deprives us of the opportunity to gain international discourse power through translation.

7.2.2 Deviation from Operational Norms

Operational norms in translation primarily refer to the micro-level decisions made by translators during the translation process. Toury (1995) further categorized these into matricial norms and textual-linguistic norms, encompassing the application of various translation techniques at lexical, syntactic, and discourse levels. Translation inevitably requires positioning within two distinct linguistic and cultural traditions. Translators may adhere to the norms of the source text, conform to the conventions of the target language, or seek a compromise between the two. Consequently, operational norms serve as restrictive frameworks that permit certain choices while prohibiting others. In the micro-decision-making process of applying translation techniques, translators must first carefully consider the overall translation strategy, which then informs the selection of translation methods. Thus, operational norms are closely linked to and influenced by initial norms.

The outcomes of translators' choices may result in retaining the stylistic features of the source text but failing to integrate the translation into the target culture, instead imposing an artificial language upon target readers. Alternatively, through adaptation, the translation may become a rendition that conforms to the linguistic and cultural standards of the target language. The ideal outcome involves achieving a compromise between "adequacy" and "acceptability" through appropriate translation techniques, allowing the translated text to find a suitable position within the target culture and fill gaps in its linguistic and cultural landscape (Hermans, 1999). Ideally, the goal of legal translation is to strike a balance between "adequacy" and "acceptability", with translators selecting appropriate techniques under the guidance of operational norms to achieve this objective.

In terms of lexical translation, laws and regulations employ a substantial number of fuzzy legislative terms with distinct Chinese linguistic and cultural characteristics. These terms, described as "unable to strictly delineate their scope of application, rendering understanding ambiguous", pose challenges to lexical translation norms (Wu, 2014: 24). Taking sentence patterns in legal translation as another example, due to the high stability of legislative institutions and the language used, legislative texts feature many recurring common sentence structures. Translators' primary task when encountering such structures is to select the correct grammar to construct sentences in the target language.

Translators play a critical role in micro-decisions regarding translation techniques, ultimately influencing the acceptance of the translated text by target readers. If translators mechanically adhere to a single strategy or ideology during the translation process without discerning appropriate techniques based on social and reader needs, the resulting translation will inevitably fail to achieve a balance between "adequacy" and "acceptability". Micro-decisions on translation techniques depend on macro-decisions regarding translation strategy and directness. Therefore, translators must accurately define the goals and strategies of their translation activities before commencing work, as this is a prerequisite for making appropriate micro-decisions. In current legal translation practice, translators often lack opportunities for in-depth communication with translation commissioners, leading to misalignment in grasping the goals and strategies of translation activities and, consequently, operational norms anomie.

Additionally, some regions outsource the translation of local regulations and rules to commercial translation agencies following standard business translation models. Due to the relatively loose regulation of the translation industry in China, it is often challenging to assess whether the professional competence and abilities of translators hired by these agencies meet the requirements of the task. Employing translators with inadequate professional proficiency to undertake the translation of regulations and rules is another cause of operational norms anomie.

7.2.3 Deviation from Relation Norms

Chesterman argues that relation norms in translation primarily require translators to ensure that an appropriate and relevant similarity is established and maintained between the target text and the source text (Chesterman, 1993). A key characteristic of this norm is its emphasis on appropriateness. Unlike previous translation standards that emphasized uniformity and closure (such as the principle of fidelity), this appropriateness is not fixed but is determined comprehensively by the translator based on factors such as the specific context of the translation activity, the client's requirements, the author's intent, the purpose of the translation, and the readers' acceptance. This characteristic of the norm aligns with the Skopos theory proposed by Vermeer (2000) and others, adopting a relativist stance and emphasizing that the purpose of translation determines the means of translation.

In the context of translating government regulations and rules, their purposes are twofold: first, external publicity, and second, regulating the behavior of foreigners within China. These two purposes determine that the appropriate degree of relevant similarity between the translated text and the source text must ensure the effectiveness of external publicity, reflect the achievements of rule of law construction, and genuinely fulfill the constraining function of the law.

The translation of laws and regulations involves cross-legal-system communication. Translation "must not only operate at the linguistic level but, more importantly, require a clear understanding of the legal culture and legal conventions underlying the language that are not explicitly articulated in the text" (Dong, 2015: 110). During the translation process, for translators to grasp its operability effectively, they must cultivate their own legal literacy, particularly regarding the legal system of the target language. Currently, China's translation workforce for laws and regulations mainly consists of translation professionals whose expertise is confined to the linguistic domain, enabling them to handle linguistic aspects of translation relatively well. However, legislative texts differ in form and function from other ordinary texts, making it difficult for translators lacking legal literacy to fully meet the demands of such translation tasks. To improve translation quality and avoid relation norms anomie, we need to provide legal professional training for existing translators or introduce interdisciplinary translators with legal backgrounds.

7.2.4 Deviation from Communication Norms

The communication norms in translation require the translator, as a mediator between the source and target languages, to optimize the communicative effectiveness of the target text according to specific contextual and audience requirements (Chesterman, 1993). The fundamental prerequisite for meeting this requirement is that the translator must have a comprehensive command of the source language, fully understand its meaning, and skillfully use the target language to express this meaning. In the translation of government regulations and rules, the communication norms anomie primarily manifests in two situations: first, the translator's insufficient or erroneous understanding of the regulations leads to deviations in the meaning of the translation; second, the translator's inappropriate use of the target language results in difficulties in comprehension for the readers.

The communication norms anomie in translation arises from the fact that legal texts are characterized by rigorous internal logic and precise terminology. Any carelessness by the translator during the translation process can lead to deviations in the transmission of information in the translated text, misleading the readers. To avoid errors such as taking phrases out of context or interpreting literally, the translator must conduct a comprehensive interpretation and thoroughly understand the intent of the regulations and rules before commencing translation. Secondly, the professionalism of legal texts is primarily reflected in terminology, including legal terms and industry-specific terminology. Government regulations and rules impose detailed provisions on various industries, often containing specialized vocabulary. Translators must conduct professional interpretations and seek standardized expressions in the target language.

7.2.5 Deviation from Accountability Norms

The accountability norms primarily require translators to adopt a faithful and trustworthy attitude in translation, prohibiting them from deviating from the original text to create their own versions or arbitrarily altering the source material (Chesterman, 1993). In essence, the accountability norm is an ethical standard in translation that prevents translators from acting without constraints or arbitrarily pursuing certain objectives during the translation process. Unlike the translation of ordinary texts, the translation of regulations and rules demands the complete and accurate reproduction of legislative intent as a fundamental requirement. Translators must subjectively strive for consistency between the translation and the legislative intent, thereby avoiding various forms of accountability norms anomie. However, due to the inherent characteristics of legal language, violations of accountability norms in translation remain relatively common (Jin & Hu, 2000).

First, translators often omit or add content to the source text due to personal oversight, thereby altering its meaning and resulting in accountability norms anomie. Although translators are expected to work diligently and meticulously to avoid omissions or errors, they are human and susceptible to various factors such as emotions, health, environment, and time constraints, which may lead to mistakes. Therefore, while the cause of anomie lies with the translators, addressing this issue cannot rely solely on them. In modern translation practice, translation tasks have become more specialized and complex, and translation is no longer solely the responsibility of individual translators. According to the relevant national standard GB/T 19363.1, the translation process requires project managers to control workflow stages and compile specialized terminology, industry experts to review the translation for content accuracy, and language experts to ensure the fluency and coherence of the translated text.

Second, accountability norms anomie in the translation of laws and regulations often results from information asymmetry faced by translators. This is particularly true for local regulations and rules, which are typically formulated to address specific issues in specific regions. Translators, and even reviewers, are often not involved in the legislative process, leading to a significant information asymmetry compared to legislators. This can result in an incomplete understanding of the meaning of legal texts or legislative intent, leading to mistranslations.

Third, the core requirement of accountability norms is for translators to adopt a faithful attitude toward the source text. However, for translators of laws and regulations, the objects of loyalty extend far beyond the source text itself. Legal texts form a rigorous system, with each new text building upon previous ones, representing "new explorations" based on existing concepts and ideas (Wu, 2014: 25). Therefore, local regulations and rules must align with their respective superior laws, and consistency must also be maintained among different local regulations and rules. As official translations of laws, regulations, and rules, their translated versions should inherit this characteristic, ensuring that translations of local regulations and rules remain consistent with the official translations of superior national laws and regulations, and that translations of regulations and rules among different local governments are also harmonized. This requires translators, particularly those working on local regulations and rules, not only to remain faithful to the source text but also to refer to the official translations of superior laws and other relevant government regulations and rules. This is essential to avoid creating translations that disrupt the consistency and uniformity of the legal system. However, this requirement poses significant practical challenges. It demands a high level of self-awareness from translators, who must proactively consult the official translations of superior laws and other relevant regulations and rules. To maintain consistency, extensive cross-referencing and comparison are necessary, making the task labor-intensive. Furthermore, access to official translations of superior laws and other relevant government regulations and rules is often limited, leaving translators frequently lacking such resources.

7.3 Factors Affecting the Standardization of Translation of Laws and Regulations

The translation of legislative texts can be divided into two categories: authoritative translation and non-authoritative translation (Šarčević, 1994). Authoritative translation refers to legally valid translations of legislative texts adopted and enacted by national legislative bodies, serving as parallel texts of the same law and constituting legal instruments in their own right. Non-authoritative translation, on the other hand, typically refers to translations produced for purposes such as dissemination and exchange, lacking legal effect. In China, the translation of laws and regulations falls under the category of non-authoritative translation. Despite its lack of legal enforceability, it is an official translation activity organized by state government agencies, representing the image and will of the state and carrying certain legal implications in foreign-related legal affairs. Therefore, it must strive for the highest translation quality and adhere strictly to relevant translation norms.

Regarding translation norms, as discussed earlier, early scholars primarily approached the topic from philological and comparative linguistic perspectives, focusing on how to produce correct translations according to specific criteria. However, such prescriptive translation norms lack systematic theory and comprehensive analysis, overlooking "the communicative function of translation within the target culture or context and its association with socio-cultural ideologies" (Han, 2004). After 40 years of development since the reform and opening-up, China's legislative work has formed a socialist legislative system with Chinese characteristics. However, the systematic translation of laws and regulations has been conducted for a relatively short period, with a limited number of translated texts. Moreover, Western countries do not use Chinese-English legal translations, so there is no established tradition of Chinese-English legal text translation to draw upon. Simultaneously, due to differences in language, culture, and social systems across countries, China's laws and regulations inevitably reflect ideologies different from those of Western countries such as the United States and the United Kingdom, which may reduce their acceptability among target readers. To maximize compliance with the operational and initial norms of legal translation, translators should first adhere to the norms applicable to general text translation and actively seek legal texts in the target society that are identical or similar to China's laws and regulations as references to explore translation norms.

As this book demonstrates, the current English translations of China's laws and regulations exhibit multifaceted and multi-layered instances of deviation from translation norms, which can be broadly categorized into four types. First, deviation from inconsistency is relatively prominent. Legislative texts constitute a complete system, and consistency should be maintained among texts within the system. However, existing translations reveal inconsistencies between local regulations and rules and their superior laws, inconsistencies among translations of different local regulations and rules, and inconsistencies within the same local regulation or rule. Such inconsistencies violate the "principle of identity" in legal texts and significantly undermine the authority of legal texts (Chen, 2000: 214). Second, deviation from professionalism exists. Current translations exhibit inappropriate use of legal and industry-specific terminology and misinterpretations of legislative intent, reflecting a lack of professionalism. Third, inaccuracy, which contravenes the requirements of accountability norms, is prevalent. This includes deviations in expression that compromise the accuracy of translations. Fourth, lack of acceptability arises from poor expressive effects, hindering reader comprehension.

As a form of legislative text translation, legal translation involves not only language conversion but also the transformation of legal systems and cultures. It is further influenced by factors such as the translation commissioner (government), the translators themselves, and translations of superior laws. From the perspective of modernizing the national governance system, the standardization of legal translation faces multiple structural constraints. As an institutional practice for the international dissemination of the nation's rule-of-law discourse, although China's current legal translation is categorized as non-authoritative, it functionally undertakes the critical tasks of constructing the country's rule-of-law image and participating in the global governance discourse system. The systematic presence of deviation from translation norms essentially reflects the state of national governance capacity in the cross-linguistic dimension: inconsistency reveals shortcomings in the coordination mechanisms between central and local legislation at the level of language conversion; deviation from professionalism highlights the scarcity of interdisciplinary legal translation talent; inaccuracy exposes the lag in standardizing translation processes; and lack of acceptability indicates the need to enhance cross-cultural governance capabilities. These complexities contribute to the multifaceted factors underlying translation anomie in China's laws and regulations. The following section attempts to explore these factors from three perspectives.

7.3.1 *Inconsistency in the Professionalization of Translation Work Mechanisms*

Inconsistency in the Professionalization of Translators

Translators are the primary agents of translation work, and the quality of translation largely depends on the selection of appropriate translators. Therefore, the professionalization of translators is the first step in ensuring translation quality from an institutional perspective. However, the uneven professionalization of translators is one of the causes of translation irregularities. For example, the composition of translators currently engaged in translating local regulations and rules in China can be broadly categorized into three types: in-house translators, that is, local legislative authorities delegating translation tasks to individuals within their departments; outsourced translation companies, that is, contracting translation work directly to external translation agencies; and specialized translation teams, that is, hiring professionals from the fields of translation and law to form dedicated translation teams, which generally ensures higher translation quality but requires significant investment in human and material resources. In practice, due to constraints such as limited resources, time, and costs, most regions fall into the first or second category, while only a few developed regions belong to the third category, organizing fixed and professional translation teams. This situation often results in translation work being carried out in an "open environment", characterized by "temporary and risky features", which is the primary cause of inconsistencies in translations (Pu & Gao, 2014).

First, the varying levels of specialization among translation practitioners have led to inconsistency between the translations of higher-level laws and those of local regulations and rules. For the same provision, if there exists an official translation of the higher-level law, the translation of local regulations and rules should maintain consistency with it. However, in the absence of a fixed and professional translation team, translators temporarily assigned to such tasks often lack a comprehensive understanding of the legal translation system, neglecting existing official translations of higher-level laws and creating independent translations for provisions that already have authoritative versions. When readers of local regulations and rules attempt to reference the corresponding higher-level laws based on these translations, they may struggle to locate the corresponding texts.

Second, the varying levels of specialization among translation practitioners have resulted in inconsistency across translations of different local regulations and rules. Legal texts form an extremely rigorous system, and their language must be consistent across documents. This requirement should also apply to the translations of local regulations and rules. However, in the absence of a fixed and professional translation team, it is difficult to expect or enforce consistency among translations of various regulations and rules produced by temporary translators.

Third, the varying levels of specialization among translation practitioners have led to inconsistency within the translations of individual local regulations and rules.

A local regulation or rule comprises multiple interconnected clauses, forming a cohesive system. Therefore, all clauses and their translations should maintain internal consistency. A fixed and professional translation team typically conducts translation work in a centralized manner, with a short time span and dedicated personnel, ensuring better internal consistency in translations. However, when translation tasks are handled by temporary or part-time translators, the lack of concentrated work time and extended project durations often leads translators to forget previous translation choices, resulting in inconsistencies within the same text. Additionally, some translation agencies, due to a lack of permanent translators or a focus on maximizing efficiency, may fragment and outsource translation tasks, sometimes even subcontracting them multiple times, further exacerbating inconsistencies and severely compromising the accuracy of the text.

Uneven Professionalization of Translation Review Project Management

Giammarresi (2011) pointed out that modern translation work is shifting from traditional models centered on individual translators to large-scale, professional project-based translation, with greater emphasis on translation environment development and project management. Currently in China, due to the deeply ingrained traditional concept of translation that prioritizes individual translators, as well as considerations of cost and budgetary constraints, the level of professionalism in translation review project management for local regulations and rules varies significantly across regions. Some areas still rely on individual translation approaches, lacking any team structure, let alone systematic management. Other regions may form teams but lack effective management, with organizers merely assigning tasks without facilitating genuine collaboration among translators. Only a few localities, in the translation of local regulations and rules, are able to provide comprehensive human and financial support, appoint dedicated personnel as project managers to coordinate efforts, and employ industry and language experts for review and proofreading, thereby establishing a complete project management mechanism.

The uneven professional level of project management in translating local regulations and rules reflects the phased characteristics of China's legal external communication system in terms of specialization and standardization. Such disparities not only affect the consistency of legal text translation quality but may also constrain the effectiveness of international dissemination of local rule-of-law achievements. To enhance the soft power of national rule of law, translation project management must be integrated into the framework of modernizing legal capacity. This requires establishing standardized processes with central-local coordination, cultivating a professional legal translation talent pool, and improving digital terminology management systems. These efforts will drive the transformation of translation work from being "dominated by individual experience" to being "driven by systematic governance", thereby enabling legal translation to serve as an effective extension of the national governance system in the international arena.

Insufficient Professional Support from Legislative Authorities

The mechanism for translating laws and regulations requires professional support from legislative authorities. However, under current circumstances, translators have very limited access to such support. Most regions have not yet established communication mechanisms between translators and legislative authorities when translating local regulations and rules. The quality of translations for local regulations and rules is influenced by the legislative intent of the regulations themselves, the legislative intent of higher-level laws, and the tradition of official translations. As specialization deepens in modern society, legislative work has become highly professional. The meanings and legislative intent of legal provisions (including translations) are often complex and profound, and sometimes legislative authorities need to issue specialized judicial interpretations. However, in translation work, translators are usually unable to participate in the legislative process (or the official translation process of higher-level laws). Many translators also lack sufficient legal expertise. Therefore, to fully understand the legislative intent of regulations and rules and produce accurate translations, they need to establish communication channels with the legislative authorities of local and higher-level laws, as well as with the institutions responsible for translating relevant legal provisions. In the absence of professional support from legislative authorities, relying solely on the composition of translation teams and project management in the translation and review process cannot fundamentally ensure the accuracy and standardization of translations. Consequently, translations are inevitably constrained by the individual professional level of translators, leading to various issues such as misinterpretation of legislative intent.

7.3.2 Insufficiency in Cultivation of Interdisciplinary Legal Translation Professionals

Legal translation is an interdisciplinary undertaking that typically encompasses linguistics, translation studies, and jurisprudence. As noted in my work Legal Text Translation, "A successful legal translator must be a high-quality interdisciplinary professional, both a jurist and a bilingual linguist" (Dong, 2011). Currently, interdisciplinary legal translators are in critically short supply across China, far from meeting the demands of legal translation work.

First, there is a shortage of specialized translation training. Within the higher education system, translation has long been treated as a subfield of foreign language and literature studies, without establishing an independent disciplinary framework. Translation instruction occupies only a small portion of foreign language curricula. Although foreign language programs have produced numerous graduates, language proficiency alone does not equate to translation competence. The number of translators trained by universities remains limited. Moreover, current translation education tends to prioritize academicization, emphasizing theoretical research over practical translation skills. As a result, some graduates still fall short of the professional standards required for translation work and are unable to meet its demands.

Second, there is a lack of professionals with multidisciplinary expertise. Competent interdisciplinary legal translators must possess knowledge across multiple disciplines. However, traditional higher education in China emphasizes specialized training, with interdisciplinary education, particularly spanning linguistics, translation studies, and jurisprudence, remaining rare. Individuals with solid expertise in all three fields are exceedingly scarce. Consequently, most translators involved in translating local regulations and rules are specialists in only one discipline. Due to the limitations of their single-disciplinary knowledge, they are prone to misunderstandings, mistranslations, and other issues stemming from a lack of expertise in other relevant fields.

Third, in the process of cultivating legal translators, insufficient attention is paid to the study of Western legislative language and culture. Translators often overlook the linguistic and cultural receptivity of the target readers (Western audiences), leading to non-standardized translations.

7.3.3 Lack of Translation Standards for Chinese Laws, Regulations, and Rules

As legislative texts, the translation of local regulations and rules must achieve more than mere functional equivalence at the linguistic level; it must prioritize the attainment of legal functional equivalence. In light of the unique characteristics of legal texts, some scholars have proposed more detailed translation guidelines. For example, Qiu (2000) outlined five principles for legal translation: the use of solemn language, accuracy, conciseness, terminological consistency, and the application of specialized terminology Li and Zhang (2006) proposed six applied operational principles for legal translation: accuracy and precision, consistency and uniformity, clarity and conciseness, specialization, linguistic standardization, and collaborative work. While these existing guidelines have further enriched and refined traditional translation standards and enhanced the practicality of legal text translation, they still exhibit certain limitations.

First, these standards remain largely within the academic sphere and lack uniformity and authority. As legal texts issued by the government, local regulations and rules represent the will of the state. Their translation standards should be formulated and promulgated by authoritative national institutions and serve as mandatory references for translators at all levels of local legislation.

Second, existing standards remain overly abstract and lack comprehensiveness and specificity, making them difficult for translators to apply in practice. To address the abstract nature of these principles, some government departments and localities have compiled reference materials that standardize the translation of common legal terms and sentence structures for translators. Examples include the *Chinese-English Glossary of Terms in the Laws and Regulations of the People's Republic of China*, jointly published in 1998 by the Department of Translation, Review, and Foreign Affairs under the Legislative Affairs Office of the State Council, and the *Handbook of Common Sentence Patterns for Legal Translation and Review*, compiled in 2005 by the same department. Unfortunately, these standards have not been updated or supplemented in subsequent years. Amid rapid social development, new vocabulary and sentence structures continue to emerge in local regulations and rules, rendering the existing translation standards insufficient for current translation needs. Translators still lack comprehensive, authoritative, and specific translation guidelines, which, to some extent, has laid the groundwork for a range of issues in the translation of local regulations and rules.

Third, existing standards in the form of handbooks still suffer from inefficiencies. As societal specialization progresses, translation increasingly involves a growing number of terms and sentence structures. The current handbook-style standards require translators to repeatedly consult standard translations during their work, which consumes considerable time and hampers efficiency. Additionally, these handbooks present challenges in usability. While terms are arranged according to the stroke count or pinyin order of the first character, making them relatively easy to locate, fixed sentence structures are randomly ordered, making them difficult to find and resulting in significant time expenditure. This often leads translators to forgo consulting the handbooks altogether, resulting in translation errors or inconsistencies.

In summary, the underlying causes of this anomie are rooted in the historical and developmental characteristics of China's legal translation. Over the 40 years since reform and opening-up, the established legislative system with Chinese characteristics has created structural tension with the relatively underdeveloped translation system. Additionally, there is a tension between the Western-centric dominance of legal discourse and the autonomous construction of socialist rule-of-law discourse with Chinese characteristics, as well as a methodological gap between traditional philological translation paradigms and the functionalist demands of modern legal translation. To overcome these constraints, it is necessary to elevate the standardization of legal translation to the strategic level of national governance capacity building. This involves constructing a systematic framework encompassing terminology management, process control, quality assessment, and talent development. Such an approach would ensure that translation practice not only faithfully represents the institutional achievements of China's rule-of-law development but also effectively contributes to the co-construction and sharing of global legal discourse, ultimately serving the governance objective of enhancing the nation's institutional discourse power.

7.4 Strategies for Standardization of Translation of Chinese Laws and Regulations

In the era of profound transformation in the global governance system and mutual learning among civilizations, legal translation has transcended its traditional role as mere linguistic conversion to become a strategic bridge for the international dissemination of a nation's rule-of-law discourse. China's laws and regulations, as the core carrier of the socialist rule-of-law system with Chinese characteristics, not only carry the institutional wisdom of modernizing national governance but also serve as key texts for showcasing the philosophical underpinnings and practical pathways of "China's governance" to the world. The new era entrusts legal translation with a threefold mission: technically, to achieve precise transmission of legal concepts and the standardized construction of terminology systems; culturally, to facilitate dialogue and integration between Chinese legal civilization and global legal cultures; and in terms of governance, to provide the international community with referential Chinese solutions and institutional public goods. Through systematic, standardized, and high-quality legal translation practices, we can not only clearly elucidate to the international community the uniqueness and effectiveness of the Chinese path to modernization under the rule of law but also actively participate in international rule-making, fostering a more inclusive, representative, and equitable global legal discourse system. This endeavor represents both a strategic investment in the nation's cultural soft power and a substantive contribution to building a community with a shared future for humanity.

7.4.1 Comprehensively Enhancing the Professionalism of Translation of Chinese Laws and Regulations

Giammarresi pointed out that modern translation work is shifting from a traditional focus on individual translation to a large-scale, professional translation model that emphasizes the construction of a translation environment. In terms of the translation environment, the traditional model operates in an "open environment", characterized by "temporality and risk" (Pu & Gao, 2014), which cannot meet the demands of translating China's laws and regulations. Professional legal translation first requires identifying "stakeholders" and establishing a relatively fixed professional team (Project Management Institute, 2008: 4). In particular, the translation of China's local regulations and rules requires the recruitment of experienced translators to form a translation team responsible for completing the initial translation. Simultaneously, it is essential to engage legal and linguistic experts to form a review panel for professional evaluation at both legal and linguistic levels. Finally, staff proficient in both English and law are needed to conduct the final review, responsible for the last round of language proofreading and polishing of the translated texts that have passed professional evaluation. By establishing a rigorous collaborative mechanism of "initial translation – professional review (first review) – final review (second review)", the quality of translations can be effectively ensured.

With social development, the division of industries has become increasingly specialized, particularly in the translation of China's local regulations and rules, which involve a growing number of legal and industry-specific terms. The limited knowledge and experience of individual translators struggle to keep pace with the rapid advancements in these fields. Simultaneously, the scale of translation has expanded, involving a large number of translators. These new trends necessitate the adoption of project management in modern translation to enhance both efficiency and quality.

In the project management process, two key nodes play a critical role in ensuring translation quality through institutional mechanisms: organizing translators and reviewers to compile specialized terminology, and arranging expert reviews in both industry-specific and linguistic fields. By coordinating all translators and reviewers to summarize specialized vocabulary, the power of professional collaboration can be fully leveraged to quickly and accurately identify corresponding translations for legal and industry-specific terms. After the initial translation phase, conducting expert reviews in relevant industries and linguistic fields ensures the accuracy of the professional content covered by the laws, thereby controlling translation quality through the management process.

The translation of laws and regulations requires the establishment of a strict project management system for translation and review, creating a favorable working environment and employing project management techniques to improve the efficiency and quality of the work. In the project management of translation and review, according to relevant national standards (GB/T 19363.1), the project manager should organize, plan, monitor, communicate, and conclude tasks at each stage of the review process. At the initiation of the translation project, the project manager should first convene the initial translators and assign translation tasks for relevant laws and regulations based on their professional backgrounds and experience. During the translation process, the project manager must organize translators to compile specialized terminology, regularly liaise with translators to monitor progress, inquire about any difficulties, and resolve issues through appropriate channels. Upon completion of the initial translation, the project manager should submit the draft to the review team for expert evaluation in both industry-specific and linguistic fields. After the professional review, the project manager will forward the reviewed draft to the final reviewers for approval. Finally, the project manager should arrange for technical personnel to typeset, print, or upload the finalized version to relevant government websites for public disclosure.

In addition to establishing an internal collaborative mechanism of "initial translation - professional review - final approval", it is also essential to create a professional support system from legislative bodies for translation projects. This includes establishing communication channels between translators/reviewers and legislative personnel, regularly inviting translation experts from higher-level legal departments or legislative authorities (such as the Legislative Affairs Office of the State Council) for guidance, and organizing exchange activities with legal translation departments in other provinces and cities. This enables translators and reviewers to gain valuable insights and experience during exchanges, thereby improving translation quality in terms of accuracy, consistency, and other aspects.

Taking the translation of local regulations and rules in Jiangsu Province as an example, since 2011, in accordance with the requirements of the translation project management system, a preliminary translation team composed of experienced translators was organized. Additionally, a professional review group consisting of senior English experts with legal education backgrounds was engaged, and final approval was conducted by professionals from the Jiangsu Provincial Legislative Affairs Office proficient in English and law. The Jiangsu Provincial Legislative Affairs Office also assigned an administrative staff member to act as the project manager, responsible for coordination and organization throughout the translation and review process. The entire translation and review project typically takes 3–5 months. Although the process is complex and time-consuming, it ensures the quality of the translations, receiving positive feedback from foreign-related institutions and enterprises. It has also been commended by relevant leaders of the State Council at national legal work conferences.

The notable achievements in the translation of local regulations and rules in Jiangsu Province, along with the new workflow of "initial translation - industry review - final approval" + "project management" + "professional support from legislative bodies" established during the translation process, can serve as a reference for other provinces and cities in carrying out standardized translation of local regulations and rules. This will promote the professionalization of local regulations and rules translation efforts nationwide.

7.4.2 Strengthening the Cultivation of Interdisciplinary Legal Translation Professionals

Given the shortage of interdisciplinary legal translation talents, enhancing the development of legal translation as a specialized academic field presents a crucial solution.

Over the past decade, some domestic higher education institutions have only begun to develop translation as an independent discipline, resulting in a gradual increase in trained translation professionals. However, the number of translation talents cultivated through formal university education, particularly through professional degree postgraduate programs such as Master of Translation and Interpreting (MTI), remains relatively small. Among these, those specializing in legal translation are even fewer. This scarcity stands in contrast to the growing demand for such professionals. Since the beginning of the twenty-first century, the deepening globalization of politics, economics, and culture, coupled with China's rising international status, has led to an increased demand for translation. Translation work is now evolving toward "providing information to the outside world, explaining concepts, and securing the right to discourse in international communication" (Li & Li, 2014). In recent years, with the decentralization of legislative powers, more regions have begun formulating local regulations and rules, necessitating a greater number of translation professionals to engage in legal translation work. This is essential for the timely, accurate, and comprehensive dissemination of legal information. To address society's demand for legal translation talents, qualified universities should strengthen the development of legal translation as an academic discipline. This can be achieved by offering professional degree postgraduate programs in translation, such as MTI, and increasing the cultivation of specialized legal translation professionals.

The cultivation of legal translation professionals can also adopt a "dual-degree" talent development model. Translating legal texts primarily requires translators to possess strong foreign language proficiency and legal literacy. Individuals with academic backgrounds in both foreign languages and law, so-called "dual-degree" talents, are particularly well-suited for translation work. In the translation of Jiangsu Province's local regulations and rules, the leading translation and review experts were English professors from the School of Foreign Languages who held doctoral degrees in law and had postdoctoral experience at prestigious American law schools. Their qualifications comprehensively met the demands of legal text translation. Given the current shortage of legal translation professionals, qualified universities may consider integrating existing educational resources and encouraging students in linguistics or law to pursue a second major. This approach can cultivate a cohort of "dual-degree" talents to meet societal needs for legal translation professionals. Practicing translators can enhance their knowledge and skills beyond their primary expertise by participating in on-the-job training, such as receiving guidance from translation experts in higher-level legal or legislative departments, or engaging in exchange activities with legal translation departments in other provinces and cities. Of course, the circumstances of each individual may vary, and they should be encouraged to pursue self-study or systematic academic programs based on their specific situations.

Furthermore, to ensure that translations of legal texts are better accepted by target readers and to strengthen the discourse power of our translations, translators must not only be familiar with domestic legal knowledge but also with Western legal systems. In legal translation education, the Content-Based Instruction (CBI) teaching approach can be adopted. This involves extensive and meticulous reading and study of Western legal texts to help translators grasp their legislative language and cultural characteristics, thereby enabling translations to better align with Western legislative language and culture.

7.4.3 Introducing Advanced Technologies

Constructing a Unified Digital Parallel Corpus for Legal Translation Standards

An authoritative, unified, operable, and efficient standard is a critical condition for ensuring translation quality. Given the need for such standards to be authoritative and consistent, national legislative bodies or state-level legal departments (such as the Ministry of Justice under the State Council) should take the lead in organizing translation departments across regions to compile standardized translations. The content should be continuously updated and expanded in line with the times. Modern society has entered the digital age, and relying solely on manual efforts without the assistance of digital technology would result in highly inefficient access to translation standards. Hasselgard's research (2012) indicates that establishing parallel corpora with the help of computer database technology can significantly improve the efficiency of translation studies. Therefore, when compiling standard translations of legal texts, they should be developed into digital parallel corpora to enhance the efficiency of translators' reference processes. When translators are uncertain about the meaning of construction A in the source language and its corresponding translation, they can clarify the semantics of the original text and the correspondence between the source and target texts by examining the scale of construction A in the corpus and its counterparts, such as construction B or C in the translations.

Utilizing Computer-Assisted Translation

The application of Computer-Assisted Translation (CAT) is one of the significant advancements in the translation field today. It differs from commonly used electronic dictionaries, which only perform simple, mechanical word or phrase translations, and from Machine Translation (MT), which attempts to "replace human translation through fully automated translation processes". CAT uses corpus-based computer-assisted translation software to "improve translation efficiency and optimize the translation workflow". Its core components mainly include translation memory systems, terminology management tools, alignment tools, and project management tools. After establishing a corpus of a certain size with Chinese-English aligned texts, CAT software can quickly compare the text to be translated with the data in the corpus, displaying identical or highly similar translations or even performing direct translations. In other words, the richer the corpus and the more regular and repetitive the text to be translated, the more effective the software's assistance will be. This characteristic makes CAT particularly suitable for translating legal texts. Currently, numerous CAT software tools are available in the international translation software market, such as Germany's Trados, France's Déjà Vu and Wordfast, and domestic products like Yaxin, Yongli, CECtrans, Snowman, and others. In Western developed countries, the usage rate of CAT software is high. According to a survey of Western translators conducted by British scholar Lagoudaki in 2006, the usage rate of Trados was 51%, Déjà Vu 23%, and Wordfast 29%, with 53% of translators even using more than one CAT software (Lagoudaki, 2006). In contrast, domestic translators and translation agencies in China have not placed much emphasis on the application of CAT software. A survey conducted by Chinese scholars in 2008 showed that only 66% of the surveyed translators used CAT tools (Hou & Yan, 2008).

The use of CAT software can reduce the workload of translators, avoid errors in manual memory, and improve translation speed and efficiency by more than twofold compared to manual translation. Since the use of CAT software relies on memory database files, promoting CAT software and sharing databases among translators can technically ensure the accuracy and consistency of terminology and sentence structures between superior laws and local regulations, as well as among local regulations of various provinces and cities. As the database continues to grow, translation speed and efficiency will also improve. This foresees that the use of CAT will provide technical support for the standardization of local regulations and rules translation.

Utilizing Generative AI in Translation Assistance

With the rapid advancement of artificial intelligence technology, generative artificial intelligence (Generative AI) has demonstrated revolutionary potential in the field of language processing, offering new technological pathways for enhancing the accuracy, efficiency, and consistency of legal translation. Generative AI, based on large-scale pre-trained language models, is capable of deeply understanding the semantic logic, stylistic features, and normative structures of legal texts, and can generate highly specialized translations through contextual learning. Its core advantages lie in:

(a) **Deep Semantic Analysis**
Pre-trained models can accurately identify the polysemy and contextual dependencies of legal terminology, such as distinguishing between easily confused concepts like "right" and "power", or "agency" and "representation".

(b) **Cross-System Conceptual Mapping**
Trained on multilingual legal corpora, AI can identify differences between unique Chinese legal concepts (e.g., "宅基地"—house sites, "行政复议"—administrative reconsideration) and approximate concepts in common law systems, generating functionally equivalent translations adapted to the target legal domain.

(c) **Dynamic Terminology Consistency Maintenance**
By leveraging real-time updated legal terminology databases, AI can automatically detect deviations in the translation of the same term across different provisions and suggest standardized alternatives, ensuring both vertical (between superior and subordinate laws) and horizontal (across regional regulations) terminology consistency.

(d) **Stylistic Standardization Adaptation**
By learning from authoritative legal translations (such as official versions issued by the Legislative Affairs Office of the State Council), AI can automatically emulate their solemn, concise, and precise stylistic features, reducing the interference of individual translator styles on the authority of the text.

In practice, AI can quickly generate initial translations based on parallel corpora, allowing translators to focus on reviewing legal logic and cultural adaptation. What's more, embedding AI terminology prompt tools during translation can automatically recommend authoritative translations and flag potential ambiguities. Additionally, AI can intelligently compare different historical or regional versions of the same regulation, revealing patterns in terminology evolution and regional variations.

However, the application of generative AI in legal translation still faces three major challenges. Firstly, incomplete coverage of training data may lead to mistranslations of emerging legal concepts (e.g., "data property rights", "digital governance"). It is essential to continuously incorporate the latest legislative and judicial interpretation corpora. Secondly, if errors in AI-generated translations lead to legal disputes, the responsibilities of translators, technology providers, and legislative authorities must be clearly defined, and mandatory human final review processes must be established. Thirdly, to prevent translators from becoming overly reliant on AI, which could lead to a decline in professional competence, a "human-machine collaboration" model should be emphasized, positioning AI as an "expert-level auxiliary tool" rather than a replacement.

Establishing a tripartite collaborative mechanism involving "legislative authorities, professional translators, and AI systems", and utilizing blockchain technology to enable full-chain traceability and verification of the translation process, will deeply integrate generative AI into the national standardization system for legal translation. This will not only enhance the efficiency of translating local regulations but also provide technological support for China's participation in the construction of a global legal discourse system, advancing the exchange of legal civilizations from "language conversion" to a new stage of "intelligent integration".

7.5 Future Prospects

Since the initiation of reform and opening-up, China has achieved remarkable accomplishments in the development of the rule of law. As the rule of law deepens and international exchanges expand, the translation of China's legislative texts (laws and regulations) faces unprecedented challenges. Academic research generally indicates that the overall quality of legal translation in China remains to be improved, with key challenges including inadequate equivalence in terminology, a lag in professional talent development, limited technological application, and a lack of systematic translation strategies (Wu, 2014; Dong, 2014; Zhao & Zheng, 2015; Li & Dong, 2015). After more than a decade of practical exploration, China's legal translation efforts have achieved phased progress but still exhibit significant shortcomings. First, the structure of the translation and review workforce is imbalanced, there is a risk of discontinuity in the external expert pool, while the professional competencies of in-house translators require systematic training. Second, the translation standards system remains incomplete, lacking mandatory normative guidelines. Unlike literary translation, which encourages diverse interpretations, legal translation is essentially the cross-linguistic reconstruction of legislative intent and must strictly adhere to textual norms and the determinacy of intent.

As China's legal system continues to improve and local legislative authority gradually decentralizes, the number of local regulations and rules continues to grow. Currently, translation efforts are not only underway across all provincial-level administrative regions but have also been initiated in many larger cities with legislative authority. Against this backdrop, the translation of local regulations and rules is poised to become a critical component of rule-of-law development. However, existing issues in translation practice, such as inconsistent terminology, stylistic irregularities, and cultural misinterpretations, significantly undermine the authority and applicability of official translations. Therefore, constructing a scientific and systematic framework for translation standards and establishing a four-in-one mechanism encompassing "terminology standardization, procedural institutionalization, talent specialization, and technological intelligence" should become the core mission for advancing the high-quality development of China's legal translation efforts. This responds to the demands of modernizing national governance and is an inevitable path toward enhancing the international discourse power of China's rule of law.

The translation of laws and regulations is a crucial component of the complex systematic project aimed at promoting the global outreach of Chinese legal discourse, requiring concerted efforts from all parties involved.

7.5.1 Efforts at the Governmental Level

From a national perspective, it is imperative to elevate the enhancement of legal translation capabilities and the cultivation of legal translation talent to a strategic level, aimed at strengthening the nation's cultural soft power and the international influence of Chinese legal culture. This must be approached as a long-term, systematic, and strategic endeavor, with comprehensive planning and scientific layout in areas such as educational resource allocation, academic discipline design, the organization of major national-level translation projects, the planning and management of translation undertakings and industries, and the establishment of translation quality evaluation systems and authoritative publication mechanisms.

On one hand, legislative, judicial, law enforcement, diplomatic, foreign trade and economic, and international communication departments must collaborate closely with academic research institutions to establish cross-departmental coordination mechanisms and develop standardized reference texts for the translation of laws and regulations, thereby ensuring the authoritative nature of translation efforts. On the other hand, increased investment should be directed toward strengthening academic research in universities and research institutions, with a focus on cultivating interdisciplinary talent proficient in both law and foreign languages. Efforts should be made to produce a cohort of legal translation experts who not only possess strong foreign language proficiency but also understand the characteristics of different legal systems and have both theoretical knowledge and practical experience in translation.

7.5.2 Efforts to Be Implemented in Talent Cultivation

Promoting the global outreach of Chinese legal discourse requires further emancipating our minds and adopting an open and inclusive international perspective on legal translation talent. When considering the question of "how Chinese legal culture can go global", it is essential to break free from conventional thinking patterns and establish a concept of global collaboration. We should fully unite and rely on sinologists, jurists, and professional translators from various countries engaged in translating Chinese works into foreign languages, building a regularized and institutionalized international academic collaboration network. It is important to transcend the limited notion that "the dissemination of legal discourse can only rely on domestic forces" and actively create platforms for dialogue between Chinese and international legal translation communities. Deepening professional exchanges through joint research, collaborative translation, international seminars, and other forms is crucial.

To achieve more effective international dissemination of Chinese legal discourse, a dual empowerment strategy should be implemented: on one hand, domestic scholars should be encouraged to strengthen systematic research on the outstanding traditional legal culture of the Chinese legal system, distill the jurisprudential essence with contemporary value, and produce original theoretical achievements that reflect Chinese characteristics while conforming to international academic norms. On the other hand, innovative modes of international cooperation should be developed, such as establishing joint training mechanisms with renowned international translation institutes and authoritative legal translation institutions, and exploring the creation of advanced training institutions focused on the specialized field of legal translation. Such institutions should design a progressive curriculum system covering modules such as an introduction to the Chinese legal system, comparative law studies, and legal language conversion. Emphasis should be placed on targeted training for overseas sinologists, jurists, and professional translators. Through immersive workshops, case studies, translation practice sessions, and other formats, their depth of understanding of China's path to rule of law, the characteristics of Chinese legal culture, and contemporary judicial practices should be systematically enhanced, while their abilities in cross-cultural conversion and mastery of specialized terminology should be strengthened.

It is worth special attention that a collaborative working mechanism between Chinese and international legal translation experts should be established. This can be achieved through projects such as establishing joint international legal translation laboratories, building multilingual legal terminology databases, and conducting parallel text comparative research, thereby integrating advantageous resources and sharing professional expertise. This deeply integrated cooperative model can not only expand the international dimension of the high-end legal translation talent pool but also provide sustainable intellectual support for building a credible system for translating Chinese legal texts into foreign languages. Ultimately, it will foster a virtuous ecosystem for the international dissemination of Chinese legal discourse.

7.5.3 *Efforts for Overall Planning*

Promoting the international dissemination of Chinese legal discourse requires the establishment of a systematic and forward-looking strategic planning framework. The development of legal translation talent should be elevated to the level of national language strategy and integrated with rule-of-law diplomacy for comprehensive deployment. It is essential to construct an institutionalized support system covering the entire chain of talent selection, professional training, project practice, and quality evaluation. Through specialized initiatives such as the "National Legal Translation Project", domestic and international academic resources should be systematically integrated to attract top global sinologists, comparative jurists, and professional translators, forming a cross-cultural collaborative network.

Innovation in legal translation project management mechanisms is also crucial. A standardized process should be established, encompassing "topic selection and argumentation, team formation, terminology unification, multi-round review, and international evaluation". Concurrently, a legal translation quality intelligent monitoring system should be developed to enable dynamic quality control throughout the translation process. In terms of institutional safeguards, the "National Standards for the Legal Translation Industry" should be formulated, clarifying the qualification certification system for high-end legal translation professionals. A National Award for Outstanding Legal Translations should be established, and exemplary translations should be incorporated into the official repository for international legal and cultural exchanges.

More importantly, a collaborative innovation platform involving government, industry, academia, and research institutions should be built. Through initiatives such as postdoctoral research stations in legal translation and international joint laboratories for legal translation, a virtuous ecosystem where theoretical innovation and practical application mutually reinforce each other should be fostered. Ultimately, this will establish a globally influential academic community for Chinese legal translation, providing a professional linguistic bridge that combines Chinese wisdom with international expression for dialogue among global rule-of-law civilizations.

7.6 Conclusion

In summary, the author's systematic research on the unification and standardization of Chinese legal translation, from multiple dimensions such as talent development, technological application, management mechanisms, and standard formulation, offers innovative insights and practical pathways for advancing the modernization of China's legal translation system. These achievements not only provide theoretical references for improving the quality control mechanisms of legal translation but also contribute professional expertise to enhancing the capacity for foreign-related rule of law within the national governance framework. However, it must be soberly recognized that, compared to mature translation fields such as literature and science and technology, the translation of Chinese laws and regulations remains in the preliminary stage of institutional development. Its professional paradigm has yet to be fully established, and the theoretical framework for cross-system transformation requires further refinement. This calls for a closer collaborative network among legal scholars, translation researchers, and practical departments, fostering continuous academic dialogue and practical exploration to jointly develop a legal translation standard system that reflects Chinese characteristics while aligning with international norms. Only through interdisciplinary and cross-sectoral collaboration can we elevate the theoretical depth and practical precision of China's legal translation, transforming it into a strategic pillar for the global dissemination of the nation's rule-of-law soft power.

References

Chen, Z. 2000. *Essays on Legal Translation*. Beijing: China Legal System Publishing House.

Chesterman, A. 1993. From "is" to "ought": translation laws, norms and strategies. *Target* 5.

Chesterman, A. 1999. The Empirical Status of Prescriptivism. *Folia Translatologica* 6.

Dong, X. 2011. *Legal Text Translation*. Beijing: University of International Business and Economics Press.

Dong, X. 2014. An analysis of several issues in the standardized English translation of China's legislative texts. *Foreign Language Learning Theory and Practice* 3.

Dong, X. 2015. On the "equivalent" translation of English-Chinese legal terminology. *Journal of Xi'an International Studies University* 3.

Giammarresi, S. 2011. *Strategic Views on Localization Project Management*. In *Translation and Localization Project Management*, ed. K. Dunne and E. Dunne. John Benjamins Publishing Company.

Han, J. 2004. On the study of translation norms in China. *Shandong Foreign Language Teaching Journal* 6.

Hasselgard, H. 2012. Using parallel corpora in contrastive studies: cross-linguistic contrast of future referring expressions in English and Norwegian. *Foreign Language Teaching and Research* 1.

Hermans, T. 1999. *Translation in System: Descriptive and Systematic Approach Explained*. Manchester: St. Jerome Publishing.

Hou, X., and Y. Yan. 2008. *Survey Report on the Application of CAT in China's Translation Industry*. Beijing: School of Software and Microelectronics, Peking University.

Jin, C., and A. Hu. 2000. On problems in current legal translation in China. *Chinese Translators Journal* 3.

Lagoudaki, L. 2006. *Translation Memory Systems: Enlightening User's Perspective*. London: Imperial College.

Li, D., and M. Hu. 2002. Legal translation studies: Current status and prospects. *Chinese Science & Technology Translators Journal* 3.

Li, J., and X. Dong. 2015. Standardization and countermeasures in the translation of local regulations and rules: A study based on translation practice in Jiangsu Province. *Southeast Academic Research* 4.

Li, K., and X. Zhang. 2006. *Legal Texts and Legal Translation*. Beijing: China Translation & Publishing Corporation.

Li, Z., and N. Li. 2014. Innovating translation talent training mode to enhance translation talent quality. *Shanghai Journal of Translators* 4.

Project Management Institute. 2008. *A Guide to the Project Management Body of Knowledge*. Project Management Institute.

Pu, X., and J. Gao. 2014. Introduction to translation project management processes. *Shanghai Journal of Translators* 2.

Qiu, G. 2000. On some principles of legal text translation. *Chinese Science & Technology Translators Journal* 2.

Šarčević, S. 1994. *Translation and the Law: An Interdisciplinary Approach*. Amsterdam/ Philadelphia: Benjamins.

Schäffner, C., and B. Adab. 2000. *Developing Translation Competence: Introduction*. In *Developing Translation Competence*, ed. Christina Schäffner and Beverly Adab. Amsterdam & Philadelphia: Benjamins.

Toury, G. 1995. *Descriptive Translation Studies and Beyond*. Amsterdam & Philadelphia: Benjamins.

Vermeer, H. J. 2000. *Skopos and Commission in Translational Action*. In *The Translation Studies Reader*, ed. Lawrence Venuti. London and New York: Routledge.

Wu, C. 2014. Translation principles for fuzzy words in legislative texts. *Shanghai Journal of Translators* 3.

Yan, M. 2009. *College English Translation Teaching: Theory and Practice*. Changchun: Jilin Publishing Group Co., Ltd.

Zhao, J., and J. Zheng. 2015. Analysis and translation strategies of legal definition clauses. *Foreign Language Research* 4.

The manufacturer's authorised representative in the EU is Springer
Nature Customer Service Centre GmbH, Europaplatz 3, 69115 Heidelberg,
Germany. If you have any concerns regarding our products, please
contact ProductSafety@springernature.com

Printed and bound by CPI Group (UK) Ltd, Croydon, CR0 4YY
21/09/2026
02219989-0003